REFERENCE

R342.085

G464v

DETROIT PUBLIC LIBRARY

3 5674 00657689 7

W9-CBC-368

PRESENTED BY

OF THE DETROIT

PUBLIC LIBRARY

THE FRIENDS

PEOPLE'S WALL, WORLD'S FAIR. QUEENS, NEW YORK, 1965.

MARTIN LUTHER KING, JR., URGES BLACKS TO VOTE FOR THE FIRST TIME IN AN
ELECTION SUPERVISED BY FEDERAL REGISTRARS. CAMDEN, ALABAMA, 1966.

VISIONS OF LIBERTY

THE BILL OF RIGHTS FOR ALL AMERICANS

BY IRA GLASSER
PHOTOGRAPHS BY BOB ADELMAN

A BOB ADELMAN BOOK
·
DESIGN BY MARY K. BAUMANN

ARCADE PUBLISHING · NEW YORK

LITTLE, BROWN AND COMPANY

Text copyright © 1991 by Ira Glasser
Photographs copyright © 1991
by Bob Adelman

All rights reserved. No part of this book may
be reproduced in any form or by any
electronic or mechanical means, including
information storage and retrieval systems,
without permission in writing from the
publisher, except by a reviewer who may
quote brief passages in a review.

First Edition

All photographs not otherwise credited
are by Bob Adelman.
The section "Including All Americans"
appeared in a slightly different form in
Doing Good, by Gaylin, Glasser, Marcus, and
Rothman, published by Pantheon Books.

Library of Congress
Cataloging-in-Publication Data

Glasser, Ira.
Visions of liberty:
the Bill of Rights for all Americans/
by Ira Glasser;
photographs by Bob Adelman
    p. cm.
Includes index.
ISBN 1-55970-104-8
1. Civil rights—United States—History.
2. United States—Constitutional law—
Amendments—1st–10th—History.
I. Adelman, Bob. II. Title.
KF4749.G53 1991
342.73′085—dc20
[347.30285]   91-16618

Published in the United States
by Arcade Publishing, Inc., New York,
a Little, Brown company

10 9 8 7 6 5 4 3 2 1

Picture research: Andrew Norman
Copyediting and computer text
preparation: David Frederickson
Photographic prints: Michael Macioce
Designer: Mary K. Baumann,
Hopkins/Baumann
Associate Designer: Wylie Nash
Design Assistant: Miyoko Baensch

Published simultaneously in Canada by
Little, Brown & Company
(Canada) Limited

Printed in Japan

ACKNOWLEDGMENTS
I should like first to thank Colleen
O'Connor, who persuaded me to write this
book when I knew my full-time job
wouldn't permit it. I told her it would kill
me. She told me I would love it. We were
both nearly right. Special thanks too to my
secretary, Maxine Lowell, who typed the
manuscript and kept track of everything, all
while doing her full-time job, too, and with
her usual unflappable competence. One
fully values such assistance only when it is
not there. I am also in the debt of my
colleagues who read the manuscript and
made many valuable suggestions and more
than a few saving corrections: Arthur
Eisenberg, who read the entire thing and
gave me his usual thoughtful reactions; and
Janet Benshoof, Jean Bond, Joel Gora,
Morton Halperin, Susan Herman, Isabelle
Katz Pinzler, William Rubenstein, Steven
Shapiro, and Nadine Strossen, each of
whom read and commented on various
sections. Rita Spillenger saved the day with
some nifty research and fact-checking, all
done cheerfully and accurately under
unreasonable time constraints. To my
family and workmates, I can only apologize.
I hope you think the product worth it.
—I.G.

Photographs of people are perforce
cooperative ventures, and I must thank my
subjects for their help and indulgence. I
am in debt to a number of attorneys for
their advice and counsel, particularly my
own lawyer, John Horan, as well as Martin
Bradley Ashare, Hon. James M. Catterson,
Jr., and James M. McCabe. For so gener-
ously lending her expertise to this project, I
am grateful to Joni Weyl. This book could
not have come into existence without the
support and wise suggestions of the editor
and publisher, Richard Seaver. In these
parlous times, a small hope that for
Samantha Adelman and David Hall the
course of their lives will be enlarged by the
principles enunciated here.
—B.A.

HOLLYWOOD, CALIFORNIA, 1989

THE AUTHORS WISH TO
THANK THE AMERICAN MASTER
AND CIVIL LIBERTARIAN
ROY LICHTENSTEIN
FOR HIS GENEROUS SUPPORT
OF THIS PROJECT.

ANTI-VIETNAM WAR DEMONSTRATORS, NEW YORK CITY, 1968.

•

A PASSION FOR LIBERTY

THIS IS A BOOK ABOUT TRADITIONAL AMERICAN VALUES, WRITTEN AT A TIME
when Americans seem deeply divided over what exactly our traditional values
are, what it means to be an American, what it means to be patriotic — even
what it means, or should mean, to be conservative.

Samuel Johnson once said, "Patriotism is the last refuge of a scoundrel."
He was referring not to patriotism that reflects "a real and generous love of
country," but rather to "that pretended patriotism" that is often used by
grasping politicians as a "cloak for self-interest" and transient political advantage. We have seen much of that brand of patriotism. Sometimes the
American flag itself has been used as such a cloak by those who wrap themselves in it even as they act to undermine what the flag represents.

But there is another kind of patriotism, too, which exhibits itself not so
much through devotion to the flag as through commitment to the two great
principles that the flag represents: democracy and liberty, the principles upon
which the United States was founded two hundred years ago. Supporting
these principles is what constitutes patriotism, and conserving them is what
ought to constitute being a conservative.

Democracy and liberty are often used today as synonyms, but they are
not; indeed, there is an inevitable tension between them. Democracy means
that people ought to have a meaningful say in the decisions that affect their
lives. They ought to be able to vote for public officials in fair elections, determine the kind of government they wish to have, and make most political
decisions by majority rule. Liberty, on the other hand, means that even in a
democracy, the majority cannot be allowed to rule everything, that people
have rights—are born with rights—that no majority should be able to take
away. There are more whites in this country than blacks, but that doesn't
mean that whites should be able to deny blacks the right to vote or other
fundamental rights. Men have more political power than women, but that
doesn't mean that women should be relegated to second-class citizenship.

Some religions have more believers than others, but that doesn't mean that adherents of minority religions may be denied their rights of conscience, or may be required to support other people's beliefs.

The original citizens of the United States were committed to this idea of inalienable rights; they set themselves the task of defining the rights they wished to secure against majoritarian rule, and they created a system for protecting those rights. For example, today we sometimes think that we are entitled to free speech because the First Amendment gives it to us. That is not how the original citizens saw it. They believed they were entitled as human beings to free speech, and they invented the First Amendment in order to protect it. The entire Bill of Rights was created to protect rights the original citizens believed were fundamentally and naturally theirs.

Before the United States was founded, struggles for liberty almost always involved efforts to establish rights against a king or tyrant. In America, for the first time, the struggle for liberty established legal boundaries for democracy itself, forbidden zones of freedom where the individual, not the majority, reigns supreme.

The Bill of Rights was the primary weapon in that struggle. It established rights by setting strict legal limits on society's power, even though society was to be governed democratically. This had never happened before, and remains America's unique contribution to the world.

But as Governor L. Douglas Wilder of Virginia, a grandson of slaves and the nation's first black governor, said in a 1991 speech at the University of North Carolina, "Not everyone in this land has been committed to following that blueprint throughout our history.... Although we have paid homage to the words 'liberty and justice for all,' throughout this country's history we have fallen far short of that ideal." That was true at the beginning, when Africans and their descendants were kept in chattel slavery by the white majority, and when women were not permitted to vote. It is still true today: although we have made great progress in two hundred years, large gaps remain between our professed ideals and the realities of many Americans' lives.

Moreover, fundamental disagreements have emerged and recently grown sharper about how best to express those ideals, about what we mean by patriotism, fairness, liberty, and the rest:

• Is the patriot the person who would force you by law to respect and salute the flag? Or is the patriot the one who argues that what the flag represents is your right not to salute it, your right not to show your faith or bend your knee to what the majority or the government thinks is orthodox in politics or religion?

• Does the commitment to equal rights require compensatory remedies to overcome the injuries imposed by centuries of unequal treatment? Or is it time for the majority to reassert itself against what some would call reverse discrimination?

• Does fundamental fairness and a concern for the innocent require strict adherence to procedural rights, even for people accused of heinous crimes? Or have such rights become an impermissible impediment to public safety and crime control?

• Does the protection of religious liberty require a strict separation between church and state? Or should the government be allowed to give religion a helping hand, so long as it does not favor one denomination over another?

• Have federal courts acted properly over the past three decades in repeatedly invoking the Constitution to limit governmental power and secure rights for people not previously protected? Or have federal judges—elected by no one and appointed for life—gone too far and intruded improperly upon legislative prerogatives?

All of these questions have often confused, and deeply divided, the American people. And the different answers have almost always reflected fundamentally different beliefs about what constitutes basic American values. It is the thesis of this book that the most fundamental American values are to be found in the vision of individual liberty that led to the adoption of the Bill of Rights in 1791.

In the pages that follow, I will attempt to describe that vision, trace its roots, and chronicle its development. The Bill of Rights—the first ten amendments to the United States Constitution—is both the starting point of that development and its single most crucial event. But this book is about basic liberties as much as it is about the Bill of Rights. Thus, a number of the first ten amendments are not discussed here, while several later amendments —especially the three adopted right after the Civil War—are extensively discussed. The focus throughout is on the great rights—freedom of conscience and expression, fundamental fairness, and equality—and how those rights have evolved over the last two centuries.

The book also seeks to relate current controversies to the original vision of the people who founded the country. The worldview of the Americans reflected, above all else, a fierce commitment to liberty and a belief that securing individual rights was the highest and most noble purpose of government.

Today, that view often seems remote from our own.

Instead, we hear a lot of talk about "too many rights," and about "restoring" government power. Studies have suggested that a majority of Americans may not even support the Bill of Rights, except perhaps in a general and abstract way, and do not understand how it protects them. Public figures have often given voice to this general feeling of unease. In the late 1960s, Vice-President Spiro Agnew spoke of the Silent Majority of Americans that was supposedly opposed to many of the rights secured by the Constitution. During the early 1980s, the reverend Jerry Falwell spoke of a Moral Majority that he said was opposed to many civil liberties and wanted to return to what he called "traditional American values." Men like Agnew and Falwell, and the movements they represented, assumed an antagonism between liberty and the common good, as if the expansion of one necessarily resulted in the reduction of the other. And they projected a candid preference for majoritarian control over claims of individual rights. This view steadily gained ground during the 1980s, and today the Supreme Court increasingly reflects it.

But for the original citizens of this country—whom one might legitimately call the First Majority—individual liberty was the fundamental social value most to be cherished and protected. Far from being antagonistic to the common good, individual liberty was seen as part of the common good, indeed as the highest common good.

As the early Americans saw it, if there was an enemy of liberty, it was not the common good but the encroachments of government power. For them, as the historian Bernard Bailyn has brilliantly shown, the ultimate explanation of every political controversy was the disposition of power. Power was defined as dominion—the dominion of some people over others, and ultimately force and compulsion.

The essential characteristic of power was its aggressiveness, what Bailyn calls "its endlessly propulsive tendency to expand itself beyond legitimate boundaries." In the pamphlets of the American Revolution, words like "trust" and "benevolence" cannot be found among the many descriptions of power. According to Bailyn, the metaphor most commonly used to express the early Americans' view of power was the act of trespassing. Power was said to have "an encroaching nature," a punishing, grasping, devouring nature. It was said to be "tenacious," "like a cancer," "restless, aspiring, and insatiable."

The natural prey of power, and its necessary victim, was liberty, or law, or individual rights. The early Americans saw the public world as divided into two innately antagonistic spheres—power and liberty, the latter delicate, passive, and above all fragile. "The one must be resisted, the other defended, and the two must never be confused."

Power was not itself evil, but it was dangerous. And power resided prominently in the hands of government. Liberty was not—as it seems sometimes to be for us today—the concern and interest of all, governors and the governed alike; rather, liberty was the concern and interest only of the governed. "The wielders of power did not speak for it, nor did they naturally serve it. Their interest was to use and develop power, no less natural and necessary than liberty, but more dangerous."

This worldview was not based on academic or theoretical ideas, but rather on a practical understanding of human nature and its "lust for self-aggrandizement." The point on which there was absolute agreement in those days was that people in general were incapable of withstanding the temptations and seductions of power. Therefore, the protection of liberty—always vulnerable—required something more than faith in the decent intentions and benevolent instincts of public officials.

Even democracy was not seen as sufficient protection. On the contrary, the power of the people was seen as no less threatening to individual rights than the power of the king. If the highest social good was the attainment of liberty, then all citizens had an interest in preventing all governments, whether democratic or regal, from exercising too much power over their lives. Not even democratic majorities or democratically elected public officials could be trusted to preserve individual rights during moments of frenzy or fear, or when the appetite for power grew too strong.

No one seemed immune from this flaw in human nature. Even such a celebrated apostle of liberty as Thomas Jefferson was much less respectful of individual rights when he was president. As Leonard Levy tells us,

Jefferson at one time or another supported loyalty oaths; countenanced internment camps for political suspects; drafted a bill of attainder; urged prosecutions for seditious libel; trampled on the Fourth Amendment; condoned military despotism; used the Army to enforce laws in time of peace; censored reading, chose professors for their political opinions; and endorsed the doctrine that the means, however odious, were justified by the ends.

Jefferson's lapses were in large part natural and to be expected. They "did not result from hypocrisy or meanness of spirit," but rather derived from the fact that when he found himself in a position of power, his libertarian ideals were often sacrificed for what he believed were "larger" and more compelling governmental ends.

Today, we may be surprised to learn of Jefferson's darker side. But to the prerevolutionary pamphleteers, nothing Jefferson or any other president did would have been surprising. Their view of human nature predicted such outcomes: one should not confuse the sphere of liberty with the sphere of power, and those who exercise power should not be entrusted or expected to protect liberty; their self-restraint is a poor safeguard. Instead, power—no matter how benevolent of intention, no matter how devoted to liberty in principle—must be restrained by law. Liberty requires, concludes Levy, that "the state must be bitted and bridled by a Bill of Rights ... its protections not to be the playthings of momentary majorities or of those in power."

That is how the early Americans saw it. For them, government was established by the consent of the governed, but government was nonetheless an adversary of the governed, and a dangerous one at that. To say that a person had a right to publish a leaflet or criticize the government or worship freely therefore required that government be explicitly denied the authority to prevent it. Virtually every right was thought of in this way. The right to be secure in one's own home from unreasonable government intrusion, for example, literally meant that not even the highest government official was authorized to enter without a court order based on adequate evidence. It was precisely to define and construct such legal protections—protections that not even Congress could override—that the Bill of Rights was added to the fledgling United States Constitution two hundred years ago.

But for all its grandeur, the Bill of Rights was a flawed document. It left much out, and proved difficult to enforce. This book tells how the courts acquired the power to interpret the Bill of Rights and to strike down legislative and executive acts on the basis of its interpretations; how such decisions gradually created a living, vibrant body of law that to this day keeps most of us free; and how the Bill of Rights was expanded, both by subsequent constitutional amendments and Supreme Court decisions, to include those who were at first left out.

It is a story full of conflict and drama, of individuals who claimed their rights, often at great personal risk, and who were at first denied; who fought on—sometimes, it seemed, unreasonably—but whose persistence and stamina helped establish many of the rights that protect us all today. It is the story of how principles of liberty were transformed into the practice of liberty. But it is also a story without an ending, because rights are always vulnerable, as the early Americans knew, to the aggressions of power.

If this book can be said to have a single purpose, it is to excite in its readers the passion for liberty that so deeply inspired those who founded this country. For in the end, individual rights depend on the willingness of citizens to insist upon them. As Judge Learned Hand once said, "Liberty lies in the hearts of men and women. When it dies there, no constitution, no law, no court can save it."

THE BIRTH OF THE
BILL OF RIGHTS

PICTURE COLLECTION, THE BRANCH LIBRARIES, THE NEW YORK PUBLIC LIBRARY

"THE BLOODY MASSACRE PERPETRATED IN KING STREET, BOSTON, ON MARCH 5, 1770... ENGRAV'D, PRINTED & SOLD BY PAUL REVERE, BOSTON." VICTIMS WERE PROTESTING HEAVY NEW TAXES.

Iohannes dei gra Rex Angl. Dns Hybn. Dux Normann. Aqmt. z Comes
Andeg. Archiepis tpis. Abbibz. Comitibz. Baronibz. Iufhc. torettar. bice
comitibz. Prepolitis. Minilris. zomnibz Balliuis z fidelibz luis Salt.
————————— Nullus liber homo capiat ut inpnlonet. aut diffaifiat. aut Vtlaget.
aut exulet. aut aliquo modo deftruat. nec lup eum ibimul nec lup eum mittemul nifi p le-
gale indum patium fuor. ut p legem terre.
————————— Data p manum nram in prato qd uocat Runnymed Inter
Windelefoy z Stdnes. Quto decimo die Iun. Anno Regni noftri Septi-
mo decimo.

TOP: PASSAGES FROM AN EARLY MANUSCRIPT COPY OF THE MAGNA CARTA.

ABOVE: YIELDING TO THREATS OF BRITISH BARONS, KING JOHN SIGNS THE MAGNA CARTA AT RUNNYMEDE, 1215 (ARTIST'S CONCEPTION).

"THE BILL OF RIGHTS OF THE PEOPLE OF GREAT BRITAIN," ENACTED BY PARLIAMENT IN 1689 AFTER THE OVERTHROW OF KING JAMES II, IS READ TO THE PRINCE AND PRINCESS OF ORANGE, SOON TO BE CROWNED AS KING WILLIAM III AND QUEEN MARY (ARTIST'S CONCEPTION).

PICTURE COLLECTION. THE BRANCH LIBRARIES. THE NEW YORK PUBLIC LIBRARY

"SONS OF LIBERTY" FORCE TEA UPON TARRED AND FEATHERED SPY FOR BRITISH CUSTOMS, WHILE OTHERS DUMP TEA LEAVES INTO BOSTON HARBOR (ENGLISH ENGRAVING, 1773).

STAMP ACT OF 1765 IMPOSED A TAX ON ALL COLONIAL DOCUMENTS AND PUBLICATIONS.

PICTURE COLLECTION. THE BRANCH LIBRARIES. THE NEW YORK PUBLIC LIBRARY

REVOLUTIONARY MASSACHUSETTS TREASURY NOTE DISPLAYS MAGNA CARTA AS A SHIELD.

LIBRARY OF CONGRESS

JAMES MADISON,
PAINTED FROM
LIFE BY CHARLES
WILLSON PEALE,
C. 1792.

THOMAS GILCREASE INSTITUTE OF AMERICAN HISTORY AND ART, TULSA,OKLAHOMA

THOMAS
JEFFERSON,
PAINTED
FROM LIFE BY
REMBRANDT
PEALE, 1805.

COURTESY OF THE NEW-YORK HISTORICAL SOCIETY, NEW YORK CITY

JAMES MADISON OPENS DEBATE ON BILL OF RIGHTS IN THE FIRST CONGRESS, NEW YORK CITY, 1789 (PAINTING BY FREDRICO CASTELLON, 1954).

JOHN MARSHALL, SECOND CHIEF JUSTICE OF THE U.S., DRAWN FROM LIFE BY GABRIEL FEVRET DE SAINT-MERNIN, 1808.

LIBRARY OF CONGRESS

"THE DESTRUC-TION OF THE ROYAL STATUE IN NEW YORK" (FRENCH ENGRAVER'S CONCEPTION, PRINTED IN GERMANY, JULY 1776).

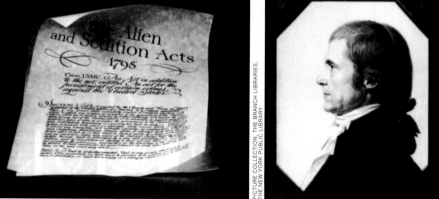

PICTURE COLLECTION, THE BRANCH LIBRARIES, THE NEW YORK PUBLIC LIBRARY

DUKE UNIVERSITY MUSEUM OF ART, DURHAM, NORTH CAROLINA

THE ALIEN & SEDITION ACTS OF 1798 (FACSIMILE).

THE BIRTH OF THE BILL OF RIGHTS

1

DECEMBER 15, 1991, MARKS THE TWO-HUNDREDTH ANNIVERSARY OF THE BILL of Rights. On that day two centuries ago, Virginia became the eleventh state to ratify the first ten amendments to the new Constitution, thus making the Bill of Rights part of the supreme law of the new American republic.

But the story of the Bill of Rights—what it included, what it left out, how it developed, and what it means for us today—stretches for hundreds of years before and after that wintry December day in 1791. It is a story often told in terms of the acts of famous people, of the speeches they made and the laws they wrote. More importantly, it is also a story of ordinary people and their daily struggles to live free of unreasonable constraints imposed by those more powerful than they. The risks they took and the suffering they endured established the rights we take for granted today.

The story behind the Bill of Rights is only part of the larger narrative of liberty and the unending struggle to define and protect the rights of the individual against the accumulated powers of society. But it is a pivotal episode: for the first time in history, people organizing a government made sure to reserve certain rights to themselves as individuals, rights that their government could not legitimately infringe or take away. In Europe, governmental power had always come first; individual rights were concessions made from time to time at the discretion of government, and they could as easily be taken away. America, on the other hand, was built on the idea that individual liberty came first and governmental powers were concessions made at the discretion of the people.

James Madison, who later would become the nation's fourth president, was the principal author of the Bill of Rights and kept the only record of the Constitutional Convention, where the original Constitution was written during four steamy summer months in 1787. Reflecting in 1792 on what had been accomplished, Madison observed that "in Europe, charters of liberty have been granted by power." But in America, he continued, "charters of power

[are] granted by liberty." He called this a "revolution in the practice of the world" and history's "most triumphant epoch." And so it was.

THE GREAT CHARTER, FORGED IN CONFLICT

Our story begins with a flashback to feudal England, at the start of the thirteenth century. Freedom meant something different back then; it mostly meant the freedom of a country's rulers to run their affairs and rule their land free from the intrusion or domination of an alien king. For virtually everyone else, freedom was as unthinkable as space travel. You survived as best you could, under circumstances dictated and determined by those with power. You had no say in who held power, and certainly no capacity to limit it.

But the king's power, while great, was not absolute. He shared it to some extent with the church and with landowning barons, who helped maintain his power through a pledge of allegiance. In return, the barons were allowed some discretion to run their affairs and exercise jurisdiction and dominion over the people who lived and worked on their land. But even this arrangement was maintained by practical considerations of power, not by laws or formal rules. If push came to shove, the king's power was limited only by the might he could summon to enforce it. Ordinary people had no part in this equation.

In 1199, Richard the Lion-Hearted died and his brother John succeeded him as king of England. Almost immediately, John got into a dispute with Pope Innocent III over who should be the archbishop of Canterbury. Although by this time the church was relatively independent of the state, John looked back to the time when the church was subservient to the king, and bishops were regarded as civil servants. When the pope defied the king and installed his own choice for archbishop of Canterbury, John responded by confiscating church property. This led to conflict with France, whose king was allied with the pope. To support the mounting costs of this conflict, John taxed the barons heavily. He also confiscated baronial estates, limited the right of landowners to bequeath property to their children, and deprived the barons of their power to hold court for their tenants. The king's officials often just took food, farm animals, wood, and equipment without payment; and when John appropriated the food reserves of the monasteries, he virtually destroyed the major means of providing relief for the poor at that time. The emerging merchant class was also heavily burdened by taxes and got little but oppression in return.

The conflict with Rome ended when John suddenly gave in to the pope and accepted his choice for archbishop, but by then he had made too many enemies, who were increasingly consolidated against him. In June of 1215, the barons united to demand that the king concede specific rights to them in writing. When John refused, they renounced their allegiance to him, thus threatening his regime. Once again he backed down, and on the banks of the Thames River, at a place called Runnymede, he accepted the barons' demands—sixty-one articles establishing their rights in writing. The document came to be known as the Magna Carta—Latin for "Great Charter."

In the centuries that followed, the Magna Carta would come to be seen as a landmark of liberty, but anyone reading it today might wonder why that should be so. The document contains no sweeping language, no idealistic rhetoric, no evidence of broad, lofty principles. Nor does it guarantee rights to ordinary people. Instead, the charter mostly defines the feudal rights of the barons, narrowly and concretely addressing highly specific grievances, like a contract between labor and management.

But there was more to the Magna Carta than meets the eye.

First, it secured rights by placing written legal limits on the king's powers. This was the first time anything like this had happened. No new limits on kingly power were created; rather, the limits that had always existed in feudal society by *custom* now were established for the first time by *law*. Whereas earlier the rules could be changed at will by the king, the Magna Carta represented the rule of law, which even the king could not in principle violate.

Second, a committee of twenty-five barons was selected to enforce the new charter. This act recognized that a legal document, no matter how grand in principle, was not self-enforcing, and it institutionalized a formal partition of governing power between the king and the barons that some have seen as the embryonic beginning of the British Parliament.

Third, although most of the sixty-one articles involve narrow operational details of the feudal system, a few touch upon farther-reaching rights.

Article 39, for example, says:

No freeman shall be taken, imprisoned, outlawed, exiled, or in any way harmed, nor will we [i.e., King John] *proceed against or prosecute him, except by the lawful judgment of his peers and by the law of the land.*

Article 39 was clearly the ancient ancestor of what today is known as "due process of law," the idea that no one should be punished by the government except under fair procedures guaranteed by law. There is a direct link between this language and the language of the Bill of Rights as it was drafted nearly six hundred years later.

Similarly, Article 40 promised that

To no one will we sell, to no one will we deny or delay, right or justice.

Other articles curtailed the power of royal officials to seize property belonging to the barons without compensation, limited the extent and severity of fines, guaranteed the free flow of travel and commerce, and even dealt with the relationship between church and state.

The Magna Carta is important, though, largely because it came to mean much more than it was originally intended to mean. The barons' interests were basically selfish. They were not acting as advocates for the ordinary people who toiled and lived on their land. They governed those people, exercised power over them, and were not interested in limiting their own power. But they *were* interested in limiting the king's power, in order to establish their own rights.

However, the barons could not keep the principles established in the Magna Carta from expanding to include others. In part this was due to the language of the document itself: it begins by declaring that all the rights that follow apply to "all the free men of our kingdom." This general language would later be invoked by other people not originally protected by the Magna Carta as a legal basis for establishing their own rights.

Just as the American Declaration of Independence in 1776 proclaimed that "all men are created equal" when it meant only white men of property, so the Magna Carta proclaimed that its rights protected "all the free men of our kingdom" when it meant only the barons. And just as that lofty phrase in our Declaration was later invoked by African slaves and their descendants, by women, and by other groups seeking to establish their own rights, so the Magna Carta's language came to be invoked by those who followed the barons' example.

As the story of liberty unfolds, we see that new rights initially established by one group of people struggling for their own narrow self-interest later evolve into broad protections for us all. The outcomes of struggles that seem to have nothing to do with the rights of ordinary people in fact end up affecting them deeply.

YOU SHALL HAVE THE BODY—AND A BILL OF RIGHTS

In the centuries that followed, the Magna Carta was reaffirmed and became an indissoluble part of English law. In 1297, it was actually incorporated into the official statute books, and in 1368, King Edward III proclaimed that copies of the charter should be available throughout the kingdom, and that no other statutes could be passed that contradicted the rights set forth in the Magna Carta. This was also a key development, for it established the Magna Carta as a law above all other laws, an early and very rudimentary example of the idea of a constitution.

By the seventeenth century, England had its Parliament, consisting of a House of Lords and a House of Commons, formally sharing governmental power with the king, in ways that the barons could scarcely have imagined back in 1215. But sharing power always invites disputes, and the seventeenth century was punctuated by power struggles between the king and Parliament. In 1626, for example, King Charles I decided to force "loans" from his subjects to pay for his military and other adventures. Ordinary people who had no money to give were forced to let soldiers live in their homes, while the knights of the realm — the descendants of the landed barons of 1215 — were required to contribute money. When some refused, claiming that the king had no legal authority to tax them without the consent of Parliament, they were imprisoned.

The knights tried to challenge the legal basis for their imprisonment in court by seeking something called a writ of habeas corpus. *Habeas corpus* is a Latin phrase that means literally "You shall have the body"; a *writ* is simply a court order. Initially developed during the late sixteenth century, the writ of habeas corpus was a court order commanding the jailer to produce the prisoner in court, so that the court could determine whether his imprisonment was legal.

The right to habeas corpus was fundamental, because it provided a means of enforcing virtually all other rights. The Magna Carta provided that no one should be imprisoned except according to law and that the king could not imprison anyone at will. But what was to be done if the king violated that provision and illegally imprisoned someone anyway? The writ of habeas corpus was an early attempt to invent a *procedural* mechanism for enforcing *substantive* rights. It was designed to force the king's representatives to produce the prisoner and answer in court to the charge that the imprisonment was illegal. The right to habeas corpus, of course, assumed that even the order of a king was not a sufficient basis to justify imprisonment. It therefore assumed the rule of law above that of the king, and was a critical development in establishing that individual rights required enforceable legal limits on kingly power. The writ of habeas corpus also presumed that the judicial review would be by a court that was to some extent independent of the king, for if the court were simply a rubber stamp for the king's action, then no meaningful legal check upon his power would be possible.

But when the imprisoned knights invoked their right to habeas corpus, the legal basis for their imprisonment was reviewed by the Court of King's Bench, which proved to be far from independent of the king. It ruled, in *Darnel's Case* in 1627, that no specific legal basis for the imprisonment was necessary because the prisoners were being held by "special command" of the king. In other words, the king's will was held to trump the law. This caused a storm of protest, for it meant that the king had the inherent authority to override the rule of law whenever he saw fit. In effect, this nullified all rights, because it allowed the king to exceed the legal limits on his power whenever he thought it important to do so.

Echoes of this kind of dispute would be heard again and again through the centuries; in 1973, for example, more than 350 years later, and a continent away, the United States Congress and the Supreme Court would be wracked by controversy over Richard Nixon's claim of inherent presidential authority to exceed constitutional limits upon his power. In 1974, in the case of *United States v. Nixon*, the United States Supreme Court reaffirmed the principle that not even the highest government official was beyond the reach of the law. Nixon had argued that, though the president was not a king because "a king rules by inheritance and for life," nonetheless the president was, during his term of office, like a king in that he was immune from certain court orders. The Supreme Court rejected that argument.

In 1627, the Court of King's Bench was neither so bold nor so independent, and it held that the king was immune from the enforcement of the law's limits upon his power to imprison his subjects. Faced with that ruling, Parliament rebelled. Resolutions were passed opposing arbitrary taxation and imprisonments, but rhetoric was not enough. In 1628, a new law was passed, the Petition of Right. Like the Magna Carta four centuries earlier, the Petition of Right sought to protect individual rights by placing strict legal limits upon the king's power. During the parliamentary debates over the new law, when the argument was made that the king should be allowed "for reasons of state" to override the right of habeas corpus, Sir Edward Coke invoked the Magna Carta and argued that not even the king was sovereign over that legal document. The Petition of Right thus greatly reinforced the general idea, first established in 1215, that the rule of law was supreme over the will of all men, including kings, and that individual rights could be secured only through written, enforceable legal limits upon governmental power.

The Petition of Right did even more. In addition to strengthening the right of habeas corpus, it specifically prohibited the king from imprisoning any freeman except according to law; it limited the use of martial law, which suspended certain legal protections, against civilians; and it prohibited compulsory loans or taxes imposed by the king "without common consent by act of Parliament." This was an early formulation of the principle of "no taxation without representation," which would be invoked resoundingly a century and a half later by the American colonists to protest the Stamp Act. The Petition of Right also outlawed the hated practice of quartering soldiers and sailors in people's homes—a provision that would also be echoed in the American Bill of Rights.

Beyond its specific provisions, though, the Petition of Right demonstrated again that the great rights that protect us all often begin with self-interest. The five knights who challenged the king's power, and risked their own imprisonment, were not inspired by broad, universal principles of liberty. Their interests, like the interests of the barons at Runnymede four centuries earlier, were narrower and more selfish. The rights established and developed by the Petition of Right in 1628 were fought for by people who wanted to advance their own interests. But the rights they won eventually protected a broader class of people and set of interests than their own.

The Petition of Right also demonstrated that rights would not be won without struggle. Rights are established by constructing limits on power, and no one has ever relinquished power without a fight. The barons' willingness in the early thirteenth century to struggle, to risk defeat and even death, in order to establish rights for themselves was a crucial factor in the creation of the Magna Carta. Similarly, the knights' willingness to confront the king, go to prison, and invoke the right of habeas corpus, as well as the willingness of the House of Commons to respond to the court's decision upholding the king's power by passing corrective legislation, were crucial factors in establishing the Petition of Right.

Finally, the events that led up to the Petition of Right showed that in order to retain rights, you have to fight for them over and over again. No new rights were established by the petition; on the contrary, for the most part it reinforced rights long since established by the Magna Carta. Until the King's Bench rejected the knights' writ of habeas corpus, they had thought themselves secure in that right. But rights once won stay won only until someone in power decides to ignore them; at that moment, they must be won again. The story of liberty is punctuated by struggles to win again rights that had been won before, to enforce, codify, or strengthen limits on power that had not proved sufficient to withstand the aggressions of government.

Although the Petition of Right did reestablish the right to habeas corpus *in principle,* officers of the crown proved very inventive in continuing to find ways around it. As a result, Parliament passed the Habeas Corpus Act of 1679, which attempted to close every imaginable loophole.

The act showed the importance of having a practical *remedy* when a right is violated. It taught us that a right without a means of enforcing it is no right at all—another lesson we would repeatedly relearn in the centuries to follow. And it showed the aggressive, voracious persistence with which government power seeks to avoid the legal limits that secure our rights. The Habeas Corpus Act of 1679 was passed a century after the right to habeas corpus had first been established in principle—but principle alone had not been enough.*

*More than three centuries later, principle again has proved insufficient. Although the right to federal habeas corpus still exists in the United States on paper, it has been severely crippled by two recent Supreme Court decisions. One erected almost insurmountable barriers to filing more than one habeas petition. The other—much more restrictive—bars people in state prisons from seeking to test the legality of their conviction in federal court even if through a lawyer's mistake their constitutional arguments were never presented in a state court. Thus, as a practical matter, access to the federal courts has been denied and the availabilty of the right to habeas corpus as a remedy for the violation of rights has been much reduced.

One might imagine that the Habeas Corpus Act of 1679 would have ended the struggle between rights and kingly power once and for all, but it did not. Charles II and James II continually sought to expand their powers beyond established limits. They tried to suspend laws and expand the king's power at the expense of Parliament's. Finally, their aggressions led to revolution — the Glorious Revolution of 1688–89 — and the enactment of the English Bill of Rights in 1689. This was the first time that "bill of rights" was used as a term of law, and the phrase would be invoked a century later in the United States.

The English Bill of Rights capped nearly five hundred years of struggle to establish rights by limiting the king's power through law. With one exception, it established no new rights, but rather codified and consolidated centuries of developing law.

Above all, the English Bill of Rights established a clear partition of power between the king and Parliament, a partition that had begun on that June day in 1215 at Runnymede. It bridled kingly power and in critical ways made the king subservient to Parliament. But neither the English Bill of Rights nor any prior law restrained Parliament itself. On the contrary, the English Bill of Rights established Parliament's supremacy. Legal limits were imposed upon the king's power, but not upon Parliament's.

After 1689, no king could legally violate the rights established in the Bill of Rights. But nothing prevented Parliament from repealing it. Because of the particular way rights developed in England, only the king's power was seen as dangerous; no one thought it necessary to restrain Parliament. To this day, British rights depend upon Parliament's willingness to maintain them. It would remain for the English settlers in America to take the development of rights that last crucial step, to establish a written constitution, a law above all other laws, that would restrain *all* branches of government, that would en-sure rights by constructing enforceable legal limits not only on the executive branch but also on the legislative branch. That achievement would turn out to be America's unique contribution to the story of liberty.

TAXES AND LIBERTY IN THE NEW WORLD

The story turns now to the shores of the New World. While the struggles to define liberty were taking place in England, English settlers were colonizing America and taking root there in ever-increasing numbers. These settlers did not see themselves as citizens of a new country; rather they saw themselves as English citizens, entitled to all their rights under English law. Steeped in the heritage of the Magna Carta, they also knew of the current struggles in England to enforce rights under law.

So when they were dissatisfied with their treatment by the king's colonial magistrates, they naturally complained as English citizens and demanded

English rights. And at first, they got what they demanded. In 1646, in the colony of Massachusetts, the king's magistrates declared that the fundamental laws of Massachusetts reflected and secured the rights guaranteed by the Magna Carta. The Magna Carta also became the model for other colonial laws, such as Pennsylvania's, and in 1687 William Penn was the first to print the Magna Carta in America.

The English idea of rights guaranteed by written and enforceable legal limits upon the king's governors in colonial America was in the air everywhere, and it was infectious. It was invoked to advance the colonists' causes and prosecute their grievances in hundreds, even thousands, of instances.

And because there was no parliament in colonial America, the settlers dealt directly and exclusively with the king's agents. No legislature intervened. As English citizens, the settlers initially saw rights as legal limits upon the *king*, but as Americans, they came to see their rights more broadly as legal limits upon the *government*, because the king's agents were the only English government there. Increasingly, the colonists saw themselves at the mercy of that government, and of what they perceived as grasping, arbitrary power, unrestrained by law, unrestrained by rights. Thus, the administrative machinery of government—what today we might call the executive branch—was perceived as the enemy of liberty, a dangerous power that needed to be legally limited if rights were to survive. It was no longer just the king that required constraint.

At the same time, the power of the English Parliament itself was a threat to the colonies. Parliament was remote, an ocean away at a time when travel was slow and communication glacial. Acts of Parliament repeatedly angered the colonists. They made their grievances known, and Parliament reacted repressively. Hitherto, Parliament had been the defender of rights, the hero of the long effort to bridle the king's power; now in America it was Parliament's power that grew too great. Therefore, to ensure rights, it would be necessary to place legal limits upon Parliament's power as well as the king's.

This new idea was a fusion of the traditional English view, of rights guaranteed by written legal limits upon royal power, with the new American view that *all* government power—whether the king's, his agents', or Parliament's—had to be legally restrained if liberty were to survive. This idea did not develop overnight. It simmered through most of the eighteenth century before boiling over into revolution in 1776.

Most historians believe that the crucial event during this period was the Stamp Act. Passed by Parliament in 1765, it imposed taxes on the American colonists, requiring them to pay a small fraction of the cost of their defense by the British army. Every legal and business document was taxed, from college diplomas to liquor licenses; ordinary items like playing cards; and all manner of printed newspapers, advertisements, books, and pamphlets.

The colonists deeply resented those taxes. Even more than the taxes themselves, they resented the fact that the taxes had been imposed by a far-off legislature, where they were not represented. Just as the knights had resisted the taxes imposed on them by Charles I in 1626, so now the colonists resisted the taxes imposed by Parliament. The knights had insisted that the king should not be able to levy taxes without the consent of Parliament. The colonists took it a step further: they insisted that not even Parliament should be able to levy taxes on them, because they were not represented there. The focus shifted from limiting the power of the king to limiting the power of the legislature.

To the colonists, the Stamp Act represented something more nefarious than taxes: a precedent for unlimited legislative power over the colonies. The revenues levied by the Stamp Act were not very large, and for that reason might have been easily paid; but paying them would have created a precedent for further and more serious incursions upon the colonists' rights.

In what the historian Bernard Bailyn has called "the most influential pamphlet published in America before 1776," John Dickinson warned:

Nothing is wanted at home but a precedent, *the force of which shall be established by the tacit submission of the colonies.… If the Parliament succeeds in this attempt, other statutes will impose other duties … and thus the Parliament will levy upon us such sums of money as they choose to take,* without any other limitation than their pleasure.

The Stamp Act was repealed within a few months, but Parliament then passed a new law confirming its authority to make any laws it wished for the American colonies, and asserting its legislative supremacy over them—precisely what Dickinson had feared. This further infuriated the colonists, who continued to argue that under English law only colonial legislatures—where they were represented—had legitimate authority to impose taxes on them.

The flames of resentment were fanned still more by the Stamp Act's imposition of taxes on newspapers, books, and pamphlets. John Adams, later to become the second president of the United States, was particularly concerned about this. He thought that "by loading the press, the colleges, and even an almanac and a newspaper with restraints and duties," the Stamp Act was stripping the colonists of their means of acquiring knowledge, and paving the way for despotism. Nearly two centuries later, echoes of John Adams's concern would be heard in a decision of the United States Supreme Court, which in 1936 struck down as unconstitutional a Louisiana tax of two percent of gross receipts on all newspapers with circulations exceeding twenty thousand copies weekly. (It was probably no coincidence that twelve of the thirteen newspapers affected had been critical of Governor Huey Long.) The Court cited English history, found the tax to be an illegal burden on freedom of the press, and called it a "tax on knowledge."

SEARCHES AND SEIZURES

The Stamp Act controversy was no academic matter in 1765. It deeply affected the lives of the colonists, and more critically, nourished their mistrust of governmental power. Mistrust was deepened by the means used to enforce the act, such as the infamous writ of assistance, which authorized customs inspectors to enter people's homes at will, even if they had no evidence of a violation, and ransack their belongings looking for contraband. These writs were authorized, not by the king, but by Parliament, and they convinced the early Americans that the right to privacy required strict legal limits on legislative, as well as executive, power.

These colonial searches, common and widespread for decades before the Revolution, had been widely condemned and resisted. Samuel Adams called them "the most pernicious attack on English liberty ever attempted." In 1761, a Boston lawyer named James Otis argued on behalf of Boston's citizens that the writs of assistance violated English legal traditions, and that no search should be authorized unless the government could show specific reasons for suspecting a particular individual. Otis lost his case, but he inspired his audience—which included the young John Adams. Nearly six decades later, looking back upon the events that led to the American Revolution and the birth of the United States, Adams would describe that day in court in dramatic terms: "Otis was a flame of Fire!… Then and there was the first scene of the First Act of Opposition to the arbitrary claims of Great Britain. Then and there the child Independence was born."

A year after Otis's unsuccessful attempt in court, the colonial legislature in Massachusetts passed a law requiring all writs to cite specific reasons before a search could be authorized. The royal governor vetoed the bill as inconsistent with Parliament's law. In 1766, a Boston merchant barricaded his home and refused entry to customs officers. Incidents like this increased, and colonial resentment against unchecked power grew.

The Fourth Amendment to our Constitution, requiring search warrants based on specific evidence, was a direct outgrowth of that resentment. The reasons for the amendment may seem abstract and remote to most Americans today, but to the early Americans, intrusive general searches were a matter of frequent and bitter experience.

Their fears about power running amok were reinforced when the Stamp Act gave jurisdiction to prosecute violations to the admiralty courts, which operated without juries and used inquisitorial methods that ignored a number of fundamental procedural rights. This outraged the early Americans because, as English citizens, they believed themselves entitled to the right to trial by jury when charged with a crime. If violations of the Stamp Act were to be tried in the admiralty courts, then the fundamental right to trial by jury would be denied.

There had been other attacks upon the colonial judiciary. In 1701, Parliament had passed a law giving judges life tenure in order to ensure their independence from the king—a direct, remedial response to the rubber-stamp courts of the seventeenth century. By the early eighteenth century, it was therefore generally recognized that an independent judiciary was crucial if legal limits were to be enforced, and rights upheld.

But in the colonies, life tenure had not been granted, partly because there were not enough properly trained lawyers there. In the 1760s, as the colonists began to feel increasingly threatened by unchecked government power, they sought refuge in the courts. Several colonial legislatures passed laws giving colonial judges the same life tenure as English judges. All these laws were disallowed by England. The issue inflamed the colonists, who well understood, from English history as well as from their own experience, why judicial independence was crucial.

Thus, taxes were being levied without representation; the press was being restrained; customs agents were entering people's homes at will; trial by jury for those resisting these depredations had been denied; and judges were being put under the king's thumb. What was going on?

What was going on, many colonists came to believe, was a systematic effort by the English government to enslave the colonies by denying them fundamental rights to which all English citizens were entitled. Like the seventeenth-century knights, imprisoned when they resisted the king's taxes, the colonists felt unfairly threatened with illegal court procedures and a systematic loss of basic legal rights if they resisted Parliament's taxes.

Again, however, the crucial difference was that in 1626, the knights in England saw Parliament as their defense against the king's excesses, while the colonists were confronted by Parliament's excesses. Parliament imposed the taxes; Parliament authorized general searches; and Parliament stripped them of their right to trial by jury. The knights had been able to turn to Parliament for help in restraining the king. To whom could the colonists turn for help in restraining Parliament? Increasingly, they began to believe that they could turn only to themselves.

Finally, discontent among the early Americans was also nourished by their resentment of the English government's colonial administrators, who were seen as petty, avaricious, and greedy. These officials were the government in colonial America, the only government the colonists knew. As Benjamin Franklin wrote, these officials were "generally strangers to the provinces they are sent to govern; have no ... relation there to give them an affection for the country;... come only to make money as fast as they can; are sometimes men of vicious characters and broken fortunes, sent by a minister [in England] merely to get them out of the way." The colonists came to regard them as an occupying force of plunderers, and it did not help their reputation that they were the ones empowered by Parliament to enforce the new taxes. Nor did it help that these were the people who used the writs of assistance to enter people's homes. Contempt developed into rage; at a Boston town meeting in 1772, this rage was pungently expressed:

Thus our houses and even our bedchambers are exposed to be ransacked, our boxes and trunks broken open, ravaged, and plundered by wretches whom no prudent man would venture to employ even as menial servants.

The early Americans view of power, and of its tendency to expand and consume the legal limits that protected liberty, was obviously influenced not only by the legislative acts of Parliament, but also by the character and behavior of the colonial officials who enforced the law, often in petty and excessively authoritarian ways.

POWER VERSUS LIBERTY

Traditional English history fused with the colonial experience to produce a new amalgam: a uniquely American view of power and liberty as natural antagonists. The early Americans came to understand, as no people quite had before, why liberty and individual rights required strict and enforceable legal limits on *all* government power—not only on the king, but on the legislature that made the laws and the executive branch that enforced them. But more than that, these Americans came to understand the devouring nature of power, how much stronger it was than the law that restrained it, and how it tended always to overreach. Containing power and protecting liberty from it thus became their most important task.

The early Americans did indeed invent a new form of government. But they did more than that: they declared a new purpose for government. That new purpose was the protection of individual rights. No government had ever before been created primarily for this purpose. Before 1787, the role of government was assumed to be "the enforcement of community consensus aimed at making citizens virtuous and moral." But the early Americans changed all that and fundamentally redefined the legal relationship between the individual and the community. For them, government's primary objective was to promote individual rights.

They were not endorsing anarchy, nor abandoning public virtue. Government was still expected to protect the safety of the community against threats foreign or domestic, to ensure economic growth, and to conduct foreign affairs. However, it was not expected to tell individuals how best to live in accordance with a state-approved political or religious truth. On the contrary, the early Americans meant to protect the rights of individuals to choose their lives by legally preventing the government from interfering. As John Stuart Mill would put it more than a half-century later: "Over himself, over his own body and mind, the individual is *sovereign*." Once, "sovereignty" was a term used only to describe the unlimited power of the king; later, it described the power of nations. In America, it came to describe the rights of individuals to decide for themselves how they should live and what they should think, how they should believe and what they should say. "To secure those rights," wrote Thomas Jefferson in the Declaration of Independence, "governments are instituted among men."

Individual rights may thus fairly be called the oldest, most traditional American values. All who wish to return to "traditional American values" must begin and end their journey in the realm of liberty.

SECURING INDIVIDUAL RIGHTS

But if the primary purpose of government was to secure individual rights, how exactly was this to be done?

First, it would be done by law. Centuries of English history, reinforced by their own recent experience, had taught the new Americans that liberty required subjecting government to the rule of law. Second, if the rule of law were to be the instrument by which rights were secured, some protection would be needed against the legislature itself. For if the legislature were supreme, it could repeal laws designed to protect rights, and pass new laws that violated those rights. To the early Americans, this threat was not speculative. They had seen it happen, repeatedly, over the decades.

Out of this experience grew a new idea, a radical idea — that some "higher" law was needed to limit the ordinary laws the legislature would be permitted to pass. What was needed was a set of fixed principles that codified individual rights and established legal superiority for liberty that no arm of government, including the legislature, could infringe: a constitution.

Though an old term, "constitution" needed a new definition. Traditionally, it had been used to describe the entire body of laws, customs, and government institutions that made up the political system — all its constituents. Parliament was part of this political system, and thus of the constitution, but in no way was it *subject* to the constitution or *controlled* by it. On the contrary, *all* laws were made by Parliament, and there was no such thing as a "higher" law.

The American idea of a constitution explored uncharted territory, cautiously at first and then more boldly. Not only did the American Constitution construct a higher set of laws limiting the legislature as well as the executive, it also reversed the notion of government itself. Where once a constitution derived its authority from the legislature, in America the legislature—indeed, all branches of government—would derive their authority from the Constitution. It would become the fundamental founding document, the ultimate authority, the highest law. It would set the limits of governmental power, thereby securing rights for all.

In this view, rights would be *recognized* and guaranteed by the Constitution, but not *granted,* because government was without legitimate power to grant or deny rights. People were born with rights, and the primary function of government was to secure them. This would be done by a written constitution that guaranteed such rights through legally enforceable limits on government power. By the time of the Revolution, this idea was widely accepted, and it heavily influenced the victorious colonists when, after the war, they came together to form a new government.

At first, the individual states refused to cede much power to a national government. Indeed, they had just fought a war against a highly centralized, remote government, and they were leery about having another one. Why give a national congress the power to tax when they had just fought to deny that power to Parliament? Why give a national congress the power to make laws affecting liberty, when they had only recently suffered so much because Parliament had that power? While it sounded good to talk about *limiting* the power of a national legislature, it would be better still if the national legislature had no power at all in certain areas. Thus Congress was denied the power to tax or regulate commerce, and each individual state remained largely sovereign over matters of personal liberty. Colonial legislatures had often clashed with Parliament and with English officials, so the protection of liberty was naturally identified with local autonomy.

As it turned out, many state governments would prove to be no friends of liberty; local power could be as voracious and aggressive in resisting legal limits and swallowing up rights as any other government power. But in the first flush of victory over England, it didn't seem that way. Although there was some dissent, those who sought to maintain state sovereignty against national sovereignty won out.

The Articles of Confederation, finally ratified in January 1781, created the first United States government. It had no power over individual rights; indeed, it had no power over much of anything, and that is why it finally didn't work. Under the Articles of Confederation, the United States as a collective entity was incapable of responding to a wide variety of serious problems. No lawmaking power was given to Congress; although it could pass resolutions and make recommendations, it had no way of making the states comply. Congress couldn't regulate commerce; it couldn't enforce treaties; it couldn't even ensure domestic peace. Gradually a consensus developed that the national government was dangerously incapable of governing and that Congress was "contemptibly weak." Some thought that this national impotence would, if left unremedied, lead to foreign domination, perhaps even to the British taking back the new republic.

The consensus led to a proposal to convene the states to revise the Articles of Confederation in order to strengthen Congress. On May 25, 1787, the Constitutional Convention convened in Philadelphia, where it met, in secret, for four months. What emerged the following September was—with one major exception—the constitutional system under which we live today. That exception was the Bill of Rights.

The decision to omit a bill of rights from the proposed new Constitution was a nearly fatal blunder, and came close to causing the new Constitution to be rejected. But the decision was understandable.

There had been no bill of rights in the Articles of Confederation. None was needed, because Congress had no power over individuals at all. The protection of liberty was therefore seen as a matter for state governments, and although enforcement of rights was often erratic, the idea of rights codified by legal limits was reflected to some extent in every state. And that was where most people believed the legal protection for liberty belonged.

For those reasons, no one thought about the problem of rights when the Constitutional Convention began in May of 1787. On the contrary, the delegates focused not on limiting the power of the national government, but on expanding it. That had been the reason for calling the convention in the first place.

Almost immediately, the convention decided to scrap the Articles of Confederation instead of amending them. Within days, they agreed on the basic structure of the new national government. There would be three branches: legislative, executive, and judicial. The radical change they proposed was that the national legislature would be superior to the states and have direct power over individuals.

This change eventually led some delegates to advocate a *national* bill of rights. As long as the national government had had no authority over individuals and no supremacy over the states, individual rights had required no protection from Congress. But under this proposed scheme, the protection of state constitutions suddenly seemed less adequate. What would happen if this newly empowered Congress one day acted as the British Parliament had? What would protect liberty then? The colonial legislatures had proved incapable of resisting Parliament; why would state legislatures be able to resist a powerful national Congress?

The framers of the Constitution during that summer of 1787 were not entirely insensitive to individual rights. The ancient right to habeas corpus was included within the body of the proposed constitution. So was the right to trial by jury in criminal cases. Similarly, both Congress and state legislatures were forbidden to issue bills of attainder—legislative acts that punished particular individuals without a judicial trial. And *ex post facto* laws—laws that punish acts that were not a crime at the time they were committed—were also banned, from either Congress or the states. Finally, the proposed constitution banned religious tests for public office. But that was all. No other guarantees of individual rights were included—no right to freedom of religion or freedom of speech or freedom of the press, and perhaps most surprisingly, no right of privacy against general searches.

Instead, liberty was protected by fragmenting national power among the three proposed branches of government. Sensitive to the fact that concentrations of national power were dangerous to the preservation of individual rights, the delegates partitioned power elaborately among the branches of government in order to prevent any branch, or any faction, from becoming too powerful. But no *substantive* limits on power were included. Nothing was said about what the *content* of rights should be. All this was left to the states.

In Philadelphia, the belief that state constitutions were sufficient to protect individual rights prevailed until the very end of the Constitutional Convention. And no great public concern over the lack of federal protection for personal rights had been expressed, because the convention was being held in closed sessions and the public had no reason to know that vast new federal powers would be created. But toward the end of the process, alarm bells began to ring. Because the new constitution proposed to give Congress legislative supremacy over the states as well as direct authority over individuals, the omission of a national bill of rights began to make several delegates uneasy.

On September 12, 1787—nearly four months after the convention had begun and only a few days before its work was completed—George Mason of Virginia rose and expressed a desire for the addition of a bill of rights. "It would give great quiet to the people," he said, and it could probably be written in "a few hours" by using the various state constitutions as models. Elbridge Gerry of Massachusetts then moved to form a committee to draft a bill of rights. Mason seconded the motion. But the delegates, voting by state, rejected Gerry's motion by a 10–0 vote, and the committee was never established.

Mason did not give up. He and others tried during the last few days to introduce a number of specific rights piecemeal. They were all unsuccessful. Even a motion to establish freedom of the press was defeated, not because anyone was against freedom of the press, but because, as Roger Sherman of

Connecticut put it, "It is unnecessary. The power of Congress does not extend to the press." This view was to be heard repeatedly over the next two years while the country debated whether to accept or reject the proposed Constitution.

On September 17, 1787, the convention voted to approve the Constitution and to submit it to the states for ratification. Three-quarters of the states had to approve the proposed Constitution before it would become the supreme law of the land. The stage was set for the struggle that would give birth to the Bill of Rights.

BATTLING FOR RATIFICATION

The opponents of ratification—who came to be called Anti-Federalists—were against the proposed Constitution for many reasons. For one, they feared that the new national government would overwhelm the states and exercise such control of commerce as to ruin the economic well-being of the states, not to mention their political independence. Many Anti-Federalists were more devoted to *states'* rights than to *individual* rights. But many Anti-Federalists also genuinely believed that the lack of a bill of rights was a serious defect. Despite his lateness in raising the issue, for example, George Mason's principled belief in a bill of rights could not be doubted; after all, he was no newcomer to the issue, having written the universally acclaimed Virginia Declaration of Rights in 1776. The Anti-Federalist campaign to defeat the new Constitution was thus based both on the lack of a bill of rights and on a desire to reserve more sovereign power to the states.

The failure to include a bill of rights was the issue that excited and alarmed ordinary people, however, and the Anti-Federalists quickly made it the centerpiece of their campaign to reject the proposed Constitution. They were joined by many Protestant churches, particularly the Presbyterians and the Baptists, who feared that without clear constitutional safeguards for religious liberty, state governments might establish other churches and tax nonbelievers to provide financial support.

Those who supported the new Constitution—who came to be known as Federalists—had badly miscalculated public opinion and found themselves on the defensive as soon as the convention's results became public. Then they compounded their error by refusing to admit to it. Perhaps because they were tired, perhaps because they had become too involved in their own work, or perhaps because there was too much at stake to risk reconvening the state delegates, the Federalists began to argue strenuously that a bill of rights was not only unnecessary, but dangerous.

In a blizzard of pamphlets and newspaper articles, the Federalists sought to calm the public's fears. As early as October 6, 1787, James Wilson pointed out that it was not necessary to secure rights by limiting powers that Congress didn't have anyway. He argued Congress would have *no* powers other than those explicitly granted to it by the Constitution. Why worry about the power of Congress to abridge freedom of the press, for example, when the Constitution grants no specific power over the press to Congress?

Others were not so sure. Responding to Wilson, Judge Samuel Bryan of Philadelphia pointed out that no specific grant of power to regulate the press was necessary. The new Constitution contained a virtually limitless grant of legislative power in a clause that allowed Congress "to make all laws that shall be necessary and proper." And Article 6 of the proposed Constitution granted legislative supremacy to all congressional acts. Under such sweeping general powers, Judge Bryan argued, Congress could without doubt restrain and suppress the press to its heart's content. All other personal rights not specifically guaranteed could likewise be lost. After all, had not the colonists recently experienced the folly of trusting Parliament?

The transfer of power to a strong central government might well be necessary for the survival of the nation, wrote Bryan, but it made a bill of rights equally necessary if liberty were to survive. "For universal experience," he continued, "demonstrates the necessity of the most express declarations and restrictions, to protect the rights and liberties of mankind, from the silent, powerful, and ever-active conspiracy of those who govern."

This sort of argument resonated in the hearts and minds of the early Americans because it fit so closely with their experience and because their sense of betrayal by the English government they had trusted was still so fresh. The more the Federalists tried to argue against the necessity of a bill of rights, the more public opinion shifted against them.

Edmund Randolph of Virginia argued that a bill of rights was not needed in America because the purpose of a bill of rights was to limit the power of the king. "Our situation is radically different from that of the people of England," he said. But this argument fell on deaf ears because it was widely believed in prerevolutionary America that the function of a constitution was to limit *all* government power. The early Americans had suffered too much at the hands of Parliament—indeed, they had fought a revolution largely to reclaim the individual rights that Parliament had stripped away—to believe Randolph. Anger grew, and the prospects for ratification became dimmer.

The Federalists would not give in. Alexander Hamilton, arguing for approval of the Constitution without a bill of rights, actually claimed that the Constitution as written "is itself, in every rational sense, and to every useful purpose, a bill of rights." What he meant was that provisions guaranteeing the right to elect public officials, the right to be represented in Congress, the partition of power among the three branches, and other such mechanisms were adequate to protect liberty.

But none of these mechanisms protected *substantive rights* such as liberty of conscience or freedom of speech or the right to be free from general searches. To this, Hamilton replied that no list of specific rights could possibly be complete, and that listing some would imply no protection for others. The day would come, Hamilton warned, when someone opposed to a particular personal right would point to its absence from the list and argue that therefore it was not constitutionally protected. (During the hearings on his nomination to the Supreme Court two hundred years later, Robert Bork would make precisely that argument, placing himself not only far outside contemporary legal thought but in stark opposition to the dominant view of the early Americans.) This argument was easily rebutted because no one believed that having no legal protections for individual rights was better than having some. Besides, the proposed Constitution already protected some rights, like habeas corpus and trial by jury in criminal cases. If Hamilton was right, he proved too much. If the inclusion of some rights implied no protection for others, then virtually all fundamental personal rights were now in jeopardy, and a bill of rights was even more necessary than had been imagined.

It is perhaps doubtful that Hamilton and the other Federalists wholly believed in their arguments. But they certainly believed that the future of the nation depended on approving the new Constitution, and they did not trust the motives of the Anti-Federalists, who after all wanted a second convention at least in part to weaken the powers of the national government and restore some measure of sovereignty to the states. This the Federalists were committed to resist.

In any case, Hamilton's arguments against having a bill of rights were decidedly unpopular with the majority of Americans at the time. These explanations, wrote Judge Bryan of Philadelphia, were "an insult on the understanding of the people." And so they were. For in those tumultuous days two centuries ago, a bill of rights was a very popular idea. Unlike Americans today, most of whom take their rights for granted, the early Americans had lived without a bill of rights, had suffered the abuses of power because of it, and were not about to do it again. Many Federalists began to believe that the Constitution would not be approved.

The Federalists seemed incapable of compromise. But support for a bill of rights continued to grow. From his diplomatic post in Paris, Thomas Jefferson wrote to James Madison in December 1787; he criticized the omission of a bill of rights and listed a number of rights, including freedom of the press and religion, that needed explicit constitutional protection. And he ended with a ringing rejection of the Federalists' arguments:

A bill of rights is what the people are entitled to against every government on earth, general or particular, and what no just government should refuse, or rest on inference.

Jefferson's view turned out to be much more in harmony with public sentiment. And as time went on, the Anti-Federalists continued to exploit that sentiment. A bill of rights, wrote James Winthrop of Massachusetts, "serves to secure the minority against the usurpations and tyranny of the majority." Power, he wrote, echoing the prevailing view of the early Americans, is inevitably used "wantonly." A bill of rights is therefore "as necessary to defend an individual against the majority in a republic as against a king in a monarchy."

But where was that bill of rights? Certainly not in the proposed Constitution, which if unamended would establish a power too dangerous to liberty to contemplate. In florid language, Luther Martin of Maryland called the "unamended" Constitution "certain death to your liberty, as arsenic could be to your bodies." In an equally vivid simile, Thomas Tredwell of New York likened government, even democratic government, to "a mad horse, which, notwithstanding all the curb you can put upon him, will sometimes run away with his rider." As a man should expect a broken neck if he rode such an unbridled horse, so the people should expect oppression if they did not insist upon legal limits to the power of this new government. To adopt the unamended Constitution, he warned, would be to destroy liberty.*

The tide began to run against the unamended Constitution. State after state ratified the Constitution, but many by very narrow votes and only by accompanying their ratification with recommended amendments for adding a bill of rights. Although these recommendations were not binding, it was understood as a political matter that a bill of rights would be added by the first Congress immediately after ratification. Each state's recommendations received wide publicity and added to the groundswell for a bill of rights. By mid-1788, eleven of the thirteen states had ratified the Constitution (North Carolina and Rhode Island would enter the Union later), thus assuring it of at least a trial run. But its success was far from certain. The Anti-Federalists continued to agitate for a second convention, and there was much mistrust concerning the promise to add a bill of rights. There is little doubt that the Constitution would not have been ratified without it. James Madison conceded as much.

*In a strange reprise of the eighteenth-century Federalist argument, President Ronald Reagan, in a 1984 article, celebrated "the unamended Constitution" as the major protection for liberty, and, without once mentioning the Bill of Rights, favorably quoted Hamilton's arguments, which had been so soundly rejected by popular opinion at the time the Constitution was adopted. During his eight years in office, President Reagan had been accused by some, including this writer, of showing hostility to the Bill of Rights and of engaging in a systematic attempt to undermine its protections; his apparent endorsement of the Federalists' discredited arguments against a bill of rights was at best curious, coming from someone claiming to conserve American traditions.

Today, Madison is justly remembered as the father of the Bill of Rights. But he was a Federalist who voted against the motion in Philadelphia to establish a committee to draft a bill of rights, and he argued against those who, after the proposed Constitution became public, believed the omission of a bill of rights fatal. And although he wrote Jefferson in Paris periodically, he never during the entire struggle over ratification answered Jefferson's letter calling for a bill of rights. What changed Madison?

Politics. He had come to realize that the omission of a bill of rights was a major strategic blunder that had endangered the Constitution itself. Even after ratification, he was afraid that the Anti-Federalists might be strong enough to succeed in convening a second convention, and thus undo the entire scheme. But most of all, he feared for his own political future.

Although he was one of the major political figures of his day, a prime architect of the Constitution, and a leading strategist of its ratification, Madison suffered a grievous political blow in his home state of Virginia when he was defeated in his attempt to become one of the state's first two United States senators. He was defeated, in fact, because he had defended the omission of a bill of rights. Two prominent Anti-Federalists, Richard Lee and William Grayson, were elected in his place. Now he was running for a seat in the new House of Representatives, and his election was in jeopardy because of the continued strength of public opinion in favor of a national bill of rights, and because of his reputation for having opposed it.

Madison knew he had to change his position, but his support for a national bill of rights still seemed lukewarm. In October 1788, shortly before his campaign for the House, Madison finally wrote to Jefferson in Paris and expressed his ambivalence. After all, he said, a bill of rights is a mere "parchment barrier." Implying that under a democratic government, legal rights would be unenforceable precisely when they were most needed, Madison wondered how useful a bill of rights would actually be.

The real danger to liberty in any society, Madison wrote, comes from the ultimate source of power. In America, the real power lies with the majority of the people. The invasion of individual rights, he claimed, was likely to come not from a legislature that was out of step with its constituents, but from a legislature acting as an "instrument" of popular majorities.

Madison had seen "overbearing majorities" in every state violate their own state bills of rights. In his home state of Virginia, he saw the Virginia Declaration of Rights "violated in every instance where it has been opposed to a popular current." A bill of rights might be useful in restraining the power of a king, but Madison didn't have much faith in its ability to restrain the tyranny of the majority in a democracy. Legislation will violate rights if popular sentiment wills it, Madison thought, and in such instances a bill of rights is not likely to be much of an obstacle.

Five months later (communication was indeed slow), Jefferson replied. He directly addressed Madison's concern about how a bill of rights would be enforced against momentary majorities. Madison had neglected one important argument for a bill of rights, Jefferson wrote. Once established, a bill of rights would provide the legal basis for an independent judiciary to strike down majoritarian excesses by ruling unconstitutional any legislative or executive act that violated individual rights as defined in the Constitution. Such legislative acts, even if committed in response to majority opinion, could be declared null and void by the courts. A bill of rights, Jefferson wrote, would put a powerful "legal check" into the hands of the judiciary, provided it remained safely independent of the other branches of government.

Jefferson's argument persuaded Madison, who later reflected it in his passionate speech to Congress proposing the constitutional amendments that ultimately became the Bill of Rights. By now Madison shrewdly saw that the new government would be strengthened if a bill of rights were added and quite possibly destroyed if it were not. He knew that some Anti-Federalists really wanted to promote a second convention to subvert the new constitutional system and expand state powers, and were using the bill-of-rights issue as a smokescreen to gain popular support. By introducing a bill of rights as promised, Madison hoped to isolate those Anti-Federalists and take the steam out of their movement.

But it wasn't easy. Many of his Federalist colleagues in the First Congress weren't much interested in a bill of rights, despite their implied promise to the states, and preferred to move on to other matters. And the Anti-Federalists, recognizing Madison's strategy, sought to subvert it first by stalling, and then by actually erecting obstacles to the rights they had for more than a year been demanding!

On June 8, 1789, Madison introduced his amendments. Taken from the various state constitutions, Madison's amendments protected freedom of religion, speech, press, and assembly; prohibited general searches; and recognized a wide variety of procedural rights belonging to a person accused of a crime. In a long speech supporting his amendments, Madison conceded the popular demand for a bill of rights and made five key points:

• First, he reflected what had become the prevailing public view: if *all* government power were not limited by a higher law, rights would be violated. Unless general searches were constitutionally prohibited, for example, Congress might someday authorize them to enforce its tax laws, just as Parliament had authorized the hated writs of assistance.

• Second, the big problem with the English Bill of Rights was that it limited the power of the king, but left Parliament's power unlimited. As all Americans knew, that had resulted in a severe loss of individual rights. Therefore, said Madison, the purpose of his amendments was to limit legislative as well as executive power, and even to limit democracy itself. For unless the community itself, "the body of the people, operating by the majority against the minority," were limited, individual rights would not be secure.

• Third, Madison adopted the key point made by Jefferson. If these constitutional amendments were approved, said Madison, they would be enforced by an independent judiciary, which would be "an impenetrable bulwark" against every assumption of unconstitutional power by either the legislative or executive branch.

• Fourth, Madison finally responded to the Federalist argument that the enumeration of certain rights in the Constitution would tend to imply that no other rights existed. This was easily remedied, he said, by what eventually would become the Ninth Amendment: a specific provision providing that "the enumeration in the Constitution of certain rights shall not be construed to deny or disparage others retained by the people."

• Finally, Madison made what would turn out to be the most prescient argument of the entire debate. Although everyone had focused up to then on the need for a national bill of rights to restrain the national government and had assumed that state constitutions were sufficient to protect rights against state governments, Madison argued that the states posed an even greater threat to individual rights than the national government, and that state constitutions were insufficient protection. Some states had no bills of rights, he said, while others were "defective." Accordingly, one of Madison's amendments read, "No state shall violate the equal rights of conscience, or the freedom of the press, or the trial by jury in criminal cases."

This last point was a startling proposal, because it turned the tables on Anti-Federalist state representatives, challenging them to apply their professed principles to their own states and to agree to limit their own powers as well as those of the national government. Madison's argument that constitutional rights should limit the power of state governments reflected the logic of popular opinion: "Every Government," he asserted, "should be disarmed of powers which trench upon" the fundamental rights of press, conscience, and jury trial. Later, a House of Representatives committee added freedom of speech to the list.

A motion soon was made by the representative from South Carolina to delete the limit on state powers. Madison now rose to say that he thought this amendment was "the most valuable amendment on the list." His argument carried the House by the required two-thirds majority.

But when Madison's amendments reached the Senate, it rejected the amendment Madison considered "the most valuable." And there died the proposed constitutional limitation on the power of states to infringe the rights of speech, press, religion, and trial by jury. Because the Senate's proceedings were secret, no one knows what the vote was except that it fell short of the necessary two-thirds. The defeat of this amendment undoubtedly altered the course of American history and for more than a century denied many American citizens rights that the early Americans believed to be fundamental.

Madison turned out to be right about the states. The most egregious and persistent denial of individual rights over the years that followed was by state and local governments, not by the national government. But because the Senate had killed Madison's "most valuable" amendment, the federal Bill of Rights offered no protection. States remained free to violate rights, unless restrained by their own state constitutions. It would take a bloody civil war before additional amendments were passed to limit the power of states to abridge individual rights. And it would be a century more before the United States Supreme Court interpreted one of those additional amendments as applying most of the original Bill of Rights to the states. Not until the 1960s would the principle of Madison's last amendment be completely realized.

Aside from the deletion of that amendment, however, Madison's other amendments were changed only slightly, consolidated, and passed by both the Senate and the House. On September 25, 1789, the Bill of Rights was submitted to the states for ratification. The approval of ten of the thirteen states was required to make the Bill of Rights part of the Constitution. Within six months, nine states had ratified. But for a variety of political reasons, Virginia, Georgia, Connecticut, and Massachusetts held out. Then, in 1791, Vermont was admitted to the Union, increasing the number of states needed to ratify to eleven. In November 1791, Vermont ratified, and on December 15, 1791, Virginia became the eleventh state to ratify. The Bill of Rights was now part of the highest law of the land.

ELITIST RADICALS AND NATURAL RIGHTS

The Bill of Rights was the culmination of decades of revolutionary thought. Yet not even its most fiery proponents were aware of just how revolutionary an impact it would eventually have upon American society. As Bernard Bailyn has pointed out, the leaders of the revolutionary movement in America were political radicals, but they were also elitists who were concerned not with the injustice of economic inequality, but rather with the need to fight against expansive political power and preserve their own individual rights. No radical transformation of the social order was contemplated, intended, or expected.

But there were unintended effects. People learned to expect their rights and to distrust authority. They saw what liberty meant, what life could be if arbitrary power were steadfastly resisted. The belief grew that when fundamental rights were violated, disobedience was an obligation. "When tyranny is abroad," wrote Andrew Eliot in 1765, "submission is a crime." Thus "the principle of justifiable disobedience and the instinct to question public authority before accepting it acquired a new sanction and new vigor," not only against a remote Parliament an ocean away, but also against local legislatures and administrative officials.

Perhaps even more significantly, the idea of *natural rights,* the "self-evident" truths of the Constitution, which became contagious in colonial America, implied *equality* in a way few people explicitly understood at the time. If people were born with rights that no government could alter or take away, then every person was entitled to have his or her rights respected. How then could slavery be accepted? How could sexual inequalities be accepted? How could economic inequalities be accepted as a basis for the stratification of rights? If rights were truly universal, wouldn't the logic of the idea of rights eventually lead to radical notions of equality? In many respects, that is precisely what happened over the next two hundred years.

Although the leaders of the Revolution and the proponents of the idea of rights had no intention of upsetting such racial, sexual, and economic distinctions, and did not do so, the ideology of natural rights was inevitably corrosive to established institutions and to traditional authority because it meant that any person could oppose, indeed was *obligated* to oppose, any king, any government, or indeed any community of people whose power intruded upon his natural rights.

In the years before the Revolution, a number of writers became alarmed about this attitude, believing that the ideology of rights would lead to instability and was incompatible with society itself.

But to others, perhaps to the majority of the early Americans, the ideology of rights offered a vision of a brighter future. As Bailyn concludes, they

found in the defiance of traditional order the firmest of all grounds for their hope for a freer life.... Faith ran high that a better world than any that had ever been known could be built where authority was distrusted and held in constant scrutiny; where the status of men flowed from their achievements and from their personal qualities, not from distinctions ascribed to them at birth; and where the use of power over the lives of men was jealously guarded and severely restricted. It was only where there was this defiance, this refusal to truckle, this distrust of all authority, political or social, that institutions would express human aspirations, not crush them.

This, then, was the original American vision of liberty. In the eighteenth century, its highest expression was the Bill of Rights, but we would see that same vision expressed over and over again in the two hundred years that followed: in the yearning of slaves to be free and equal, of women to vote, of factory workers to organize unions; in the struggle of black Americans to end segregation; in the demand of homosexuals for the same rights as everyone else; in the refusal of conscientious objectors to be conscripted to go to war; in the pain of Japanese-American citizens interned in camps during World War II; in the resistance of Jehovah's Witness children against public-school requirements to salute the flag in violation of their religious beliefs; and in the courage of tens of thousands of ordinary people, most of them unknown to history, who were willing to confront authority and risk punishment in order to preserve their rights.

The Bill of Rights was a pivotal development in the long story of liberty. But, as Madison feared, the rights it sought to protect did not follow automatically or easily from the text. In the years that followed, more struggle would be required before Madison's "parchment barrier" would in fact bring the great rights to life.

JUDICIAL REVIEW

No provision of law, especially law that attempts to state broad, general principles, can possibly anticipate the many circumstances to which the law may arguably apply. Although the Bill of Rights established soaring principles that guaranteed a variety of fundamental rights in general terms, from the beginning cases arose that raised difficult questions about exactly how the Bill of Rights applied, or even if it applied. Before the *paper* rights could become *actual* rights, therefore, someone had to *interpret* what the general language of the Bill of Rights required in specific situations.

Who was to be the final arbiter was unclear at the start. In his March 1789 letter to James Madison, Thomas Jefferson had suggested that the courts should have that power. He thought the judicial branch should remain independent of the other branches of government, in order to be able to act as a kind of umpire, an arbiter of liberty that would interpret the constitutional ground rules, and curb the actions of the legislative and executive branches whenever they violated rights. Madison echoed Jefferson's view in his ringing speech to the House of Representatives, when he endorsed the notion that a system of independent courts would be "an impenetrable bulwark" of liberty and have the power to strike down as unconstitutional all legislative or executive acts that violated the Bill of Rights.

But nowhere in the Constitution was such power explicitly given to the courts. And even Madison and Jefferson expressed concern about the supremacy of the courts on other occasions. For example, Jefferson was much less an advocate of the independent power of judges to declare government acts unconstitutional when he was president than when he was a diplomat in Paris, looking at the problem in a more disinterested way. As president, feeling his own power curbed, he criticized the idea of "judges as the ultimate arbiters of all constitutional questions," calling such an idea "a very dangerous doctrine indeed."

In fact, President Jefferson actually recommended a constitutional amendment that would have made judges removable by the president! The proposal never made it out of committee, but it showed how correct the early Americans were to mistrust *all* government power. If even so fervent an apostle of liberty as Thomas Jefferson, who in 1789 had vigorously argued that an independent judiciary was the key to enforcing rights, only eight years later could reverse himself when his own power was at stake, how could liberty ever be entrusted to the discretion of any government official? The unique American idea that the rule of *law*—written, enforceable limits on *all* government power—was the only trustworthy guarantor of individual rights clearly implied the need for an independent judiciary to enforce those rights.

Freedom of speech, for example, is protected by the First Amendment, which says, "Congress shall make no law ... abridging the freedom of speech." But suppose that, despite the First Amendment, Congress were to pass a law abridging freedom of speech. Unless the courts were authorized to strike down that law, the First Amendment would have no force.

Unlike the legislative and executive branches, however, the courts were not given the power to initiate action by themselves. Congress may decide to pass an unconstitutional law, but the courts have no authority to strike it down on their own initiative. No act of Congress—indeed, no act of any government official—requires the approval of the federal courts, either in advance or afterward, and no matter how illegal such an act may be, the courts are powerless to review it on their own. Nor may they give legal advice.

Federal courts exist only to settle live disputes. If Congress did pass a law abridging freedom of speech, for example, the only way a court could get its hands on that law would be if someone were injured by it, and complained.

Suppose Congress were to pass a law making it a crime to peacefully distribute leaflets criticizing the government. No court would have the power to do anything, except under either of two circumstances. If someone were arrested under that law, she could defend herself in court by claiming that the law was unconstitutional because the First Amendment prohibits such laws. A court could then rule, in response to this defense, that the law is unconstitutional, and could dismiss the criminal charges. Alternatively, someone who wanted to distribute a leaflet criticizing the government, but did not want to expose himself to criminal charges, could bring a lawsuit against the government challenging the constitutionality of the law. The court could then respond to the lawsuit by ruling that the law violates the First Amendment, and declaring it null and void. Both sides would have the right to appeal an unfavorable decision, and the case could eventually end up being decided by the United States Supreme Court, whose decision would then determine what the First Amendment meant in that particular context. If the Court upheld the law, it would mean that other such laws could, and probably would, be passed. If the Court struck down the law, it would mean that all such laws, now and in the future, would probably be similarly vulnerable to constitutional challenge.

The key point is that no court may measure any law, or any government act, against what the Constitution requires, except to resolve an actual dispute between parties who have something to gain or lose by the outcome. But not even this much was clear in 1791, or in the decade that followed. If the courts had the power to hold acts of Congress unconstitutional, they didn't use it until 1803, in a case called *Marbury v. Madison,* when the United States Supreme Court struck down an act of Congress, thereby establishing its judicial power. The case itself involved no fundamental right, no great principle of personal liberty. The dispute was entirely political, involving the refusal of James Madison, who was then Secretary of State, to deliver the commissions of four judges appointed and confirmed by the Senate during the prior administration.

The new president, Thomas Jefferson, wanted to block these appointments. William Marbury, one of the four, sued Madison, seeking a court order compelling him to issue the commissions. The dispute was intricate and would have grave implication for the emerging relationships among the legislative, executive, and judicial branches. The Supreme Court was in a difficult position. Whether it agreed with Marbury or not, serious political consequences would have resulted. So the Court evaded that dilemma by declaring unconstitutional the law that gave it the authority to issue such an order in the first place, thus avoiding a decision on the merits of the case. Madison won the case because the order was never issued, even though the question of who was right was never legally decided. Instead, the law giving the Court the authority to issue such an order was struck down. Nonetheless, because this was the first time the Court had ever struck down an act of Congress, its judicial power, which before had been in doubt, was established.

At the time, the precedent this set was hardly noticed. More attention was paid to the merits of the dispute between the executive branch and its political enemies. In the long run, however, the significance of *Marbury v. Madison* had nothing to do with that dispute, nor is there any reason now to care whether it was right to have withheld Marbury's appointment. The overriding significance of the case is that it established the independent power of the judiciary to strike down acts of Congress that violated constitutional limits. It would be another five decades before the Supreme Court would do so again; thus it is fair to say that but for the *Marbury* case, the principle of judicial review might never have been established, and the history of liberty in America would almost certainly have been radically different.

Marbury v. Madison showed again that great principles affecting the liberties of all of us often emerge from narrow, petty disputes. There was little immediately at stake in the *Marbury* case except the self-interest of grasping politicians. But the enduring legal principle established in *Marbury*, almost as an unintended side-effect, turned out to be the key to the development and protection of most of the rights we enjoy today. For if the Supreme Court had not early in its history established its power to nullify acts of Congress that violated the Constitution, a great many of the personal rights we take for granted today might never have been secured. This is not to suggest that the courts have exercised this power often; they have not. Throughout our history—now over two hundred years—the Supreme Court has struck down fewer than 125 acts of Congress. But the Court has also invalidated executive branch actions and, especially during the last forty years, many laws and actions of state and local officials. Had it not been for the principle of judicial review, established almost without notice in *Marbury v. Madison,* much of this might not have happened.

ACTIVISM AND THE SUPREME COURT

Today, the power of courts to invalidate government actions when they exceed constitutional limits is firmly entrenched in our system of government. Although this judicial power has been attacked periodically, usually by those who oppose the substance of the rights being protected, it has survived for nearly two centuries. The most powerful challenges to it have come from presidents. Thomas Jefferson was not the only president who felt restricted by Supreme Court decisions and tried to dilute the Court's power.

During the 1930s, President Franklin D. Roosevelt, furious because a conservative and activist Supreme Court had invalidated key New Deal legislation, sought legislation to increase the number of Supreme Court justices, which would have allowed him to "pack" the Court with his appointees. The plan provoked heavy debate and was criticized both by conservatives opposed to Roosevelt's politics and by some of his liberal supporters. The plan failed.

In the late 1950s and early 1960s, the Supreme Court, under the leadership of Chief Justice Earl Warren, a former Republican governor of California, struck down state-enforced school segregation and issued a series of other decisions upholding individual rights against government power. Southern

Democrats—outraged by what they saw as an unwarranted federal intrusion into the power of Southern states to maintain racial separation, and supported by right-wing groups opposed to many of the individual rights that were increasingly being protected by the Supreme Court—introduced bills in Congress to prohibit the Supreme Court from hearing appeals in certain classes of cases. A number of these bills were supported by the Conference of Chief Justices of the States—an organization of judges who resented the intrusion of the federal courts and the Bill of Rights, which, they said, denied "the power [of states] to keep order." But none of these bills passed.

As the Warren Court continued to apply the Bill of Rights to limit government powers and secure individual rights, conservative opposition intensified. When conservatives were opposed to Roosevelt's New Deal legislation, they applauded an activist Supreme Court, cheering as the Court repeatedly struck down acts of Congress designed to regulate the economy. Now, however, conservatives attacked the Court for too actively expanding individual rights, and advocated judicial deference to legislatures, particularly state legislatures. At the same time, liberals who had denounced the Supreme Court's activism in the thirties now applauded the Warren Court's activism, as it repeatedly limited the states' powers in behalf of individual rights. Although the debate continued, and continues today, in terms of abstract notions of *judicial activism* versus *judicial restraint,* the underlying debate has always been mostly over the substance of Supreme Court decisions.

The Supreme Court has, from the beginning, been activist on many occasions and has often reached out beyond the narrow meanings of constitutional text. From the time of *Marbury v. Madison,* in 1803, when an activist Supreme Court first created the power of judicial review, through the nineteenth-century decisions that validated slavery and stripped the post–Civil War amendments of their force, through the conservative activist Court of the 1930s, which blocked New Deal economic programs in behalf of business interests, the Court has frequently been activist. Indeed, the current Supreme Court—although dominated by "conservative" justices who advocated judicial restraint before being appointed—has actively reached out, in decision after decision, to cut back on long-established rights. In its activism, the Warren Court was no different. Its reasoning was no more or less specious, its grasp of power no more far-reaching. What was different about the Warren Court, what it did that no Supreme Court had ever systematically done before, was to invoke the Bill of Rights to protect the rights of vulnerable, powerless minorities: blacks at the mercy of racist Southern states; disadvantaged voters; people expressing unpopular religious or political beliefs; people accused of crimes; and people whose poverty hindered their access to fundamental legal rights. What was unique about the Warren Court was not its activism, but the beneficiaries of its activism.

Throughout the sixties the debate raged between those who thought it was proper for the Supreme Court to protect such rights by imposing strict limits on government power and those who thought the Court ought to defer to democratically elected legislatures. By the early seventies, a substantial backlash against the expansion of rights had begun to find political expression. By 1980, a powerful political coalition had formed that included conservative Republicans, former Democrats in the South, and a strong, highly organized fundamentalist religious movement. The political figure who came to symbolize the hopes of this coalition was another former governor of California, Ronald Reagan. In 1980 he was elected president.

During the 1980s, a concerted attack upon the scope of judicial review —and indeed upon many of the rights now protected by the Bill of Rights— was mounted by President Reagan. Besides publishing an article championing "the unamended Constitution"—that is, the Constitution without a Bill of Rights—Reagan initiated a series of actions to dilute judicial review and undermine a number of the substantive rights it protected. During the first two years of the Reagan administration, for example, forty bills were introduced in Congress to strip federal courts of their authority *even to hear* cases involving constitutional rights that Reagan opposed. None of the bills passed. If any of them had passed, and had been held constitutional, both Congress and state legislatures could have enacted laws violating the Bill of Rights, and no federal court (though some of the bills excepted the Supreme Court) would have had the authority to strike them down. Although state courts would still have retained such authority, the removal of federal-court jurisdiction would have crippled our system's ability to maintain a uniform check on the abuse of government power. The substance of our rights would have remained intact, but the means of enforcing them would have been substantially, perhaps fatally, weakened.

Then, in 1987, President Reagan nominated Robert Bork for a vacant seat on the United States Supreme Court. This culminating effort of the Reagan administration to dilute the scope of judicial review triggered a furious nationwide debate.

Bork was a law professor who had been made a federal judge by President Reagan a few years earlier. For over twenty-five years, he had been the leading conservative critic of the Supreme Court and the architect of a theory of judicial review that, if adopted, would have drastically narrowed the scope of the Court's authority. Bork's vision of the role of the courts was exceedingly narrow; he stood for the proposition that the courts had gone entirely too far in invalidating legislative actions. He was opposed to the idea, so popular among the early Americans, that government was not to be trusted with the people's liberties. In fact, he had written that one of the disadvantages of courts striking down majoritarian laws was that it tended to "teach the lesson that democratic processes are suspect, essentially unprincipled and untrustworthy." Bork's view would have surprised the early Americans, who *assumed* that all government processes, even democratic ones, were untrustworthy, at least as far as protecting their liberties was concerned; that is why they sought to restrain the excesses of democracy by strict legal limits: to assure their own rights.

Bork reflected very little of this mistrust. He was willing, even anxious, to place considerably more power in the hands of legislatures and considerably less in the hands of courts. Although he recognized the essential tension between power and liberty, he did not share the early Americans' view that power would inevitably and aggressively try to restrict liberty, and that individual rights would be in danger if power were not firmly bridled.

Bork's approach was perhaps best exemplified by his severe criticism of a 1965 case called *Griswold v. Connecticut.* At that time—less than three decades ago—an old Connecticut law still made it a crime for a married couple to go down to their corner drugstore and buy contraceptives. In fact, using contraceptives was entirely forbidden. In 1961, the operators of a birth-control clinic were prosecuted for advising married couples about contraceptives and for actually providing them with contraceptives. They were convicted, and appealed to the Supreme Court. The Court ruled, 7–2, that the Connecticut law was unconstitutional. Bork made that decision the centerpiece of his campaign to restrict the scope of judicial review.

The Court had struck down the law because it authorized an intolerable legislative intrusion into marital privacy. Although the right to privacy was nowhere explicitly mentioned in the Bill of Rights, the Court ruled that it was clearly implied by a number of "fundamental constitutional guarantees," including the much-neglected Ninth Amendment.

The Ninth Amendment was the one that Madison had invented to satisfy those critics of the Bill of Rights who believed that any enumeration of specific rights guaranteed by it might imply that other, equally fundamental rights were not protected. It says, "The enumeration in the Constitution, of certain rights, shall not be construed to deny or disparage others retained by the people." In the *Griswold* case, Justice William O. Douglas relied heavily on the Ninth Amendment to support his decision to invalidate the Connecticut law. If the Ninth Amendment meant anything, he said, certainly it meant to protect so obvious a right as the right to marital privacy, which was "older than the Bill of Rights."

But Bork disagreed. His position was that the Court had exceeded its powers, since the right to marital privacy is nowhere specifically mentioned in the Constitution. The Ninth Amendment is meaningless, Bork argued, because no one can know what it means or what it protects.

Bork was precisely what some eighteenth-century Federalists had feared: a man who argued that only those rights specifically enumerated in the Constitution could be protected by the courts. Despite the fact that the Ninth Amendment was unarguably intended to rebut that argument, Bork pressed on. Setting himself firmly against the political ideas of America's original citizens, he built a career upon his opposition to the *Griswold* decision and came to represent a theory of judicial review that would have required the Supreme Court to leave such matters in the hands of state legislatures. Bork saw the question of whether a married couple could be prosecuted and convicted for using contraceptives as a question to be decided by a legislature, not by a court. For Bork, therefore, the *right* to marital privacy, established by the Supreme Court in *Griswold,* did not exist: instead, it was up to the discretion of the legislature. This view, once understood, alarmed many Americans. After a major televised national debate on the proper scope of judicial review, Bork's candidacy was rejected by the United States Senate, by a vote of 58 to 42.

Although it is always difficult to ascribe specific meaning to such outcomes, the decisive vote against Judge Bork, and the strong public support for the Senate's action, amounted to a rejection of his attempt to narrow the scope of judicial power. A number of historians have noted that judicial review could never have flourished as it has if the people had been opposed to it. That is undoubtedly true. Although particular Supreme Court decisions have been opposed by large segments of the public (IMPEACH EARL WARREN billboards were fairly common in the late fifties), the principle of a strong and independent judiciary, acting as a brake upon the excesses of government power, has generally been broadly supported. Without independent judicial review, many of the rights we wake up with each morning, and take for granted, would not exist.

THE BILL OF THE RIGHTS AND THE POWER OF THE STATES

Although the power of judicial review was established almost immediately—in 1803—the Supreme Court virtually never used that power to protect individual rights until well into the twentieth century. There were a number of reasons for this—including the Court's longstanding tendency to show more concern for the property rights of corporations than for individual liberties—but the major reason may be found in the original design of the Bill of Rights itself. Although it was a grand statement of lofty legal principles, the original Bill of Rights contained several glaring, nearly fatal flaws.

First, and most importantly, it did not apply to state governments. The First Amendment, for example, prohibited *Congress* from abridging the right to free speech or freedom of the press, but it didn't prohibit any state—or, for that matter, local—government from censoring speech or banning newspapers or restricting the freedom of religion. James Madison's proposed amendment prohibiting states from violating certain fundamental rights, such as freedom of the press and religion and the right to trial by jury, was the only amendment rejected by the Senate. As a result, state governments were left unrestricted, free to violate individual rights as they pleased. They could imprison people for their religious or political beliefs, abolish trial by jury, even torture suspects to extort confessions. However grand the Bill of Rights sounded, at the outset it provided no legal protection against the states.

This was a major flaw, to put it mildly, since most government activity affecting the lives of ordinary people was carried out by state and local governments. That was where people lived. To lack protection against state and local government was to be without rights. That is why Madison called his proposed amendment "the most valuable" of all.

In 1833, a man named John Barron tried to use the Bill of Rights in a dispute he had with the city of Baltimore. The city had seized some of Barron's property, and he claimed that under the Fifth Amendment he was entitled to "just compensation." The Fifth Amendment did in fact appear to support his claim, since it prohibited the government from taking "private property ... for public use, without just compensation." But the Supreme Court ruled that the Fifth Amendment, and indeed the entire Bill of Rights, applied only to the federal government, not to state or local governments.

That the Supreme Court hardly ever used its power to protect individual rights during the early years of our nation's history should thus come as no surprise. Most often, rights were violated by state and local governments, and they were completely immune from the legal restraints in the Bill of Rights. It would take a civil war to change the situation.

In 1868, the Fourteenth Amendment was passed; it was one of three constitutional amendments passed after the Civil War to address the rights of the newly freed slaves. The Thirteenth Amendment permanently prohibited "slavery and involuntary servitude" and gave Congress the power to enforce that prohibition through legislation. The Fifteenth Amendment forbade both federal *and* state governments from abridging the right to vote "on account of race, color, or previous condition of servitude"; it, too, gave Congress the power of enforcement.

But the Fourteenth Amendment was more complex and far-reaching. It provided, in part, that

No state shall ... abridge the privileges or immunities of citizens of the United States; nor shall any state deprive any person of life, liberty, or property without due process of law; nor deny to any person within its jurisdiction the equal protection of the laws.

This language appears to be a more general form of Madison's rejected amendment and would seem to mean that no state can legally violate the rights of its citizens, including the rights guaranteed by the Bill of Rights. Indeed, some historians and some Supreme Court justices believe that the Fourteenth Amendment was explicitly intended by its authors to overrule *Barron v. Baltimore.* Other historians disagree, and think the historical record is "probably inconclusive." But ultimately any constitutional provision means what the Supreme Court says it means, and for a long time the Court ruled that the Fourteenth Amendment did *not* apply the Bill of Rights to the states.

In 1873, five years after the Fourteenth Amendment was adopted, the Supreme Court rendered its first decision interpreting its meaning. The case grew out of a commercial controversy that seemed at first to have very little to do with the lives of most Americans. In 1869, the state of Louisiana, through its licensing power, had granted a monopoly on butchering to a single company, the Crescent City Stock Landing and Slaughterhouse Company. Butchers who were excluded claimed discrimination and a deprivation of their livelihood, and argued that Louisiana's actions violated the second clause of the new Fourteenth Amendment, which prohibited states from abridging the rights (or, in the language of the amendment, the "privileges and immunities") of United States citizens.

The Supreme Court ruled that the Fourteenth Amendment did not apply. Though it did clearly prohibit states from violating the rights of United States citizens, the Court ruled that the "privileges and immunities" of United States citizens did not include the full range of individual liberties set forth in the Bill of Rights. Instead, the Court ruled that the only rights protected by the "privileges and immunities" clause of the Fourteenth Amendment were rights of *national* citizenship, such as the right to travel or the right to go to Washington and petition the *national* government.

By settling a commercial dispute between butchers and the state of Louisiana the way it did, the Supreme Court in effect nullified the capacity of the Fourteenth Amendment to correct the restrictive interpretation of the Bill of Rights rendered by the Court's 1833 decision in *Barron v. Baltimore.* Therefore, despite the Fourteenth Amendment, the Bill of Rights still provided no protection in the circumstances where it was most needed.

It took another half-century before the Court began to use the other clauses of the Fourteenth Amendment to apply the Bill of Rights to state and local governments. But it would be a slow process. Not until the 1960s — nearly a century after the Fourteenth Amendment was passed — would the Bill of Rights be applied comprehensively to the states. A narrow commercial dispute turned out to diminish the rights of tens of millions of Americans for almost a hundred years.

WHO THE BILL OF RIGHTS LEFT OUT

The failure to apply any part of the Bill of Rights to the states was a serious omission in 1791, but it wasn't the only omission. At its inception, the Bill of Rights was not intended to protect everyone. Whole groups of people were left out. Women were seen as second-class citizens, at best. The prevailing social view was that women were the property of their husbands, and this was in part reflected in the new Constitution. The very language of our early declarations of principles was exclusionary. When in the Declaration of Independence the principle of equality was announced, by its own terms it was exclusionary: "All *men* are created equal," it said. In a system designed grandly to ensure people the right to have a say, through elections, in how they would be governed, women were not even entitled to vote.

The right to vote, of course, derived in large part from property qualifications. "All men are created equal" excluded more than just women: it also excluded most men. The consent of the governed was commonly understood to be limited to the consent of property owners. Later, property qualifications for voting were abandoned, often to be replaced by taxpayer qualifications. In time, many of these were abandoned as well. But even after such tests were abolished, women continued to be denied the vote. The Bill of Rights was in force for nearly 130 years before the right of women to vote was recognized and guaranteed by the Nineteenth Amendment.

If women were partially unprotected by the original Constitution, others were completely unprotected. American Indians, for example, were entirely outside the constitutional system, since they were defined by the United States as an alien people within their own land, decimated, militarily defeated, and confined to reservations. They were not American citizens, and thus were governed, not by ordinary American laws, but by federal treaties and statutes that stripped tribes of most of their land and much of their authority. In 1924, Congress belatedly granted all Indians United States citizenship, but it has never completely resolved the issue of tribal sovereignty. To this day, the degree to which individual Americans of Indian descent are protected by the Bill of Rights against the powers of *tribal* governments remains ambiguous.

But the group most grievously excluded from the protections of the original Bill of Rights were African slaves and their descendants. Their exclusion was not inadvertent, and it indelibly stained the Constitution and the ideals of liberty it claimed to protect and symbolize.

By the time of the Revolution in 1776, slavery was nearly universally believed to be "the absolute political evil." It is not difficult to see why. The philosophical force driving the fight for freedom from English rule was the belief that individual rights were God-given *to every human being;* that the attainment of liberty was the highest social good; and that the mortal enemy of liberty was unlimited power, the *dominion* of some people over others. The most propulsive political force at the time was the idea that power must be sharply limited. The polar opposite of sharply limited power was *slavery,* what one pamphleteer defined as "being wholly under the power and control of another," and what a newspaper writer in 1747 described as "a force … by which a man is obliged to act, or not to act, according to the arbitrary will and pleasure of another." Thus defined, slavery represented the death of liberty, the end result of the failure to limit power.

The early Americans were so sensitive to the horror and degradation of slavery that they were quick to see it lurking in every illegitimate reach of government power. The Stamp Act was seen as a step toward slavery. Denial of the right to trial by jury was seen as a step toward slavery. The unlimited power to search was seen as paving the way toward slavery. In this context, the presence of a completely enslaved African population in America inescapably created a cancerous contradiction in the body politic. How could political leaders in the colonies seek liberty for themselves while they tolerated or even imposed the complete denial of liberty to others? If slavery was the ultimate evil, to be resisted even at its earliest stages, how could it be permitted in its extreme form? As one American pamphleteer put it, "What is a trifling three-penny tax on tea compared to the inestimable blessings of liberty to a captive?" In 1765, the Reverend John Camm put it pointedly: What does "all *men* are *born free*" mean? he asked. Does it mean "that Negroes are not … *born slaves*, or that the said slaves are not men?" In 1770, Samuel Cooke pled "the cause of our African slaves," and in 1773, Benjamin Rush begged "advocates of American liberty" to rouse themselves to oppose slavery. "The plant of liberty is of so tender a nature that it cannot thrive long in the neighborhood of slavery," he wrote.

As the conflict with England deepened and liberty became a rallying cry against unjust exercises of power, the contradiction of slavery became harder to ignore. The "slavery we suffer," Samuel Hopkins wrote in 1776, "is lighter than a feather" compared to the "heavy doom" of the African slaves. A colonial printer who was loyal to Great Britain attacked the hypocrisy: How could the rebels ground their rebellion in their professed love for liberty, he asked, and yet "themselves own two thousand Negro slaves"? There was no good answer to this question.

The contradiction may have become impossible to ignore, but it was not resolved. In the end, it was tolerated. Thomas Jefferson wrote that "the abolition of domestic slavery is the great object of desire," but he owned slaves himself and took no serious steps to outlaw the slave trade even when he was president. Patrick Henry, the fiery Anti-Federalist who refused to accept the original Constitution without a bill of rights, wrote that he looked forward to a time "when an opportunity will be offered to abolish this lamentable evil." But that time would have to wait because, Henry said, "the general inconvenience of living here without them" made freeing the slaves impractical.

And so the great apostles of liberty came to tolerate the greatest possible denial of liberty in their midst. Believing that they could not both abolish slavery *and* form a strong Union, they accepted political reality. The word "slavery" nowhere appears in the Constitution. Where the slaves are referred to, euphemisms are used, such as "persons held to service." Until after the Civil War, nearly eighty years later, the word "race" did not appear in the Constitution. Some historians believe that this omission was intended, by at least some of the delegates, to maintain the great constitutional ideals of liberty and equality without any explicit exceptions, in the hope that one day the lack of stated exceptions would provide the basis for extending the principles to everyone, regardless of race. Others believe that the use of euphemisms was primarily "meant to shield the consciences of the delegates just as the clauses themselves were meant to protect the institution of slavery."

Whatever the intent may have been, the general principles of liberty and equality upon which the Constitution was based did, as we shall see, provide some impetus years later to extend the Bill of Rights to those initially excluded. The contradictions between the ideals expressed by the Bill of Rights and the realities of American life have been steadily, if slowly and unevenly, resolved in favor of the ideals.

But if the price of the new Constitution was the legitimization of slavery and racial discrimination, it was a steep price indeed, paid in pain and blood and suffocated hopes, not only then but now as well. The price included maintaining the fiction that skin color matters, that it is a legitimate distinction among people. Over the years, that fiction became embedded in our social and political structures; it created and nourished sharp limits on opportunity, and therefore on achievement. Differential levels of achievement in employment, in education, in politics — themselves the product of discrimination — became, ironically, so associated with skin color that they have furnished additional justifications for discrimination. Like a cancer, the fiction that skin color matters spread throughout the body politic, seeped below the surface of our professed ideals, and corroded them from within.

Slavery was America's original sin: it infected the Constitution at its conception. The new nation, conceived in liberty, was born with a defect that we have never been able entirely to correct. Years of struggle and a bloody civil war would be required before additional constitutional amendments were passed — amendents that were intended to bring black Americans within the Constitution's protections.

But even after those amendments were passed, liberty and equality did not follow. On the contrary, within a short time, the postwar hopes and aspirations of black Americans were snuffed out and white dominion was restored. Slavery had been abolished, but subjugation remained, supported by laws designed to deny the most fundamental rights to black citizens and to maintain white supremacy. It would take another century before the struggles of black people began even minimally to redeem the promise of the post–Civil War amendments, much less the original eighteenth-century vision of liberty.

During all those years, racial discrimination became deeply entrenched, not only in our laws, but also in our political and social institutions, in our personal habits, in our instincts, and in our culture. Racial violence against blacks was common and irremediable, and black people, especially and tragically young black people, learned to limit their aspirations and suppress their dreams. Most whites accepted this, and nearly all whites benefitted from it. And until 1954, the United States Supreme Court—the institution James Madison had thought would be "an impenetrable bulwark" for liberty—mostly legitimized it.

On July 5, 1852, more than a half-century after the Bill of Rights became law, Frederick Douglass, a former slave, told a white audience celebrating Independence Day:

The rich inheritance of justice, liberty, prosperity, and independence, bequeathed by your fathers, is shared by you, not me. The sunlight that brought light and healing to you, has brought stripes and death to me. This Fourth of July is yours, *not* mine. *You may rejoice.* I *must mourn.*

But America did not listen. Five years after Douglass spoke, the Supreme Court decided the case of Dred Scott. It was the first time since 1803 that the Court had exercised its power of judicial review to strike down a federal law on constitutional grounds. It did so, however, not to protect individual liberty, but to protect its polar opposite, slavery.

Dred Scott was a Missouri slave who had traveled with his owner to federal territory outside of Missouri. Congress had banned slavery in that federal territory, and Scott sued, arguing that his residence on free soil had emancipated him. During the previous twenty years, antislavery advocates had succeeded in making this argument, and there was growing judicial acceptance of it. But the Supreme Court ruled against him, 7–2.

In his opinion, Chief Justice Roger Taney not only ruled that Scott had no right to bring the suit because he was not a citizen, but he also said that the federal law prohibiting slavery in the territories was unconstitutional. The decision committed the full weight of the judiciary to the institution of slavery, and to the proposition that blacks "had no rights which the white man was bound to respect." As a result of this decision, blacks—including free blacks—were excluded both from citizenship and from all constitutional protections.

The *Dred Scott* decision did not endure, because it was overruled by the Thirteenth and Fourteenth Amendments after the Civil War. But the case stands as a sorry monument to the state of liberty in mid-nineteenth-century America, and as a landmark in the crisis that was leading inexorably to war.

The *Dred Scott* case also showed the corrosive effect of the original decision to tolerate slavery. The failure of those who founded America to resolve the contradiction between liberty and slavery at the outset left the nation with a tragic legacy. And despite the constitutional abolition of slavery after the Civil War, the race exception to the Constitution would persist as a matter of fact for yet another century.

During the middle of the twentieth century, a civil-rights movement arose that finally succeeded in striking down the crudest barriers to equal rights. But it could not strike down the effects of centuries of slavery and legalized, persistent racial discrimination. It could not strike down the institutionalized economic disadvantages that still fell disproportionately upon black people. And it could not strike down what W. E. B. Du Bois once called "centuries of instinct, habit, and thought."

FREEDOM
OF RELIGION

SAYING GRACE,
FAMILY DINNER.
SUMTER, SOUTH
CAROLINA, 1967.

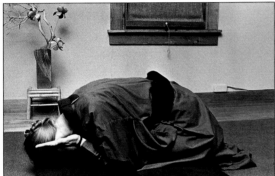

TOP: JAMES
HICKEY, ROMAN
CATHOLIC
ARCHBISHOP OF
WASHINGTON, IN
HIS STUDY. 1985.

MIDDLE:
ZEN BUDDHIST
AT PRAYER.
ROCHESTER,
NEW YORK, 1979.

ABOVE:
BORN-AGAIN
PROTESTANT
MINISTER.
NEW YORK
CITY, 1976.

"TESTIFYING"
DURING BAPTIST
SERVICE. NEAR
EUTAW,
ALABAMA, 1983.

HARE KRISHNA
CELEBRANTS.
NEW YORK CITY,
1967.

LEFT: OPPONENT OF RIGHT TO ABORTION DEMONSTRATES HER COMMITMENT TO ROMAN CATHOLIC FAITH BEFORE SUPREME COURT. WASHINGTON, 1991.

TOP: ON-STREET BAPTISM. NEW ORLEANS, 1964.

ABOVE: WALTER HOVING, CHIEF EXECUTIVE OF TIFFANY & CO., IN HIS OFFICE. NEW YORK CITY, 1976.

FACING PAGE: HOLOCAUST SURVIVOR DISPLAYS YELLOW STAR OF DAVID ALL JEWS WERE REQUIRED TO WEAR IN NAZI GERMANY. NEW YORK CITY, 1979.

LEFT: RUSSELL CANTWELL SOLICITS CONTRIBUTIONS FOR JEHOVAH'S WITNESSES, IN BROOKLYN, 1991. HIS AND HIS FATHER'S CONVICTIONS FOR SOLICITING WITHOUT LICENSE IN NEW HAVEN WERE OVERTURNED BY SUPREME COURT IN 1940; DECISION IS REPRINTED, LEFT, WITH SUMMARY ADDED BY JEHOVAH'S WITNESSES.

BELOW: A. GREGORY FRAZIER'S SUIT AGAINST CHRISTMAS CRECHE ON PUBLIC PROPERTY WAS REJECTED BY SUPREME COURT BECAUSE THE RELIGIOUS SYMBOLS WERE PART OF A LARGER, MAINLY SECULAR, DISPLAY. PAWTUCKET, RHODE ISLAND, 1990.

SUPREME COURT OF THE UNITED STATES

No. 632.—OCTOBER TERM, 1939.

[310 U.S. 296]

Jesse Cantwell, Newton Cantwell, and Russell Cantwell, Appellants,

vs.

The State of Connecticut.

On Appeal from and Certiorari to the Supreme Court of Errors of the State of Connecticut.

To enforce and apply against

Jehovah's witnesses

a statute requiring a permit to solicit for a charitable or philanthropic or "religious" cause, is unconstitutional and unlawful. In going from house to house offering to residents literature explaining the purposes of ALMIGHTY GOD and His Government under Christ Jesus described in the Bible, and accepting contributions for this work, Jehovah's witnesses use their liberty to worship Almighty God as He has commanded. Under the United States Constitution (First and Fourteenth Amendments) such activity is shielded against all governmental invasion.

Playing in the hearing of Catholics a phonograph record containing a strong attack upon all religion and particularly Roman Catholicism, is right conduct fully secured by the United States Constitution and does not amount to a breach of the peace or incitement to commit a breach of the peace.

[May 20, 1940.]

Mr. Justice ROBERTS delivered the opinion of the court.

Newton Cantwell and his two sons, Jesse and Russell, members of a group known as Jehovah's witnesses, and claiming to be ordained ministers, were arrested in New Haven, Connecticut, and each was charged by information in five counts, with statutory and common law offenses. After trial in the Court of Common Pleas of New Haven

JEHOVAH'S
WITNESS RYAN
MCCABE STANDS
SILENTLY
DURING PLEDGE
OF ALLEGIANCE
IN HIS PUBLIC
SCHOOL. THE
SUPREME COURT
RULED IN 1943
THAT ONE OF
THE THINGS THE
AMERICAN FLAG
STANDS FOR IS
THE RIGHT NOT
TO SALUTE IT.
NEW YORK CITY,
1991.

HALLOWEEN.
BROOKLYN,
NEW YORK,
1966.

FREEDOM OF RELIGION
2

THE ENGLISH CITIZENS WHO CAME TO THE NEW WORLD WERE DEEPLY FAMILIAR with the denials of religious freedom that arose when the power of the state became fused with the beliefs of the church. In sixteenth-century England, it was common for laws to regulate religion, sometimes promoting one creed, sometimes suppressing it and promoting another. The power to do one necessarily carried with it the power to do the other. At one time or another, the clergy were forbidden by law to promote belief in miracles, required to teach Protestant creeds, and prohibited from lighting candles in certain religious ceremonies. Laws were passed making heresy a crime, punishable by burning. At one period it was heretical to deny that the body and blood of Christ were actually present in the form of bread and wine during communion; at another time it was heretical to maintain that they were present. In 1538, a law required the clergy to provide each church with a Bible and to encourage people to read it; a few years later, a new law prohibited reading the Bible in church. People eventually understood that if the government had the power to promote religion, it also had the power to destroy it, and that true religious liberty required the government to stay out of religion completely. But this understanding was slow in coming.

In England in the 1680s, less than a hundred years before the American Revolution, it was a crime not to go to the Protestant Church of England, or not to receive the sacrament. Most Protestants rejoiced; Catholics and Puritans suffered.

Then James II, a Catholic, became king. He issued the Declaration for Liberty of Conscience. The declaration suspended the criminal laws supporting the official church and proclaimed tolerance for religious diversity. Those aims were laudable, but the declaration was widely understood as an effort to bring the king's party to power and as a step toward returning England to submission to Rome. When King James ordered the declaration to be read aloud in all churches, seven bishops, including the archbishop of Canterbury, refused, and wrote the king explaining why. For this they were arrested and prosecuted for seditious libel—for criticizing the king, disturbing the government, and stirring up the people. They were acquitted by a jury from which, as a matter of longstanding law, all Catholics had been excluded, and the king soon fled to exile. Under his successor, William of Orange, the established church was secure.

There were incidents of religious intolerance in the colonies as well. In 1637, a woman named Anne Hutchinson, who openly disagreed with the Calvinist ministers of the Massachusetts Bay Colony about how to achieve salvation, was tried for heresy, convicted, and banished to the wilderness. And right up to the Revolution in 1776, the colonies imposed religious tests for public office. Pennsylvania mandated every legislator to "believe in one God" and "acknowledge the Scriptures … given by Divine inspiration." That was one of the more liberal provisions. Delaware required a belief "in Jesus Christ … and the Holy Ghost"; Massachusetts obliged all state officials to swear to "believe in the Christian religion"; Georgia required legislators to be "of the Protestant religion"; and North Carolina disqualified anyone from public office who denied "the being of God or the truth of the Protestant religion, or the divine authority of either the Old or New Testament."

Such laws establishing official religion became a problem in early America, however, in part because of the diversity of religious beliefs and sects that flourished there. But opposition to established religion was not strong, because in practice many of the offensive laws were ignored. For example, when Thomas Jefferson was growing up in Virginia, the Church of England was the official church. Laws forced other churches to register with the government; laws punished those who failed to attend Anglican communion and imposed taxes on nonbelievers to support the official church; and laws prohibited non-Anglicans from holding office. Yet these laws were rarely enforced. Few people, if any, were actually punished for not attending Anglican communion. Exemptions from taxes to support the Church of England were common, and even Catholics held public office. The same was largely true in other colonies. John Adams called this "the most mild and equitable establishment of religion that was known in the world."

Nonetheless, there was episodic resistance to it. New Light Presbyterians and members of some Congregationalist groups felt discriminated against; many chose to go to prison rather than pay taxes to support another church. Then, in 1752, a Church of England college was founded in New York with financial support from the government. This produced a furious controversy, complete with heavy pamphleteering. For the first time in American history, the idea arose that public institutions should be secular or at least nondenominational. The movement for complete separation of church and state had begun.

In 1759, in Massachusetts, a similar incident strengthened that movement. Once again, the Church of England sparked a controversy, this time by sending a mission for the propagation of its official faith to a historically and dominantly Puritan colony. The head of that mission, a man named East Apthorp, vigorously attacked dissent and nonconformity. To the colonists, who already feared for their political liberties at the hands of England, Apthorp's assaults seemed like the beginning of an effort to transport the English establishment of religion to the colonies. Should that happen, warned Jonathan Mayhew in a popular pamphlet published in Boston in 1763, religious oaths would be required of all colonists and they would all be taxed to support Anglican bishops.

For people already inflamed about Parliament's unjust civil taxes, the prospect of religious taxes seemed both possible and intolerable. The two fears merged, and Mayhew explicitly connected them:

From what we hear of ... Parliamentary acts and bills for raising money on the poor colonies without their consent, [we fear] that provisions might also be made for the support of these bishops, if not all the church clergy also, in the same way.

More than half a century later, John Adams recalled that the Mayhew-Apthorp dispute

spread a universal alarm against the authority of Parliament. It excited a general and just apprehension that bishops, and dioceses, and churches, and priests, and tithes, were to be imposed on us by Parliament.... If Parliament could tax us, they could establish the Church of England with all its creeds, articles, tests, ceremonies, and tithes, and prohibit all other churches.

The fear of Parliament's legislative power began to create in the colonists a belief that their civil liberties and their religious liberties were inextricably related, and that to protect both, strict legal limits on legislative power would be needed. This growing belief eventually led to the conviction that the preservation of religious liberty required that the government stay neutral, that it neither support nor oppose religious practices of any kind, that the power to prefer religion also meant the power to suppress it, and that money raised through taxes on *all* citizens should never be used to support the religious beliefs of *some* citizens. This theme—especially opposition to the expenditure of tax-raised money to support religious activities—echoes throughout American history, and remains today a source of serious debate.

In the years leading up to the Revolution, the fear of Parliament's power over religious liberty quickly spread to local colonial legislatures. Many radical religious sects arose, and they used the same arguments against local governments that local governments had used against Parliament. New Light Presbyterians, Separate Baptists, Strict Congregationalists, and Methodists all were deeply hostile to local orthodoxies. In 1772, a bill was introduced in the Virginia legislature that would have required nonconforming religious believers to meet only during the daytime and only in meetinghouses licensed by the state; baptizing or preaching to slaves was forbidden, and nonbelievers could under certain conditions be forced to swear allegiance to the Church of England. The bill was dropped after widespread protest. But after the Revolution, this incident and the issues it raised helped determine the climate in which the original American principle of separation of church and state was written into the Bill of Rights. James Madison, for example, admitted to having been influenced by the protests of the Presbyterians and the Baptists.

Still, like John Adams, many argued that despite these episodes, America remained a remarkably tolerant place. And to a large extent, that was true, at least relative to other nations. Laws might exist requiring taxes from nonbelievers to support the official religion, but in practice nonbelievers were often exempted from such taxes. For the Baptists and others, however, this wasn't enough. They did not think that religious freedom was a *favor*, to be granted by the government. Nor did they think that *tolerance* was the same as having the *right* not to be taxed to support someone else's religion. Liberty, they argued, meant that local legislatures should have no legal power to tax them to support a church. If legislatures did have such power, but out of a spirit of open-mindedness chose not to exercise it, Baptists would still have no religious liberty, for they would be at the mercy of the majority's discretion.

This view of religious liberty was compelling, and hard to argue with, because it mirrored the popular ideas then being used to defend political liberty against the English Parliament. John Allen, in a pamphlet entitled *The American Alarm*, put it precisely:

You tell your governor that the Parliament of England has no right to tax the Americans ... because they are not the representatives of America; and will you dare to tax the Baptists for a religion they deny?

The Baptists picked up this theme and pressed it home, comparing the protest in Boston against the British tax on tea—the protest that produced the famous Boston Tea Party—to their own plight, and accusing the colonists of hypocrisy. A tax of three pence a pound on tea had made a great noise in the world, they proclaimed,

but your law of last June laid a tax of the same sum every year upon the Baptists in each parish.... All America are alarmed at the tea tax, though, if they please, they can avoid it by not buying the tea; but we have no such liberty.

This contradiction would not go away. And unlike the African slaves, who were in no position to press their grievances, religious minorities in colonial America had power and numbers enough to press theirs, as well as a more sympathetic audience.

The question of whether to separate church and state completely became impossible to avoid. Proponents of separation began to argue that unless the civil authorities were stripped altogether of the power to act for or against religion, religious liberty could not flourish. If a legislature were empowered to favor *any* religious practice, it was argued, its decision about *which* religious practice to support would have to be made by majority vote. Inevitably, minority religious beliefs would suffer. Some would be tolerated, others would not, and therefore the process of deciding which is which should not be made by the government. The uniquely American idea of religious liberty protected by a high wall of separation between church and state was forged during the time of the Revolution and ultimately codified in the Bill of Rights in 1791. Ever since, however, its exact meaning has been in dispute.

MAY THE GOVERNMENT FOSTER RELIGION IN GENERAL?

The first question is whether the Bill of Rights only prohibits the government from taking actions that *prefer* one religion over another, or more broadly prohibits it from aiding *all* religion, even if nonpreferentially. This is not merely a matter of historical interest; the question is very much alive today.

During the early 1980s, the state of Alabama passed a law requiring public-school children to observe a period of prayer each day in school. No particular prayer was required; in fact, the prayer was intended to be silent, so that each child could choose his or her own prayer. Though the law did not express a preference for one religion over another, the Supreme Court ruled, 6–3, that the law was unconstitutional because the government prohibited by the First Amendment from endorsing or sponsoring or mandating any religious exercise. William Rehnquist, the chief justice, was one of the three dissenters. His view was that the First Amendment certainly prohibited Alabama from preferring one religion over another but did not prohibit aid to religion in general. Was he right? The language of the First Amendment by itself doesn't tell us, because it merely prohibits any law "respecting an establishment of religion."

But as Leonard Levy's historical research shows, a fairly strong case can be made against Rehnquist's view.

The author of the First Amendment was not ambiguous. Madison firmly believed in what he called "perfect separation" between religion and government. He said repeatedly that religion would flourish more freely without the aid of government because the power of government to aid religion necessarily implied the power of government to suppress religion. Madison also believed that the main purpose of the Bill of Rights was to make certain that the government had no power to act at all in forbidden fields such as religion. In his own state of Virginia, Madison opposed a 1784 tax bill that would have subsidized religion *without preference.* As often happens today, those who supported the bill said they were on the side of God and recounted the many benefits of religion, implying that Madison somehow was opposed to God and religion. Madison replied, just as defenders of religious liberty do today when they oppose state aid, that the question wasn't whether religion was good, but whether state aid was good for religion. He thought not. The proposal for a general, nonpreferential tax for supporting religion failed, and two years later, the Virginia Statute of Religious Freedom completely separated church and state.

Second, when the Senate was originally considering the First Amendment, it *defeated* three motions that would have changed its language to prohibit laws that established "one religious sect or society in preference to others." The defeat of such a substitute for Madison's language weighs heavily against Rehnquist's view.

Finally, in attempting to understand what the framers had in mind when they passed the First Amendment, it is important to understand the times. During the Revolution, nine of the thirteen states had established religion, that is, government support of religion. After the Revolution, three of them — North Carolina, New York, and Virginia — strictly separated church and state. The remaining six converted their laws to provide for *nonpreferential support only.* When the First Amendment was enacted, *no* state had an established state church or supported one religion over another, and the six that supported religion at all did so on a nondenominational basis. What "establishment of religion" meant in America in 1791 was precisely nonpreferential aid. When the First Amendment prohibited the federal government from establishing religion, it was undoubtedly these nonpreferential establishments that the framers had in mind.

MAY STATES DENY RELIGIOUS RIGHTS?

For a very long time after 1791, no religious disputes arose that invoked the Bill of Rights. The federal government virtually never acted in the field of religion back then, so most of the violations of religious freedom were committed by state and local governments. But the Bill of Rights was, once again, powerless to limit state and local governments, because Madison's "most valuable" amendment had failed in 1789, and because the Supreme Court's 1873 decision in the *Slaughterhouse* cases destroyed the effectiveness of the Fourteenth Amendment as an instrument for applying the Bill of Rights to the states for nearly another century.

It was not until 1940—a century and a half after the Bill of Rights became law—that the Supreme Court first used the First Amendment to protect a religious right. In that case, three Jehovah's Witnesses—a man named Newton Cantwell and his sons—were arrested in Connecticut for distributing pamphlets in the street, soliciting contributions for their church, and criticizing the Catholic Church. They were convicted of a breach of the peace and also of violating a Connecticut law prohibiting the solicitation of money without a license.

The Supreme Court unanimously overturned their convictions. Although, to some extent, the issues in this case did not turn only on the fact that the Cantwells were engaged in *religious* speech—some of the Court's ruling applied more generally to any speech, whether religious or not—for the first time the Supreme Court clearly applied the First Amendment to the states to protect freedom of religion from *state* action. This was one of many cases over the next twenty-five years in which the Court ruled that the Fourteenth Amendment did in fact limit the states from abridging rights guaranteed by the Bill of Rights, and in that respect it was a vindication of James Madison's original view.

Over the next few years, the Court extended the protection of the Bill of Rights for religious freedom by ruling that state and local governments could not prohibit religious parades in public parks and streets, could not prohibit distribution of religious literature in public bus or railroad terminals, and could not prohibit Jehovah's Witnesses from door-to-door solicitations. All of these decisions, however, also made plain that the state had the power to make reasonable rules governing when, where, and how such activities could take place, in order to regulate traffic, for example, or to control noise. But such rules could not be based on the *content* of what the speakers or demonstrators had to say.

Those decisions, though they involved the religious rights of relatively small sects, ended up enlarging the rights of all Americans. The legal standards first imposed in these cases became the basis for many of the decisions upholding the rights of Martin Luther King, Jr., and his colleagues to parade and demonstrate, and limiting the power of local Southern towns and sheriffs to stop them. Few Americans understood at the time that their own rights would be determined by what happened to the Jehovah's Witnesses in these cases, yet that is how it turned out. Once again, narrow self-interest, initially affecting only the rights of parties to a particular dispute, was transformed into broad principles of liberty protecting large numbers of Americans.

That the Supreme Court issued these rulings, however, did not mean that all state and local governments immediately complied. A decade later, a New York street preacher who strenuously denounced other religions was prevented from doing so by a local law requiring a permit to hold religious meetings in public places. There were no standards for issuing such permits, so in effect the law gave local officials the discretion to decide. Not surprisingly, the street preacher was denied his permit. But the Supreme Court struck down the permit law and ruled that New York could not control the right to speak on religious subjects by allowing an administrative official to decide with no legal standards to restrain him. This, said the Court, would allow the official to pick and choose who should speak depending on what they were saying, and perhaps on whether he agreed with them or not.

Nearly two decades later, this decision was used by the Supreme Court to protect the rights of Fred Shuttlesworth, a black minister and civil-rights leader in Alabama, who was arrested and convicted for leading an orderly parade through the streets of Birmingham. The arrest was based on a law that allowed local officials to use an arbitrary permit system to censor speech.

Throughout the history of the Bill of Rights, we will see that in order for a right to stay alive, it must be won over and over again. This is partly because government power is decentralized in America. A court ruling limiting the power of the state of Connecticut in 1940 does not automatically prevent the state of New York in 1951 or the state of Alabama in 1969 from trying to use their power in the same way. But it does provide the basis for a challenge to that power. Beginning in the 1940s, cases involving the exercise of religious freedom in public places, and later the more general rights of free speech and assembly, helped prove this point. *Persistence* by citizens exercising their rights, as well as the text of the Bill of Rights, was responsible for establishing these basic liberties.

The development of religious liberty in America involved more than the right to preach and solicit in public places. One of the most fundamental religious rights the early Americans meant to protect was the right not to be subjected to a religious test for public office. Even before the Bill of Rights was adopted, the Constitution banned religious tests for public office. That ban applied only to federal offices. The First Amendment was meant to bar all government endorsement of religion, not only religious tests for public office, but for 150 years it didn't apply to state governments either.

The state of Maryland, as late as 1961, still required public officeholders to declare a belief in the existence of God. The Supreme Court struck down that law, ruling that the First Amendment prohibited state governments from forcing a person "to profess a belief ... in any religion." The Court ruled that the First Amendment not only prevented the state from preferring theistic religions to nontheistic religions such as Buddhism, Taoism, or Ethical Culture, but also from preferring religion to nonreligion. Nor may states discriminate against religion in setting qualifications for public office. In 1978, the Supreme Court struck down state laws that disqualified members of the clergy from holding public office.

IS SUNDAY THE ONLY PERMISSIBLE SABBATH?

Protecting religious liberty by keeping the state entirely out of religion is not always easy. In America's early years, many states passed laws requiring all stores to be closed on Sundays, in observance of the Christian Sabbath. The origin of these laws was undoubtedly religious, and represented government support of a religious belief. But since the Bill of Rights didn't apply to the states for a very long time, the First Amendment was not invoked to challenge any of these laws until 1961, when the Supreme Court decided four cases at once. Two of those were brought by the owners of stores who wanted to stay open for business seven days a week. The Court ruled against them. By then, Sunday-closing laws had acquired a strong secular purpose as well, and for that reason, the Court upheld those laws as a valid exercise of government power, ruling that such laws, whatever their origin, no longer represented government support of religious belief.

The two other cases decided that day were brought by Orthodox Jews, and raised a different question. Since they observed Saturday as the Sabbath, Sunday-closing laws penalized them for their exercise of religion by effectively requiring them to close their businesses for two days. Unless they were permitted to stay open on Sunday, they argued, the law created a discriminatory preference for Christians. The Court rejected this claim too, holding that although states were free to exempt, from the Sunday-closing laws, those who observed Saturday as their Sabbath, the First Amendment did not require them to do so.

Two years later, however, the Court confronted the same issue in a slightly different context and came to the opposite conclusion. A Seventh-Day Adventist who also observed the Sabbath on Saturday was denied government unemployment benefits because she had refused the offer of a job that required working on Saturday. The Court overruled the government and said that it could not force the applicant to choose between violating her religion and forfeiting government benefits. In effect, said the Court, that was like fining someone for worshipping on Saturday instead of Sunday. That, of course, was precisely the result for the Orthodox Jews who were penalized by the Sunday-closing laws. For worshipping on Saturday instead of Sunday, they were limited to a five-day business week, while the state permitted a six-day week only for Sunday observers. It is not easy to reconcile the different outcomes in these two cases.

Nonetheless, the Seventh-Day Adventist case was a landmark victory for the rights of religious minorities. Even though the obligation to be available for Saturday work was equally applied to everyone as a condition of receiving unemployment benefits, and was not intended to discriminate against Sabbatarians, the effect of the requirement restricted their freedom to exercise their religious beliefs, and for that reason it was struck down. For more than a quarter-century, that ruling prevailed.

Then, in 1990, the Court radically reversed itself. Two members of the Native American Church in Oregon used peyote during a sacramental ceremony of the church. They were both fired from their jobs, and applied for unemployment benefits. Oregon law made it a crime to use peyote, and made no exemptions for religious sacramental use. As a result, the state denied unemployment benefits because the applicants had been discharged for "misconduct." The Oregon Supreme Court reinstated the benefits, ruling that their denial violated the religious rights of the dismissed employees. Citing the Seventh-Day Adventist case, the Oregon court said that although the state's general practice of denying unemployment benefits to people discharged for misconduct was legitimate, its effect in this instance was to force the applicants to choose between violating their religion and forfeiting government benefits.

On appeal, the United States Supreme Court reversed the Oregon court and announced a new rule: from now on, an individual's religious beliefs would not excuse him from compliance with an otherwise valid law, as long as the law was not intentionally designed to discriminate against a particular religion. The applicants were thus forced to give up their religion or expose themselves to criminal penalties as well as the loss of unemployment benefits.

This new rule robbed the First Amendment of much of its ability to protect the free exercise of religion from majoritarian preferences. The Court acknowledged as much when it admitted that "religious practices that are not widely engaged in" would place religious minorities "at a relative disadvantage" and subject them to the discretion of legislative majorities. This, said the Court, is an "unavoidable consequence of democratic government."

This cavalier language seemed remarkably insensitive to the very purpose of the Bill of Rights. Forty-seven years earlier, the Supreme Court had described that purpose eloquently:

The very purpose of the Bill of Rights was to withdraw certain subjects from the vicissitudes of political controversy, to place them beyond the reach of majorities and officials, and to establish them as legal principles to be applied by the courts. One's right to life, liberty, and property, to free speech, a free press, freedom of worship and assembly, and other fundamental rights may not be submitted to vote; they depend on the outcome of no elections.

But in 1990, that vision of liberty was blurred by the Court's opinion. Perhaps the ruling would have been different if the sacramental drug had been wine. During the time of Prohibition, the National Prohibition Act contained an explicit exemption for the sacramental use of wine, so the constitutional issue was never raised in the courts. But the statutory exemption for wine demonstrated a sensitivity to a majority religion that Oregon did not show for the Native American Church. Because peyote was less familiar than wine, and the religion a distinctly minority one, no exemption was made, and the First Amendment provided no relief.

IS TAX EXEMPTION AN IMPERMISSIBLE SUBSIDY?

The question of using taxes to benefit or burden religion often provoked passionate controversy in colonial America. Similar questions have reverberated in modern times. A New York law exempted from real-estate taxes church-owned property that was used exclusively for religious purposes. This law was challenged in 1969 by a citizen who believed that tax exemption was the equivalent of a government subsidy. Exempting the church from taxes, he claimed, was like giving the church a direct government grant, which would be clearly unconstitutional. Only one Supreme Court justice agreed with this argument. The tax exemption was upheld, in large part because it was not limited to churches. The law granted tax exemptions to a wide variety of nonprofit organizations engaged in religious, educational, or charitable work, such as hospitals, libraries, playgrounds, and a variety of scientific, professional, historical, and civic groups. Several justices, including Chief Justice Warren Burger, who wrote the opinion for the Court, implied that if the tax exemption had by law or in practice resulted in benefitting churches exclusively, their decision might have been different. But insofar as churches were part of a much broader class of beneficiaries, the tax exemption did not represent government support of religion, any more than did the extension to churches of the privilege of postage discounts on nonprofit bulk mail.

On the other hand, the Court has upheld the power of the government to exact social-security and unemployment-insurance taxes from religious employers. In 1982, Amish employers brought suit to challenge such government taxes on the grounds that they violated their First Amendment right to free exercise of religion. They were commanded by the Bible to provide for their own workers, they argued, citing 1 Timothy 5:8: "But if any provide not

... for those of his own house, he hath denied the faith, and is worse than an infidel." The Court upheld the government's power to tax in this situation, again arguing that the law applied uniformly to all employers and did not single out the Amish or any other religious group.

In 1983 the Court decided a very controversial case involving Bob Jones University, which accepted black students but restricted interracial dating, and Goldsboro Christian Schools, which practiced racial segregation. Both schools would normally have been eligible for federal income-tax exemption, meaning they would not normally have had to pay taxes on the income they derived from tuition payments or contributions. Since 1969, though, such tax exemptions had been denied to schools that discriminated on the basis of race, but the schools claimed that their policies of racial separation were based on religious beliefs and that therefore they were being punished by the government for those beliefs. They sued to have their tax exemption restored, on First Amendment grounds.

The Supreme Court rejected their argument, 8–1, ruling that the policy of withholding tax exemptions from schools that discriminated on the basis of race was a valid exercise of government power. Again, religious institutions were grouped within a larger class of schools to which the tax policy applied, and were not singled out. Just as the churches granted property-tax exemptions in New York could not be singled out from the larger class of beneficiaries and denied tax exemptions because of their religious activities, so these schools could not be singled out and exempted from a valid policy that applied to everyone else. Their religious beliefs provided no special protection.

Though the Bill of Rights ensures the liberty of Americans to exercise their religious beliefs freely, religious belief does not immunize all conduct from government restrictions. A person could not escape a charge of murder by claiming a religious belief in human sacrifice. Similarly, religious belief cannot be invoked to protect against other validly proscribed conduct, such as theft or embezzlement. In the Bob Jones University case, the Supreme Court ruled that religious belief did not protect conduct—racial discrimination—that the government had a valid interest in prohibiting.

RELIGIOUS FREEDOM AND CONSCIENTIOUS OBJECTION

How much the government must accommodate religious freedom can also be a difficult question. In 1972, the Supreme Court considered the claim of a Buddhist prisoner in Texas who said that prison officials were discriminating against him by denying him use of the prison chapel, punishing him for distributing Buddhist literature to other prisoners, and denying him the credit for attending religious services that would increase his chances for early parole. Prison officials argued that prisoners cannot have the same freedom of religion as ordinary citizens and that the requirements of prison security prevented them from accommodating his beliefs. While accepting these arguments in general, and conceding some practical limitations on constitutional rights in the context of prisons, the Court ruled in favor of the prisoner and said that reasonable opportunities must be given even to prisoners to exercise their religion without penalty.

This decision had broader implications for ordinary citizens than might at first appear. The larger question is whether rights ordinarily available to civilians need to be restricted when people are under the jurisdiction of special institutions, such as prisons or the military. At about the same time as the prison case was being decided, the Supreme Court let stand a lower-court ruling that had struck down the Defense Department's policy of requiring cadets in government military academies to attend chapel. Whatever the special powers of the military might be, the court ruled, they did not include compelling religious belief and practice.

Of course, the major claim of the military upon individual liberty is when there is a draft. In 1918, the Supreme Court ruled that the Thirteenth Amendment's prohibition of involuntary servitude was not meant to prohibit the government from drafting soldiers. Still, it is hard to imagine a more complete interruption of individual liberty than when a person is required by law to put a moratorium on his life and kill other people at the bidding of the government. A key question of *religious* liberty, therefore — assuming that the government has the power to compel military service — is whether an individual who is conscientiously opposed to killing can be exempted.

James Madison thought the answer was clearly yes. His original proposal for a Bill of Rights contained a specific exemption from compulsory military service for religious objectors. This was not a radical proposal. In fact, the idea that conscientious objectors should be exempt from military service was widely held at the time. Nonetheless, Madison's proposed exemption was dropped by Congress, perhaps because the Bill of Rights wasn't intended to apply to the states, and military conscription was then viewed as a state, not a federal, function. When the Supreme Court first confronted this question, it could have ruled that the First Amendment prevented the government from drafting people whose religious beliefs prohibited killing, but it did not. On the other hand, Congress has always provided for some religious exemptions from military service. During both the Civil War and World War I, federal draft laws included religious exemptions, although these were limited to members of particular denominations whose doctrines explicitly prohibited participation in war.

In 1940, Congress specified criteria for a religious exemption: first, in order to be excused from combat, you had to derive your religious belief from a traditional, theistic religion; and second, you had to oppose all wars "in any form," not just a particular war. These criteria clearly discriminated among religions, and set up a conflict that was resolved by the Supreme Court during the Vietnam War. In 1965, the Court ruled that belief in God or in a traditional religion was not necessary. If an applicant could show that his conscientious opposition to war was based on a "purely ethical creed" that occupied a place in his life similar to that occupied by more traditional religious beliefs for others, he could be exempted. Five years later, the Court reaffirmed its decision, though in a somewhat confusing opinion that appeared to suggest that any attempt to distinguish religious objectors from nonreligious objectors was itself an unconstitutional distinction. A year later, the Court upheld the requirement that to be eligible, you had to oppose all war and not just a specific one.

Thus, although there is no constitutional right to conscientious objection, as Madison wished there to be, there is a long-recognized legal right established by Congress and not likely to be repealed. And the Bill of Rights has led the Supreme Court to expand that right by eliminating distinctions among the sources of belief that justify exemption. In practice, by a combination of legislative act and judicial construction, the right that Madison originally proposed has finally been guaranteed.

MAY COMMUNITY INTERESTS OVERCOME RELIGIOUS FREEDOM?

One of the most troubling conflicts between individual religious freedom and the power of the state occurs when the government decides to require certain measures to protect the health of the community. The classic example is compulsory vaccination against communicable diseases. What happens when an individual claims that his religion forbids vaccination? The Supreme Court settled this question back in 1905, by ruling in favor of the government: if the danger to the community is substantial, religious beliefs can be overridden.

It's a different matter, however, when only the individual's health or life is at risk. A competent adult, for example, has the right to decide against having a blood transfusion or an amputation, despite medical evidence and the advice of doctors that such procedures are necessary to save his life. This right rests only partially on religious freedom; the Bill of Rights more generally protects the right of competent adults to maintain autonomy—what John Stuart Mill called *sovereignty*—over their own bodies, provided that the larger community is not placed at risk.

But this freedom exists only for adults. An adult Jehovah's Witness, for example, who refuses a blood transfusion because he believes the procedure violates the biblical prohibition against the drinking of blood, has the right to do so. But he does not have the right to refuse a life-saving blood transfusion for his child. Courts have often intervened in such situations to order blood transfusions for children over the religiously based objections of their parents. In effect, the courts have ruled that when parents deny life-saving medical treatment to children, it is a form of parental neglect or abuse that cannot be justified by religious beliefs any more than beating a child could be.

This issue may seem fairly clear in extreme circumstances; it can be much more difficult when a child's life is not at stake and when there is a difference of medical opinion about what treatment is appropriate. Under such circumstances, the parents' right to decide what is best for their children normally prevails over the power of the state. Here again, such a right rests only partially on religious freedom: all parents are presumed, under normal circumstances, to have the right to decide what is best for their children. The government is not allowed to meddle unless it can prove neglect or abuse by the parent. Virtually all American parents would agree with this principle, and would deeply resent government interference with their right to raise their children as they see fit. But the law establishing this general right has largely been developed in extreme cases involving the religious beliefs of relatively tiny sects.

A difficult and still-unsettled question is whether a child under the age of eighteen has religious rights independent of his or her parents. In 1972, the state of Wisconsin prosecuted and convicted several Amish parents for violating a state law requiring all children to attend an accredited school (either public or private). The Amish religion commands its adherents not to conform to this world, to keep themselves separated from worldly influences, and to maintain a simple, agrarian existence, close to nature and the soil, in a tight-knit, church-oriented community. Amish people have lived this way for centuries. They send their children to school until the eighth grade, after which Amish children are expected to take their place in the religious community; what education takes place from this point is unconventional and integrated with the Amish way of life. But the state of Wisconsin required all children to attend conventional, accredited schools until the age of sixteen. In defending its prosecution of the Amish parents, the state argued that the government had a duty to protect children from ignorance, and that conventional education was necessary to prepare children to function as self-supporting citizens. The Court ruled, nearly unanimously, in favor of the parents, holding that their religious freedom trumped the interests of the state. In this instance, the Amish religious belief in a separate way of life overcame the government's otherwise valid interest—in this case, in promoting a given level of formal education.

The hidden issue in this case was what the children wanted. Although they had not reached the age of majority, neither were they infants. They were old enough to express preferences and to have views about what they might want to do with their lives. One of the Amish teenagers had testified at the trial, and indicated a desire to follow the Amish religion. But what of the others? Frieda Yoder had not testified. What if she were less inclined? What about *her* religious liberty? Must she wait until she turned eighteen? Would she then be handicapped by the lack of a formal education if she wanted to live in the outside world? No one knew, because Frieda Yoder never testified.

Justice William O. Douglas therefore dissented, in part, from the otherwise unanimous decision of the Court. He agreed with the other judges and voted to uphold the religious rights of the parents whose child had testified. But as to the parents of Frieda Yoder and the other children who hadn't testified, he said he would have returned the case to the trial court, so it could hear what these children believed. Upholding these parents' religious rights inevitably imposed religious beliefs upon their children, without even offering them an opportunity to express possibly different religious beliefs. "Where the child is mature enough," Douglas wrote, "it would be an invasion of the child's rights to permit such an imposition without canvassing his views."

Douglas's opinion received no support from any of the other judges, and the question he raised has never been decided. The issue still ticks quietly like a time-bomb in constitutional law: to what extent does a mature child below the age of eighteen have constitutional rights independent of her parents? Though it arose initially in the context of religious rights, this issue remains unresolved within the relatively new area of children's rights. The problem, of course, is that any legal right a child has independent of his parents can be enforced only by the government. This necessarily forces governmental power to intrude into the presumptively forbidden field of parental child-rearing authority. It is one thing to permit the state to intervene in cases of neglect or abuse, quite another to permit it in cases involving religious beliefs or other matters normally within the province of parental powers. Having the government routinely decide what is best for children, and imposing such decisions on parents, is not something most Americans would relish. But the idea that children have rights that grow as they grow and that should be increasingly respected as they approach the age of majority will not go away. Douglas's dissent in the *Yoder* case may yet influence future cases.

RELIGION IN THE SCHOOLS

Though the *Yoder* case raised unusual questions, in some ways it was typical of the many conflicts involving the principle of separation of church and state that had taken place in the schools during the latter half of the twentieth century. This is not surprising. Nothing matters more to parents than how their children are brought up, what values they are taught, and what kind of people they become. Schools have a major influence on these outcomes, and when parents give their children to the schools, they do so with both great trepidation and great expectation. What children are taught in the schools and how that relates to what they are taught at home is therefore a matter of deep concern to most parents.

For this reason, most parents have wanted the schools to reflect their own attitudes and beliefs. In America's early days, there was no problem because there was no system of public education. Formal education was church education, and as schools developed in America, education inevitably reflected religious beliefs and included religious training. As public schools developed, it was natural for them to continue to reflect the religious environment that had always characterized schools, and in America that environment was Protestant. As immigration brought more Catholics and Jews to America, this created a problem, because Catholic and Jewish parents felt increasingly oppressed by what they saw as the imposition of other religious beliefs on their children. And, of course, all this was taking place in *public* schools, that is, schools run and paid for by the government, using taxpayers' money.

The original American principle of not using the taxes of *all* Americans to support the religious beliefs of *some* Americans began to be implicated. Catholic parents unhappy with Protestant religious instruction in public schools brought lawsuits to challenge their constitutionality. At first these lawsuits were unsuccessful, in large part because the Supreme Court had not yet applied the First Amendment to the states, and it was the states, not the federal government, that ran public schools. So non-Protestant parents had to rely on political pressure. In 1914, responding to the pressure, public schools in Gary, Indiana, began for the first time to provide for separate classes of religious instruction for Protestants, Catholics, and Jews. These programs were called *released-time* programs, because with the consent of the parents, the public schools released children for a period of time to go to their own churches or synagogues for religious instruction.

By the 1940s, such programs were fairly widespread. Then, in the town of Champaign-Urbana, Illinois, a new twist was added. It was decided that it was inefficient to send children to religious classes elsewhere. So, working closely with churches and synagogues, the schools of Champaign-Urbana decided to conduct the religious instruction in the public schools themselves. Students whose parents had approved were released from their regular classes to attend religious classes conducted by religious teachers elsewhere in the public-school building. The dominance of the Protestant faith was reflected in how this arrangement worked. Protestant instruction was conducted in the regular classroom, so Protestant children didn't have to leave. They were clearly the norm. Catholic and Jewish children went to other classrooms, as did nonparticipating students and the regular teachers.

Terry McCollum was a fifth-grader in a Champaign-Urbana school. His mother filed a lawsuit challenging the program as a violation of the First

Amendment. Government schools should not be supporting religion, she said. School authorities argued that the First Amendment didn't apply to the states, and that even if it did, the ban on "establishment of religion" was not violated because the program was not preferential but rather respected all religious faiths in the school.

The Supreme Court rejected these arguments and ruled 8–1 in favor of Mrs. McCollum. The First Amendment does apply to the states, said the Court, and the ban on establishment of religion meant that government was prohibited from aiding religion at all; whether it did so preferentially or not was irrelevant. Echoing James Madison's view 150 years earlier, the Court said that the protection of religious liberty requires the state to stay out of religious matters entirely, neither to support nor to oppose religion; that's what *separation* of church and state means. In this case, ruled the Court, by making children—who are there because of the state's compulsory school-attendance law—and classrooms available to churches and synagogues, the government was clearly providing strong and invaluable aid to religion.

That was in 1948. Four years later, in a case arising in New York City, the Court substantially cut back the scope of its decision in *McCollum*. In this case, the New York City released-time program was challenged. New York's system, however, merely released children, at the request of their parents, to leave the school for religious instruction. By a 6–3 vote, with Justice William O. Douglas writing the majority opinion, the Court upheld New York's program because public school buildings and facilities were not used and the government was much less involved. The schools were merely rearranging schedules in order to accommodate the religious beliefs of parents, ruled the Court. One of the three dissenters in the case, Justice Hugo Black, had written the Court's opinion in the *McCollum* case. He argued, unsuccessfully, that the New York program was also unconstitutional, because it used the compulsory school attendance laws to make the children available in the first place. But the majority disagreed.

And that is where the law remains today. Released-time programs are constitutional, but only if religious instruction takes place outside the public schools, and school authorities are involved only to the extent of administering the release of children whose parents request it.

The Court's view that the principle of separation of church and state requires all religious activities to take place off the premises was substantially modified in 1981 in a case from Kansas City, Missouri. Students at the University of Missouri had organized a student religious club and wanted to meet on campus, just like other clubs. The University wouldn't let them, because the students wanted to worship and engage in such religious activities as praying, singing hymns, and reading from the Bible. University officials believed that the separation of church and state barred such activities from the campus of a state school, just as released-time religious instruction was barred from public schools.

But by an 8–1 vote, the Supreme Court disagreed. Colleges are different from elementary schools and high schools, the Court ruled, because college students are both more mature and less likely to be coerced or influenced by official school activities. If the government permits other clubs to meet and allows speakers to be invited on campus to speak on all kinds of subjects, it would be discrimination to single out religious activities for exclusion.

A few years later, Congress passed the Equal Access Act, a law applying the same standard to student clubs at public schools below the college level. Supporters of this legislation argued that voluntary student clubs are different from formal religious-instruction programs, and that it would be discrimination to prohibit religious students from having a prayer club on the school premises, while permitting a political club to meet. The argument on the other side was that at schools below the college level, all student clubs require faculty advisers and that therefore public officials are inevitably involved to a degree that young children will see as indicating official approval. This argument was rejected by Congress, and the law went into effect.

Shortly thereafter, a public high school in Omaha, Nebraska, refused to allow a group of students to form a religious club to read and discuss the Bible and pray together. The club was to be open to all and would meet, like other school clubs, after school hours on the school premises. School officials denied the students' request on the grounds that all student clubs required a faculty sponsor, which they believed would constitute an impermissible government endorsement of religion in violation of the First Amendment. The students and their parents sued, claiming that the Equal Access Act required the school to allow a religious club on the same basis as all other clubs.

When the case reached the Supreme Court, the Court upheld the students. Eight of the nine justices ruled that the Equal Access Act did not necessarily violate the First Amendment, although they could not agree on the reasons why. In this particular case, school officials appeared to play only an administrative role that could not be reasonably construed to constitute an endorsement. No other cases have yet reached the Court, but if public-school officials are involved in more than an administrative way and can reasonably be perceived as sponsoring religious beliefs, such practices may be struck down; if evidence of such official sponsorship and assistance is not clear and the student religious group is entirely voluntary, its freedom to meet on the same basis as other clubs will almost certainly be upheld.

These issues demonstrate the difficulty, under certain circumstances, of making sure the government neither aids nor hinders the practice of religion.

The cases discussed above have arisen only relatively recently. For most of our history, government pervasively and unambiguously promoted religious beliefs in public schools, despite the clear ban in the Bill of Rights against doing so. Official, government-sponsored prayers were a regular feature of many, perhaps most, public schools, and children whose families did not share the beliefs expressed in those prayers had little choice in the matter. Such children, including very small children, were made to feel as if their government did not like them as well as other children, whose religion was preferred.

These practices went unchallenged for many years, because once again the First Amendment hadn't been applied to the states. Meanwhile, the complaints from Catholics and Jews about Protestant prayers in the schools began to grow, and increasing numbers of people began to feel that it was inappropriate and unconstitutional to have any form of government-sponsored religious exercises in public schools. Partly in response to this protest, the state of New York promulgated an official school prayer. It was short, fairly bland, and approved by the three major religious faiths in New York at the time: "Almighty God, we acknowledge our dependence upon Thee, and beg Thy blessings upon us, our teachers, and our country." No school had to use it, but if any prayer was used, the law required this one.

Several local school boards chose to use this prayer, including the one in New Hyde Park, a suburban Long Island town. The school board directed the principals of each school in the district to have the prayer said aloud by each class in the presence of a teacher at the beginning of each school day. Children whose parents did not wish them to participate could remain silent or leave the room. Stephen Engel challenged the prayer program, and in 1962 the Supreme Court struck it down by an 8–1 vote, as a clear violation of the First Amendment bar against any government establishment of religion. The Court's decision was applauded by those whose religious beliefs were offended by the state's prayer and by those who, regardless of their religious beliefs, felt that it was wrong for the government to take sides on the question of religion. But the Court's decision also provoked a storm of opposition from many religious believers, who saw it as an insult to their religion and to religion in general.

Justice Hugo Black, writing for the Court, tried to explain that the First Amendment was intended to protect religious liberty by guaranteeing that the power and prestige of the government would never be used "to control, support, or influence the kinds of prayers the American people can say." He reminded us about our history: how many of the early Americans had migrated to America precisely to avoid government-established prayers in England; how some of them, once here, had established laws making their own religion or their own prayers the official one; how intense opposition to such government interference with religion had developed among the early Americans; and how this opposition had led to the principle, reflected in the First

Amendment, that the best way to protect everyone's religious liberty was to keep church and state apart so that all religious beliefs remained "on an equal footing so far as the state was concerned."

New York's official prayer violated that principle, the Court ruled, and put the children of parents with nonconforming religious beliefs at precisely the disadvantage the First Amendment was intended to prevent. By permitting such children, and especially small children, to remain silent or, worse, leave the room during the majority's prayer session, the government sent a clear message to these children that their religious beliefs were not preferred by their own government.

Justice Black also firmly rejected the idea that the Court's decision reflected hostility toward religion and prayer in general. On the contrary, he asserted, the decision reflected respect for religion and for the diversity of religious beliefs in America. When government gets involved in the promotion of religion, he wrote, it degrades religion by suggesting that religious belief requires government support to sustain it. When asked to comment on the Court's decision, President John F. Kennedy, a Catholic — and the first Catholic ever to be elected president — agreed. The place for prayer, he said, was in the home and in the church. But those who wanted their own religious beliefs strengthened by government support were not mollified, and the decision continued to be controversial.

A year later, the Court struck down a slightly different program in Pennsylvania. No state-written prayer was imposed there, but Pennsylvania had passed a law requiring that "at least ten verses from the Holy Bible shall be read, without comment, at the opening of each public school on each school day." Upon a written request of a parent, children could be excused. The Schempp family, who were members of the Unitarian Church, challenged the law, and the Supreme Court struck it down, again with only one justice dissenting. The Court ruled that it didn't make any difference whether or not the government had written a specific prayer to be recited. The First Amendment prohibited *any* government action that had the primary effect of either advancing or inhibiting religion. The majority may not "use the machinery of the state to practice its beliefs," said the Court. The government must protect all religious liberty by neither preferring nor disparaging any religious belief.

In a separate concurring opinion, Justice William Brennan dealt with the question of whether Jefferson and Madison would have prohibited state-imposed religious exercises in public schools. This question is "futile and misdirected," he said. There was no comparable system of public schools at the time, nor was there as much religious diversity. The proper question, he said, was whether laws like the Pennsylvania law create the result — government support of religion — that the First Amendment was designed to prevent. Justice Brennan's answer to that question was yes.

For many years following these decisions, local school districts and some state legislatures continued to try to "use the machinery of the state" to impose the practice of their own religious beliefs, or the religious beliefs of the majority, in violation of the religious freedom of others. A large number of these practices escaped scrutiny. But some did not.

In 1980, the Supreme Court struck down a Kentucky law requiring the posting of the Ten Commandments on the walls of every public-school classroom. And in 1985, the Court struck down an Alabama law requiring all public-school children to observe a daily period of silence for the explicit purpose of praying. The Court ruled, 6–3, that the state could require periods of silence or quiet, which children could choose to use in any way they wished, including prayer. But Alabama already had an unobjectionable law requiring a period of silence; this new law added an objectionable ingredient by specifying that a preferred purpose of the period of silence was to pray. The new law had no valid secular purpose, said the Court, but instead was yet another attempt to impose a religious practice, and it was struck down.

WHEN THE FLAG IS A GRAVEN IMAGE

It is important to note here that the Court has allowed the state to require certain patriotic ceremonies, such as flag salutes, because these have what the Court has called a "valid secular purpose" and do not impose or endorse a *religious* belief. Such patriotic exercises have been challenged, however, on grounds other than religious freedom. For example, the government's power to compel loyalty or to require anyone to affirm a particular *political* belief is also limited by the First Amendment's guarantee of freedom of speech. But even where patriotic ceremonies are permitted, students have been allowed since 1943 to be excused from such ceremonies if the ceremonies conflict with their religious beliefs.

In that 1943 case, several Jehovah's Witness children and their parents sued the state of West Virginia, seeking exemption from the state's requirement that each public school begin the day with a salute to the flag. They claimed that their religion commanded them not to worship any "graven images," including flags. This small religious sect had resisted public-school flag-salute ceremonies, mostly without success, ever since they first began to be used in 1898. Interestingly, such ceremonies were not required by law, and not thought to be necessary, for more than a hundred years after the founding of America, not even at the outset, when the flag and the nation were new.

In 1943—in the middle of World War II, when one might have expected the Supreme Court to have been extremely deferential to symbolic patriotic ceremonies—the Court, by a 6–3 vote, and in ringing language, upheld the claims of the Jehovah's Witnesses, and struck down the state's requirement.

One of the things that the flag stands for, the Court said that day, was the right not to salute it. In words that expressed the American way of life as well as any ever have, the Court said:

If there is any fixed star in our constitutional constellation, it is that no official, high or petty, can prescribe what shall be orthodox in politics, nationalism, religion, or other matters of opinion, or force citizens to confess by word or act their faith therein. If there are any circumstances which permit an exception, they do not now occur to us.

This was no abstract philosophical argument at the time. Real people, including thousands of small, vulnerable children, were affected. In the years prior to the Court's decision, approximately two thousand Jehovah's Witness children had been expelled from school for refusing to salute the flag because it was against their religion. They thought that as Americans they had a right to refuse. They thought that having such a right was what it meant to be an American. But the laws said no, and punished them. The Supreme Court had upheld these laws when it first considered them in 1940. Following that decision, majoritarian hysteria compounded the violation. Many Jehovah's Witness children were followed home, taunted, abused, called traitors. A Jehovah's Witness church was burned. In Wyoming, Jehovah's Witnesses were tarred and feathered; in Nebraska, one was castrated. The Supreme Court's 1943 ruling provided constitutional shelter, and helped end the persecution of Jehovah's Witnesses.

For many years, the West Virginia case, though frequently cited by courts and constitutional lawyers, remained unknown to most Americans. Then, during the 1988 presidential campaign, Vice-President George Bush attacked his opponent, Governor Michael Dukakis of Massachusetts, for vetoing a bill that would have prohibited teachers from refusing to conduct flag-salute ceremonies. Dukakis issued that veto on the basis of the Supreme Court's West Virginia decision. But Bush tried to suggest that in aligning himself with the Supreme Court's decision in the Jehovah's Witness case, Governor Dukakis was showing a lack of respect for the flag, and for traditional American values. Others suggested at the time that perhaps it was Mr. Bush who did not understand what traditional American values were all about. They identified instead with the patriotism expressed by the Supreme Court's affirmation of religious and political liberty in the West Virginia case, and saw Mr. Bush's attack as another example of "pretended patriotism, used as a cloak for self-interest."

But while this dramatic political dispute was going on, a more poignant personal drama unfolded. One enterprising reporter for the *New York Times* thought it would be interesting to look up the Jehovah's Witnesses who, as children at the time of the West Virginia case in 1943, had been expelled from school for refusing to salute the flag. Most of them were still alive, and the pain of what had happened to them forty-five years before was reflected in their reactions now. They took no position on the politics of the moment, but the pain of the abuse they had suffered so long ago still sounded fresh when they spoke of it, and they wondered aloud why anyone would want to raise the question again, would want to stir up those mean spirits that had hurt and tormented them because of their beliefs.

The incident was revealing, because it showed that lofty debates about fundamental rights often ignore the ordinary people who are grievously hurt when rights are denied. The Bill of Rights began with abstract public debates during the period of constitutional ratification in 1787; the debate continued during the First Congress in 1789; and throughout the two centuries that have followed, the development of the great rights has been etched by landmark Supreme Court decisions. But rights are not, have never been, mere legal questions. They only seem that way to people who have not yet lost them, or suffered their violation.

EVOLUTION AND "CREATION SCIENCE"

The school-prayer and Bible-reading cases represented attempts by the state to impose religious beliefs or practices by law on all public-school children and their families. But states have also tried to impose religious beliefs by censoring secular teaching that contradicted or threatened religious tenets. In the early 1920s, during a time of fundamentalist religious revival, the state of Tennessee attempted to give that revival a helping hand by passing a law making it a crime for public-school teachers to teach the theory of evolution, or any other scientific theory that contradicted the biblical teachings of Genesis. Specifically, the law banned "any theory that denies the story of the Divine Creation of man as taught in the Bible, and teaches instead that man has descended from a lower order of animals."

In 1925, a young man named John Scopes was arrested in Dayton, Tennessee, for violating that law. He admitted teaching about evolution and challenged the Tennessee law as a violation of the Bill of Rights. The Scopes case, known at the time as "the Monkey Trial," became a nationwide *cause célèbre,* and even today remains one of the most famous trials in our history, helped no doubt by the 1955 play and the 1960 movie about the case, both called *Inherit the Wind.*

The case quickly became a stage for major national figures. The local prosecution was joined by William Jennings Bryan, a three-time presidential candidate, celebrated orator, and fervent fundamentalist who believed that every word in the Bible was literally true and that the law should enforce that belief. On the other side, young Scopes was defended, free of charge, by Clarence

Darrow, perhaps the most famous criminal lawyer of his time, who had been recruited as a volunteer lawyer by a then-new organization called the American Civil Liberties Union. He argued that the Tennessee law was as gross a violation of religious liberty and free speech as the framers could have imagined. The case was chronicled by H. L. Mencken, the acerbic journalist from Baltimore who viewed the conflict as a dramatic confrontation between rural, fundamentalist Christians and the urban forces of civil liberties and modern science.

The trial judge did not allow Scopes's lawyers to make the argument that the Tennessee law violated the Bill of Rights, nor did he allow testimony by either religious or scientific experts. The only issue, he instructed the jury, was whether John Scopes had done what he was accused of doing, and this Scopes had never denied. Scopes was convicted and fined $100.

On appeal, Scopes's lawyers hoped for a Supreme Court ruling. But the case never reached the Supreme Court. The state supreme court upheld the law, but threw out Scopes's conviction because Tennessee law prohibited fines in excess of $50 without a specific recommendation of the jury. Scopes could have been retried, but he was not. The law remained on Tennessee's books for many decades, though it was never enforced again.

Not until 1968 did the United States Supreme Court have an opportunity to rule on a similar law enacted in Arkansas. The Court unanimously struck down the law as a violation of the Bill of Rights. Somewhere in heaven, John Scopes may have smiled. But not for long.

During the next fundamentalist revival, in the early 1980s, more than a dozen states passed "creationism" laws. These laws endorsed the idea that the Book of Genesis was in fact supported by a scientific theory called creationism, which, they claimed, was a valid scientific alternative to the theory of evolution and should be taught as such in the public schools. Again, supporters of this view thought the assistance of the government would be helpful, so laws were passed requiring public schools to teach creationism wherever and whenever evolution was taught. The first of these laws was passed in 1981 by the state of Arkansas, whose antievolution law had been struck down by the Supreme Court a few years earlier.

Clarence Darrow, William Jennings Bryan, H. L. Mencken, and John Scopes were all long since dead, but Roger Baldwin, who was the American Civil Liberties Union's first executive director in 1925, when the Scopes case took place, was still alive, and then nearly ninety-eight years old. He issued a press release denouncing the Arkansas law, and the ACLU offered to represent anyone who wanted to challenge it in court.

A number of Arkansas residents took up the ACLU's offer. Among them were leading clergymen, including high officials of the Catholic, Methodist,

Episcopalian, Presbyterian, and other churches. They argued that if the legislature of Arkansas were allowed to compel the teaching of certain religious beliefs, then it would also have the power to prohibit them. Their religious freedom, they claimed, depended upon keeping the government out of the practice of religion.

After a two-week trial that nearly rivaled the Scopes case in drama, the federal court struck down Arkansas's creationism law, ruling that it was just a dodge to mandate the teaching of a particular religious belief—biblical literalism—which the First Amendment clearly prohibited the government from doing. The state of Arkansas decided not to appeal the decision. Again, the case never reached the Supreme Court, and as a result, the Arkansas decision didn't apply to other states. A few years later, Louisiana passed a similar law; it was challenged, again by a coalition of parents, teachers, and religious leaders, and struck down by a federal court in Louisiana. This time the state appealed, and the case was heard by the Supreme Court.

In 1987, by a 7–2 vote, the Court ruled that the Louisiana creationism law was an impermissible endorsement by the government of a particular religious belief—that a supernatural being created the world in seven days, literally as described in the Book of Genesis. The use of the term "creation science" was intended to embrace this particular religious belief as a matter of faith and was not in fact a scientific theory, which would be subject to empirical test and to change with new evidence. The primary purpose of the law, ruled the Court, was to use the public-school curriculum as a way of providing a distinct advantage to this particular religious belief. The Court's decision in the Louisiana case put an end to the latest effort to impose religious beliefs by law upon public-school students. No other creationism laws were passed.

TAX-RAISED MONEY FOR RELIGIOUS SCHOOLS

But if the government is not permitted to impose religious beliefs, instruction, and practices upon public schools, what about parents who want their children to receive a religiously oriented education? Do they have that right?

In the early twentieth century, Oregon passed a law requiring all children to attend *public* schools. Parents who wanted to send their children to church schools challenged the law, and in 1925 the Supreme Court upheld their right to do so. Without this decision, religious schools could not have flourished. The decision, of course, assumed that religious schools would be entirely supported by private contributions and payments. At the time, this was so obvious that it was not even an issue. If there was any single practice the early Americans meant to prohibit when they passed the First Amendment in 1791, it was forcing people to support other people's religion through compulsory taxation. Jefferson called this practice "sinful and tyrannical," and Madison denounced it as well. Public funds raised through taxation could not be used to support religious schools.

But as the cost of running religious schools mounted, pressure began to build to use tax-raised money to help support religious education. In New Jersey, a law was passed to reimburse parents for the cost of transporting their children on public buses to both public schools and private schools, including religious schools. The law was challenged by a New Jersey taxpayer who did not want his taxes to support someone else's religion. In 1947, the Supreme Court rejected this challenge. The Court unanimously agreed that the First Amendment barred the government from levying any tax, however small, to support religious activities or institutions. If the bar against an "establishment of religion" means anything, the Court said, it means that. Yet a narrow 5–4 majority upheld the New Jersey law. They said—as they were to say nearly a quarter of a century later in the New York real-estate tax case—that the New Jersey law was permissible because it provided aid to all students using public transportation to get to school—to public schools as well as private schools, nonsectarian as well as parochial. To exclude only religious-school students, said the Court, would be to discriminate against them because of their religious beliefs. It would be comparable to excluding parochial schools from other general services provided by the state, such as police and fire protection or street maintenance. These services, paid for by general taxes, certainly aid the church, but surely the First Amendment did not require the government to handicap churches by denying them services provided to everyone else.

The New Jersey transportation case stirred up a hornet's nest of questions that to this day have not been resolved. If the government can use tax money to pay for buses to take children to parochial schools, what can't it do? For twenty years, the Supreme Court was not called upon to answer that question. Then, New York passed a law allowing the government to lend textbooks on secular subjects like mathematics to children attending religious schools. The textbooks to be lent had to be authorized for use in public schools. This law was challenged by New York taxpayers who said that permitting religious schools to use textbooks paid for by general taxes constituted direct aid. Justice Hugo Black, the author of the Court's decision in the New Jersey transportation case, agreed and switched his vote. Providing textbooks went too far, he said, and was unquestionably the sort of direct financial aid prohibited by the First Amendment. By that time, however—twenty-one years after the transportation case—several Supreme Court justices had left the Court and been replaced. Had this question come up in 1947, at the same time as the transportation case, the textbook-loan program would probably have been struck down. But in 1968, by a 6–3 vote, the Court upheld it.

Despite Justice Black's dissent, the majority believed the textbook case was essentially the same as the transportation case: since textbooks were supplied to public-school children free of charge, they could also be supplied to parochial-school children free of charge. This decision permitted direct and substantial aid to church schools, because it allowed church funds that would otherwise have been used to purchase textbooks to be used for religious purposes, thereby funneling taxes collected from all Americans into church coffers. The decision also led to a long series of attempts by religious groups to find other ways of gaining government support for religious institutions.

Since 1968, several state legislatures have passed bills providing various forms of general aid to religious schools, though many of these schemes have been struck down. In 1971, for example, the Court considered two programs, one in Rhode Island and the other in Pennsylvania, that reimbursed a portion of the salaries of parochial-school teachers of secular subjects. If secular-subject textbooks could be subsidized with public funds, these states reasoned, why not secular-subject teachers? The Court struck both programs down, in part because they would have required the government to audit the books and monitor the classrooms of the religious schools involved. This, said the Court, would inevitably require the government to become too "entangled" in the affairs of the church, and for that reason would violate the principle of separation of church and state.

The Court has also struck down state laws that reimbursed religious schools for the costs of preparing, conducting, and grading tests, for repairing school buildings, for transporting children on field trips, and for purchasing equipment. On the other hand, the Court has upheld laws reimbursing religious schools for certain noninstructional health services provided by the schools, such as medical and dental care and diagnostic services for speech, hearing, and psychological problems. And in 1980, the Court allowed New York to reimburse religious schools for the cost of administering tests prepared and required by the state.

In 1983, during a major fundamentalist revival in America and with a White House strongly committed to weakening the wall between church and state, the Supreme Court took a major step further toward allowing public funds to be used to pay for religious schools. The state of Minnesota had established a program to provide income-tax deductions to parents for expenses they incurred sending their children to school. Eligible expenses included tuition, transportation, textbooks, and instructional materials on secular subjects. A decade earlier, the Supreme Court had struck down a similar program in New York because it had the effect of financially assisting the religious functions of parochial schools. But it upheld the Minnesota program, even though it conceded that the result — providing financial assistance to religious activities — was not much different from the New York case.

The Court justified its decision in part because the New York program was available only to parents who sent their children to private schools, whereas the Minnesota program was available to parents of public-school students as well. To some, the Court's reasoning seemed disingenuous. The major tax-deductible expense was tuition, which parents of public-school students didn't pay; 96 percent of the Minnesota tax deductions were taken by parents sending their children to religious schools. The Minnesota case therefore represented a major reversal and resulted in significant amounts of tax-raised public funds being diverted to religious institutions.

Establishing a clear, principled basis for distinguishing all these religious-school cases is not easy. The Supreme Court's legal theories have hardly been models of clarity or coherence, and many aspects of these decisions are mutually inconsistent. But the drift since 1968 has been steadily toward providing public funds for at least some expenses of religious schools. For states clever enough to devise programs in accordance with prior Supreme Court decisions, substantial financial assistance, raised from general taxes, is available to religious institutions. In 1991, President George Bush proposed a new federal law providing direct government payments to parents through a voucher system that could be used to pay for tuition at any school, including religious schools. If this bill passes and is upheld by the Supreme Court on the same grounds it used to sustain the Minnesota program, vast amounts of federal tax money will become available to religious institutions.

To the early Americans, who so fiercely resented having any portion of their taxes used to support someone else's church, this result would been a glaring departure from the principle of separation of church and state. But for now this original principle has been at least modified—some would say violated. Certainly, there have been breaches in the wall of separation, because some religious believers have succeeded in their efforts to harness the power of the state to assist them. Whenever they do, religious liberty for everyone else is diminished, as the early Americans knew.

Yet overall, the principle of separation of church and state in America, even though imperfectly enforced, provides more religious freedom than in any other country in the world. And this country has suffered less from religious strife than those nations where church and state remain fused or closely related, and where the power of government is routinely available to enforce the religious beliefs of the majority.

But it is well to remember how vulnerable we still remain to religious strife, and how close to the surface religious persecution can still be. Only a few years ago, in a town called Little Axe, Oklahoma, the local school board authorized religious activities and ceremonies in public schools, in clear violation of the Bill of Rights, as interpreted by the Supreme Court. Two parents, one a Nazarene and the other a member of the Church of Christ, complained because students were being harassed for not participating. One student said he was accused of being "a devil-worshipper." Another reported that an upside-down cross had been affixed to his locker door. The two parents brought suit to protect their religious freedom and their children's.

Shortly afterward, they began receiving death threats. There was a bomb threat at the school. One of the parents who had sued was attacked in the school parking lot. Later, her home was burned to the ground. All this happened in 1981, nearly two centuries after the First Amendment was adopted. At times like these, one wonders just how far we have come since that day in 1637 when Anne Hutchinson was tried for heresy in Massachusetts and banished to the wilderness.

FREEDOM
OF EXPRESSION

ARMY TROOPS
GUARD TELEVISION
CREW AT MEMO-
RIAL SERVICE
FOLLOWING THE
ASSASSINATION OF
MARTIN LUTHER
KING, JR. MEMPHIS,
TENNESSEE, 1968.

NEWSSTAND.
NEW YORK
CITY, 1991.

PICTURE COLLECTION, THE BRANCH LIBRARIES, THE NEW YORK PUBLIC LIBRARY

THE
TRIAL
OF
John Peter Zenger,
OF
NEW-YORK, PRINTER;

Who was Tried and Acquitted,

For PRINTING and PUBLISHING a LIBEL
against the Government,

WITH
The PLEADINGS and ARGUMENTS on both Sides.

Ita CUIQUE *eveniat, ut de* REPUBLICA *meruit.* CIC.

LONDON:
Printed for P. BROWN, in *Fleet-Street.* MDCCLII.
[Price One Shilling and Sixpence.]

THE EDITOR AND PUBLISHER OF THE NEW-YORK WEEKLY JOURNAL WAS TRIED IN 1735 FOR PRINTING A "FALSE, SCANDALOUS AND SEDITIOUS LIBEL" PORTRAYING THE COLONIAL GOVERNOR "AS A PERSON WHO HAS NO REGARD TO LAW NOR JUSTICE." HE WAS ACQUITTED BY A NEW YORK CITY JURY (TITLE PAGE OF A PRIVATELY PRINTED TRIAL TRANSCRIPT).

IN A LIVING ROOM, YAKIMA, WASHINGTON, 1989.

"All the News That's Fit to Print"

The New York Times

LATE CITY EDITION

VOL. CXX...No. 41,431   NEW YORK, THURSDAY, JULY 1, 1971   15 CENTS

SUPREME COURT, 6-3, UPHOLDS NEWSPAPERS ON PUBLICATION OF THE PENTAGON REPORT; TIMES RESUMES ITS SERIES, HALTED 15 DAYS

Nixon Says Turks Agree To Ban the Opium Poppy

By JOHN HERBERS

PRESIDENT CALLS STEEL AND LABOR TO WHITE HOUSE
He Asks Both Sides to Meet With Him Tuesday Before Contract Talks Start

By PHILIP SHABECOFF

Pentagon Papers: Study Reports Kennedy Made 'Gamble' Into a 'Broad Commitment'

By HEDRICK SMITH

BURGER DISSENTS
'First Amendment Rule Held to Block Most Prior Restraints'

By FRED P. GRAHAM

THE NEW YORK TIMES TRIUMPHANTLY HAILS DECISION UPHOLDING ITS RIGHT TO PRINT A SECRET GOVERNMENT REPORT ON THE VIETNAM WAR DESPITE

NIXON ADMINISTRATION ARGUMENT THAT PUBLICATION MIGHT CAUSE IRREPARABLE HARM TO NATIONAL SECURITY.

CLOCKWISE
FROM TOP:
BILLBOARD.
NEAR TOPEKA,
KANSAS,
1986.

STORE-WINDOW
SATIRE DURING
WATERGATE
HEARINGS. NEW
YORK CITY,
1973.

WALL GRAFFITI
CONCERNING
AIDS. NEW YORK,
1990.

WALL GRAFFITI
DURING PERSIAN
GULF WAR.
NEW YORK,
1991.

SIGNATURE IN
SIDEWALK OF
MANN'S CHINESE
THEATER.
HOLLYWOOD,
1989.

WALL POSTER
DENIGRATING
ROBERT BORK
DURING HIS
SUPREME COURT
CONFIRMATION
HEARINGS.
NEW YORK,
1987.

ROADSIDE
BILLBOARD
CALLING FOR
OUSTER OF THE
CHIEF JUSTICE
OF THE SUPREME
COURT.
NEAR CLINTON,
LOUISIANA,
1964.

CAMPAIGN CAR
LEFT IN FIELD
BESIDE ROAD.
NORTH OF
BATON ROUGE,
LOUISIANA,
1964.

DEMONSTRATION
IN FRONT OF
THE WHITE
HOUSE AGAINST
THE VIETNAM
WAR. 1969.

LEFT: "SIT-
DOWN" STRIKE
IN A GENERAL
MOTORS
FACTORY.
FLINT,
MICHIGAN,
1937.

UPI/BETTMANN NEWSPHOTOS

RIGHT: CLASS-
MATES OF
COLLEGE
FOOTBALL STAR
DICK KAZMAIER,
AT THEIR 25TH
REUNION,
CELEBRATE HIS
PORTRAYAL
ON A 1951 TIME
MAGAZINE
COVER. PRINCE-
TON, NEW
JERSEY, 1977.

THE MARCH ON
WASHINGTON
FOR CIVIL
RIGHTS. 1963.

HECKLERS AT
ANTI-VIETNAM
WAR MARCH.
WASHINGTON,
1968.

MASKED
VIETNAM VET
VIOLATES
FEDERAL FLAG-
BURNING LAW A
FEW MINUTES
AFTER IT WENT
INTO EFFECT.
THE LAW WAS
HELD UNCONSTI-
TUTIONAL A FEW
MONTHS LATER.
SEATTLE,
WASHINGTON,
1989.

DEMONSTRATOR
FOR FREE
PUBLIC ACCESS
TO BEACHES.
MADISON,
CONNECTICUT,
1975.

AP/WIDEWORLD PHOTOS

SUPPORTER OF
THE VIETNAM
WAR AT AN ANTI-
WAR DEMONSTRA-
TION. NEW YORK
CITY, 1968.

CAPITOL POLICE
ARREST YIPPIE
LEADER ABBIE
HOFFMAN FOR
"CASTING
CONTEMPT"
ON THE FLAG.
WASHINGTON,
1968.

COURTESY OF AMERICAN CIVIL LIBERTIES UNION FOUNDATION

WOMAN DISPLAYS
RUBBING OF A
NAME FROM THE
VIETNAM WAR
MEMORIAL.
WASHINGTON,
1985.

DEMONSTRATOR
OUTSIDE THE
DEMOCRATIC
NATIONAL
CONVENTION,
MADISON
SQUARE
GARDEN. NEW
YORK CITY,
1976.

PARTICIPANT IN
PEACE MARCH,
CENTRAL PARK.
NEW YORK CITY,
1966.

RIGHT: A NEW
YORKER. 1986.

© 1980, ROBERT MAPPLETHORPE. COURTESY OF ESTATE OF ROBERT MAPPLETHORPE.

SELF-PORTRAIT BY PHOTOGRA- PHER ROBERT MAPPLETHORPE. A POSTHUMOUS SHOW OF HIS WORK IN 1990 LED TO THE TRIAL AND ACQUITTAL OF THE DIRECTOR OF THE CINCINNATI ART MUSEUM UNDER A LOCAL OBSCENITY LAW.

2 LIVE CREW RAP GROUP AND STORES THAT SOLD THIS ALBUM WERE TRIED IN FLORIDA AND ALABAMA IN 1990 ON OBSCENITY CHARGES. ALL EXCEPT ONE RECORD STORE WERE ACQUITTED.

TIME RUNS
BACKWARD ON
WRISTWATCH
WORN BY
SENATOR JESSE
HELMS (R-N.C.),
WHO ATTACKED
NATIONAL
ENDOWMENT
FOR THE ARTS
FOR SPONSOR-
ING EXHIBITION
BY MAPPLE-
THORPE AND
OTHER ARTISTS.
LAKE GASTON,
NORTH CARO-
LINA, 1983.

FOUR OF THE
COUNTLESS
NUMBER OF
BOOKS THAT
LOCAL GROUPS
AND PUBLIC
OFFICIALS HAVE
SOUGHT TO BAN.

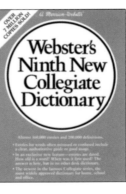

FREEDOM OF EXPRESSION

3

IN ADDITION TO FREEDOM OF RELIGION, THE FIRST AMENDMENT PROTECTS A wide range of other rights: freedom of speech, freedom of the press, and the right to assemble in the street, hold meetings, and petition the government. In practice, these rights tend naturally to work together and may be thought of in general as the right to freedom of expression. Although a major purpose of the First Amendment is to protect *political* speech, to guarantee the right to criticize the government, and to assure a free and open exchange of ideas and information concerning public policy, it also protects artistic expression — literature, music, art, drama, and dance — from government restrictions.

But when the Bill of Rights was adopted in 1791, the concept of a free press was much narrower than it is today. The struggle to establish freedom of the press originated in fifteenth-century England, when the printing press first came into use. The very language we use to express this right — freedom of the *press* — derives from that early method of publishing, though today it covers radio, television, and all other forms of electronic "publishing."

PRIOR CENSORSHIP AND SEDITIOUS LIBEL

The invention of the printing press had a revolutionary impact. Suddenly, speech and opinion could be widely disseminated. Before, speech and opinion had been audible only to listeners in the immediate vicinity of a speaker; now, ideas could be spread by anyone with access to a printing press to anyone who could read. The potential of such a means of communication was incendiary, and the British government was not slow to recognize the threat. Almost immediately, Parliament enacted laws to control what could be published. Censorship was imposed through various mechanisms: printing presses were required to be registered with the government as if they were dangerous weapons; the number of printers was limited; books could not be sold without a government license; and broad powers to search for illegal publications were established. In short, nothing could be printed unless approved in advance by either the government or the church.

These laws were harshly enforced by special courts called the High Commission, which was the supreme ecclesiastical tribunal, and the Star Chamber, which was the highest royal court. People could be arrested without any formal charges and brought before these courts to be interrogated, often without the right to a lawyer or any other guarantee of fairness. Torture was a royal prerogative until 1641, and the Star Chamber even had the power to fine and imprison juries in other courts that returned verdicts that displeased it. To this day, the phrase "Star Chamber proceeding" brands a process as tyrannical and unfair, although the Star Chamber's procedures were normally not as bad as the High Commission's. The Star Chamber came to be used to punish critics of the king, or those who published or circulated unorthodox literature. Playwrights were fined heavily for plays that made fun of the church. And fines were not the only punishments meted out by the Star Chamber: ears were cut off, cheeks branded, noses slit, tongues drilled, bodies whipped and pilloried.

Those who championed freedom of the press sought naturally to resist and abolish the laws requiring *advance* approval of printed matter by the government. Freedom of the press became synonymous with the idea that no advance approval should be required, and that anybody should be able to publish anything. In 1695, the English licensing law expired and was not renewed. The system of *prior* censorship was ended.

However, it was still illegal to criticize the crown, the government, and the church; such criticism was called "seditious libel." Although advance approval was no longer required, it was perilous to be critical of both state and church. In fifteenth-century England, seditious-libel laws made it a crime to call the king a fool, predict his death, or otherwise damage his reputation. All were regarded as treason, and punishable by death. Methods of putting people to death were not antiseptic, nor did they pretend to be humane. As late as the end of the seventeenth century, it was fairly common to sentence people to be

hanged up by the neck, to be cut down while ye are yet alive, to have your hearts and bowels taken out before your faces, and your members cut off and burnt, your heads severed from your bodies, your bodies divided into four quarters, your heads and bodies respectively to be disposed of according to the King's will and pleasure; and the Lord have mercy upon your souls.

Our English ancestors obviously did not take kindly to criticism.

By the eighteenth century, seditious libel was no longer considered treason, and punishments were reduced. Nonetheless, it remained a crime to criticize the government, and for 150 years after the licensing laws requiring prior approval were abandoned, people were prosecuted, convicted, and punished in England for their words. They were free to speak and publish, but they risked punishment *afterward*. William Blackstone, the most influential legal scholar of his time, put it this way:

The liberty of the press is indeed essential to the nature of a free state; but this consists in laying no previous restraints upon public actions, and not in freedom from censure for criminal matter when published. Every free man has an undoubted right to lay what sentiments he pleases before the public; to forbid this, is to destroy the freedom of the press; but if he publishes what is improper, mischievous, or illegal, he must take the consequences.

That was written in 1769. Thus, in the years just before the American Revolution, freedom of expression meant only than the absence of *prior* censorship. It would take more time and more experience before people came to understand that the power of the government to punish speech *after* publication also had to be sharply limited in order to protect freedom of expression.

TRUTH IS A DEFENSE

As English citizens, the American colonists carried all these attitudes with them to the New World. Throughout the eighteenth century, prosecutions for seditious libel were common in the colonies. One case became famous.

John Peter Zenger was the publisher of a newspaper called the *New York Weekly Journal.* He published ballads satirizing the governor of New York, William Cosby, and nearly every week attacked him and his administration. In 1735, Zenger was indicted and tried for seditious libel. Under the law, Zenger had no defense. He had not been censored in advance, and the law clearly prohibited what he had done. His conviction seemed assured, and like others similarly convicted, he seemed unlikely to escape a jail sentence.

Then Zenger's lawyer, Andrew Hamilton, made a new and intriguing argument. He said that criticism of the government should not be a crime *if the criticism was true.* How could freedom of the press mean anything, Hamilton argued, if it did not include the right to print truthful criticism? Hamilton did not go so far as to suggest that seditious-libel laws themselves were inconsistent with freedom of the press, but only that criticism, if accurate, should not be considered a crime.

The court quickly rejected this argument, pointing out with powerful logic that if it was legitimately a crime to criticize the governor, and damage his reputation, the crime was *worse* if the criticism was true. If what Zenger had said about the governor was false, that could at least be pointed out, saving the governor's reputation. If what Zenger said was true, there was no way to repair the damage. True criticism wounds more deeply than false, the court ruled, rejecting Hamilton's argument. The case went to the jury.

But Hamilton wasn't finished. Ignoring the judge's ruling, he appealed directly to the jury, which normally was supposed to accept the judge's legal ruling and limit its verdict to the facts: did Zenger do what he was accused of doing? Zenger, of course, did not deny criticizing the governor, so once the judge ruled against Hamilton's legal argument, the jury was expected to render a guilty verdict quickly.

Hamilton had other ideas. He repeated his legal argument directly to the jury, and urged them to take the law into their own hands and return a verdict of not guilty. Truth should be a defense, regardless of what the judge had ruled. The jury was persuaded — probably because Governor Cosby and his administration were unpopular — and acquitted Zenger. The case provided an early example of the principle of jury nullification — that a jury could acquit even when the defendant was clearly guilty, if it thought the law unjust. The jury's decision also supported the then-novel idea that even after publication, criticism of the government should be immune from punishment if the criticism was true, an idea that defined the avant-garde of late-eighteenth-century libertarian thought.

The Zenger decision was an aberration, however, and the law of seditious libel remained unchanged. Although Zenger himself was freed, the jury's decision affected only him, not the law: seditious libel was still a crime, and truth was no defense. But the case made Zenger and his lawyer heroes throughout the colonies; after the acquittal, seditious-libel laws were rarely used successfully to punish criticism. The law of seditious libel remained on the books until the nineteenth century, but in practice, criticism and dissent were widespread and vigorous, and even scurrilous criticism was common.

At the time that the Bill of Rights was proposed, debated, and adopted, therefore, the prevailing *practice* was of a press that functioned freely, but the prevailing *law* still prohibited criticism of the government, and no one seemed to think the law improper. Benjamin Franklin never criticized the seditious-libel law, and at the time that the Bill of Rights was adopted, neither did James Madison. Even Thomas Jefferson, in 1776, helped write a law that punished anyone who defended the British cause. They all subscribed to the traditional English view that freedom of the press meant no advance licensing or censorship, but not immunity from prosecution and punishment after publication. During the period between the Revolution and the adoption of the Bill of Rights, no state abolished the law of seditious libel; neither did any state adopt the principle of truth as a defense.

Only the most avant-garde libertarians thought that the Zenger standard of truth as a defense should modify the law, and even most of them continued to support the idea that seditious-libel laws could properly be used to punish false statements. Jefferson, for example, in 1783 and again in 1788, explicitly wrote and endorsed laws that permitted the government to prosecute people for printing "false facts." If some Americans were beginning to believe that the press should be completely immunized from prosecution, Jefferson was not among them. In a letter to Madison in 1789, he actually proposed a revision of Madison's draft Bill of Rights to allow explicitly for the punishment of false facts. Jefferson's suggestion was not accepted, and the First Amendment passed without any such loophole.

Interestingly, a number of states applied a much more generous standard to the protection of religious speech. In ringing words, Jefferson himself wrote that *any* restriction on religious belief or expression would destroy religious liberty. Government should restrict itself to punishing disorderly *conduct* that threatens the peace, he wrote, and leave opinion alone. "It is time enough," Jefferson said, "for the rightful purposes of civil government for its officers to interfere when principles break out into overt acts against peace and good order." A century and a half later that standard would guide the Supreme Court in interpreting the First Amendment and the degree to which it protected political speech. But in 1786, that generous standard applied only to freedom of *religious* expression; political expression remained vulnerable to the power of the government. And even religious expression could be punished if it "irreverently or seditiously" criticized the state.

Throughout the period following the adoption of the Constitution and the Bill of Rights, however, the law of seditious libel continued to have little bearing on how the press actually conducted itself. As Leonard Levy has pointed out, the "actual freedom of the press had slight relationship to the fact that, as a legal concept, freedom of the press was a cluster of constraints. The law threatened repression; yet the press conducted itself as if the law scarcely existed." Moreover, the level and tone of the criticism were neither refined nor temperate. It was, Levy tells us, often "foul-tempered," "mean-spirited," openly hostile, and intending to damage the public officials it criticized. The public supported it, understanding that "scummy journalism unavoidably accompanied the benefits to be gained from a free press."

THE FIRST FEDERAL SEDITION ACT AND THOSE IT PUNISHED

Then, in 1798—scarcely seven years after the Bill of Rights was ratified—a major event transformed the early Americans' understanding of what it took to protect the right to criticize. At the time, war with France seemed imminent. There were many French refugees in the country, and they were feared as a potentially subversive and traitorous element. John Adams, who before the Revolution had been a rock of libertarian thought, was then president, and he encouraged this prejudice by opposing the visit of a group of French scientists, calling them "incompatible with social order." Thus encouraged, war hysteria mounted, national origin became a proxy for real evidence of criminality or espionage, and the French became targets of fear and hate. In a prelude to similar frenzies during World War I (against German and Italian immigrants), World War II (against Japanese-Americans), and most recently, the Persian Gulf War (against Arab-Americans), Congress quickly passed four laws. Three targeted aliens: one increased the residence requirement from five to fourteen years before an alien could be considered for citizenship; another authorized the president to deport aliens thought to be dangerous; the third authorized incarceration and banishment of aliens during wartime.

The fourth law became the first federal sedition act ever passed by Congress. It was aimed at "domestic traitors," by which was meant anyone who criticized the government. The Sedition Act made it a crime, punishable by both a fine and a prison term, to publish "false, scandalous, and malicious" criticism of the government, Congress, or the president, "with intent to defame" them or to heap contempt upon them or damage their reputations.

Although the hysteria that produced these laws was primarily fear of aliens, American citizens and their rights were its only casualties. The war with France never came, and the fear of the French quickly subsided. No alien was ever deported or incarcerated, and a few years later the residence requirement for citizenship reverted to five years. But the Sedition Act was widely enforced against American citizens, all of them Republicans and political opponents of President Adams and his administration who had publicly criticized him. Editors, scientists, pamphleteers, and even one congressman were tried and convicted; all were fined and imprisoned.

The First Amendment was no help. In Congress, members opposed to the Sedition Act had pointed out that the First Amendment said "Congress shall make *no* law" abridging freedom of the press. No law meant no law, they said. But the act passed the Senate, 18–6, and the House, 44–41. And in a climate of fear and rampant suspicion, encouraged by the government, judges and juries proved no more respectful of the Bill of Rights. Hysteria prevailed, and the fundamental rights of Americans — particularly dissenting Americans — were trampled.

Republicans were shocked by this, because in some respects the Sedition Act was a model of libertarian principles. It punished speech only after publication, imposed no advance censorship, *and authorized truth as a defense.* This last protection was seen as a great advance, because it codified John Peter Zenger's old argument and limited the government's power to prosecuting only *false* facts, which was what Jefferson had said he wanted.

But Jefferson and others now realized that allowing for truth as a defense had created a trap for their Republican colleagues, not a safeguard. A government seeking to suppress criticism could indict anyone it wished to silence, exposing him to the cost of a trial and the risk of a serious penalty. Moreover, who would decide what was true and what was false? These were necessarily highly subjective judgments, vulnerable to precisely the kind of prejudice that led to the prosecutions in the first place. Judges and juries, who would as often reflect the general hysteria as be likely to curb it, would have the power to decide what was true and what was not. As conviction after conviction piled up, it became clear that the power to prosecute speech itself was the problem; the defense of truth was no defense at all.

A new idea of freedom of expression began to emerge. If the right to free speech was to be protected against government attempts to suppress criticism, legal limits on government power would have to extend to punishment after publication as well as to previewing and censorship before. People began to see that a law allowing the government to impose punishment after publication would have precisely the same effect as a law allowing the government to censor speech before publication. Madison expressed this growing idea pungently: "It would seem a mockery to say that no laws shall be passed preventing publications from being made, but that laws might be passed for punishing them in case they should be made."

That the government should not be able to punish speech after publication meant that even scurrilous speech, including false accusations and misrepresentations of fact, would not only be tolerated, but be protected by law — a radical departure. Before, even advanced libertarians had assumed that freedom of the press meant only the legal freedom to publish the truth; falsehoods could and should be punishable. But after the experience with the Sedition Act of 1798, people began to realize that if the government had the power to punish false speech, it would inevitably use that power to silence its critics.

John Thomson expressed this new idea in a book he wrote in 1801, *An Enquiry into the Liberty and Licentiousness of the Press.* Any laws prohibiting "licentious" speech, he wrote, would inevitably be used by those who wished "nobody to enjoy the Liberty of the Press but such as were of their own opinion." That was what had happened in 1798. Under the pretext of protecting America against a foreign menace, the Adams administration had in fact targeted its domestic political critics: all ten men convicted under the Sedition Act of 1798 were Republicans who had criticized the Adams administration and its policies, and all were pardoned by the next Republican president, Thomas Jefferson.

It may have seemed abstractly logical to protect truthful criticism while allowing the law to punish false or malicious criticism, but in the world of political power, that wasn't the way it worked. Often, the very purpose of criticism was to damage the reputation and undermine the credibility of the party in power. Permitting the target of criticism to prosecute his critics would inevitably destroy freedom of expression. In practice, there was no way to separate truth neatly from error. Political truth was often a matter of subjective judgment, not scientific determination. How would a jury evaluate political truths? It was, said John Thomson, rather like letting a jury decide which was the most tasty food or the most beautiful color, and then allowing it to punish anyone who had a different view. If government were given the power to punish false or malicious speech, would it not naturally use that power to punish any speech it found too critical? That was exactly what had just happened with the Sedition Act; why should it ever be any different?

And how could the accused prove to his accusers that what he said was true? The experience with the Sedition Act had shown beyond doubt that the defense of truth, long thought to be a safeguard, was no safeguard at all. It could never protect a critic against prosecution; and it would hardly ever protect him against conviction. Republicans who had been sent to jail by the Adams administration for their malicious speech came to understand that the only important question was who had the power to decide. Since they could not be certain of always holding political power, they began to believe that the best way to protect their own freedom of expression was to prohibit *any* government from prosecuting *any* speech.

The Republicans developed this theory initially out of blatant self-interest. They were a political minority trying to gain political power by persuading people first of the folly of the party in power and second of their own virtue. When they did this, they were prosecuted for seditious libel—for maliciously criticizing the government. They therefore championed the right to freedom of speech because they *needed* it to defend themselves. They were not political philosophers so much as practical politicians, activists hoping to advance their own cause. Nor is it likely that they would have behaved any more magnanimously toward their opponents had they themselves been in power. Indeed, when they gained power a few years later, they did not always respect the free-speech rights of their opponents. Even Jefferson himself, when he became president, urged that his opponents be prosecuted under state sedition laws.

CHALLENGING THE IDEA OF SEDITIOUS LIBEL

Nonetheless, as the result of the experience under the 1798 Sedition Act, for the first time the concept of seditious libel itself was challenged. For the first time, the truly radical idea was advanced that in a democracy the people must have the same right as the government to voice any opinion and express any thought without fear of prosecution. However harsh, however unjust, however "false," speech had to be legally protected, because the power to prosecute any opinion was the power to prosecute all opinion. There could be no such thing as a verbal crime. This new idea advocated nothing less than an absolute right to freedom of political expression. The line between what should be legally protected and what could be criminally punished was no longer to be drawn between categories of speech, true or false, but between speech and overt acts.

Not only was this a radical *libertarian* idea at the time; it was also a radical *democratic* idea. It meant, at bottom, that the government could never tell a citizen what to think or what to say, or punish him for his words. It implied an equality between citizens and their government: a king might insulate himself from criticism by his subjects, but in a democracy, the concept of seditious libel was a contradiction because *citizens are not subjects;* their relationship to the government is or ought to be a legally egalitarian one. Unlike in a monarchy, where political power was permanently vested in a single family, political power in a democracy was fluid, intended to pass from party to party, as the people saw fit. And how were the people to decide, if not by being exposed to the full flow of competing ideas and opinion, and even to competing views of the facts? If the party in power were allowed to skew the debate by punishing its critics and controlling which views became available to the public, could it not thus manipulate public opinion and entrench its own political power?

The idea thus grew that democracy itself required absolute freedom of political expression. And because this was not possible, as a practical matter, without also protecting false and malicious speech, all political speech would have to be protected from government restriction. Error could be tolerated, Jefferson said, so long as truth was left free to combat it, and, he might have added, so long as government was not permitted to decide which was which. What began as an idea rooted in the narrow self-interest of the Republican minority thus grew into a general theory of free expression that today broadly protects all Americans.

In the immediate aftermath of the Sedition Act of 1798, the new belief in an absolute right to freedom of political expression transformed political thought, but it did not transform constitutional law. The new theory of free speech was never even tested in the Supreme Court, because the Sedition Act was repealed before any case involving it reached the Court and because Jefferson had pardoned all those convicted under it. After the 1798 law was repealed, no *federal* sedition act would be passed again for more than a hundred years. So the Supreme Court never had the opportunity to decide whether the First Amendment provided the kind of absolute protection for speech advocated by the new libertarians.

Meanwhile, *state* sedition laws remained on the books, and continued to be enforced. The legal standard that had been codified in the 1798 Sedition Act continued to be reflected in these state laws. Criticizing state and local governments could still be made a crime, unless the accused could prove to a jury that what he had said about the government was true. State courts continued to uphold these laws, and because at that time the Bill of Rights did not apply to state governments, the First Amendment was not available to challenge them in federal courts. As a result, freedom of speech did not exist in many states: people could be prosecuted for expressing the wrong opinion, and many of them were.

This happened especially in the South, where antislavery opinion was ruthlessly suppressed. Beginning in the 1830s, many Southern states passed laws making it a crime to advocate abolition of slavery or to criticize a master's property rights over his slaves. Antislavery publications were even barred from the mails. Looking back upon that time, one member of Congress said in 1864, "Liberty of speech [and] freedom of the press ... had disappeared in the slave states." Another said that "the press has been padlocked, and men's lips have been sealed." Once again, the original decision to tolerate slavery had stained the Constitution and diminished the rights of all Americans even as it abolished the rights of black Americans. As black Americans continued to be bound by the chains of slavery, so white Americans lost their freedom of speech. Suppression of antislavery advocacy grew widespread, and the First Amendment was not available to challenge it. The wisdom of James Madison's attempt in 1789 to include in the Bill of Rights an amendment prohibiting state governments from passing any laws restricting freedom of speech is again apparent. And one wonders what a different country this might have been if that "most valuable" amendment had been passed in 1789.

Then, after the Civil War, the Fourteenth Amendment was passed. It seemed to say, and some still believe it was intended to say, that no state government could take away from its citizens the rights guaranteed by the Bill of Rights. Many thought at the time that once the Fourteenth Amendment was adopted, state legislatures would be prohibited by the First Amendment from restricting freedom of expression. But only five years later, as we have seen, the United State Supreme Court ruled otherwise, and generally restored the power of state governments to deny rights apparently guaranteed by the Bill of Rights. Once again, freedom of expression was vulnerable to state restriction without protection from the First Amendment. And it would stay that way for nearly another sixty years. The right to freedom of expression was guaranteed on paper, but no one had yet found a way to transform those paper rights into actual legal protections.

Eugene V. Debs made this discovery repeatedly in the course of his long career as a labor leader and political activist. During the late nineteenth century, Debs was the head of the American Railway Union, at a time when the railroads were becoming the first great interstate corporate enterprise. Debs led a strike against the Pullman Palace Car Company in 1894 and was sued in federal court. The court issued an order prohibiting Debs and his union from striking and from "persuading" workers to strike. Debs defied the order and was sentenced to six months' imprisonment for contempt of court. He challenged the legal grounds for his sentence, and the case reached the United States Supreme Court, which unanimously upheld Debs's imprisonment, although it cited no law authorizing it. Instead, it merely said that the "supremacy" of the national government was sufficient to allow the court to protect interstate commerce by removing "obstructions," such as Debs's organizing activities. Debs's right to "persuade"—a right that today would clearly be protected by the First Amendment—was swept aside. The railroads' power to crush labor unions by prohibiting their speech was upheld. Debs's union never recovered and soon fell apart.

Thus, on one of the rare occasions during the Bill of Rights' first hundred years when the Supreme Court had an opportunity to invoke the First Amendment to protect free speech, it didn't do so. Power and politics subdued liberty. This happened repeatedly during the late nineteenth century and the first two decades of the twentieth. The country was rapidly changing from a rural, agricultural economy to an urban, industrial economy, and the accompanying economic and social dislocation caused labor unrest to mount. Militant labor-union tactics disrupted the evolving corporate economy, and even though many of the early union actions would today be protected by the First Amendment—leafletting, meeting, speaking, organizing, and striking—back then they were seen as dangerously radical and subversive, and the states moved swiftly to suppress them.

SQUELCHING CRITICS DURING WORLD WAR I

As World War I approached, opposition to the United States' entry into the war provided an additional source of political protest and unrest. Just as the fear of war with France had in 1798 led to the nation's first federal sedition law, so now, for the first time in over a hundred years, World War I led to the nation's second federal sedition law. Congress had already passed an Espionage Act in 1917, only nine weeks after declaring war on Germany. Fear of French spies had served as the pretext in 1798 for the prosecution and imprisonment of domestic critics; in 1917, fear of German agents led to the same result. Although Woodrow Wilson's request for power to censor the press was rejected by Congress, the Espionage Act was broadly enough worded to permit prosecution for nothing more than a critical opinion.

The war went on, and popular support for it grew while tolerance for dissent diminished. A year after the Espionage Act was passed, it was amended by a new act called the Sedition Act, which left nothing to chance: it became a crime to print, speak, write, or publish any words that heaped contempt or scorn upon the government, used scurrilous or abusive language, or in any way damaged the reputation of the government, its flag, or even its military uniforms. Nor were the penalties trivial: twenty years in prison, and a $10,000 fine, for each separate offense. Fifteenth-century England, where reverence for the crown was considered essential to the security of the state, and where it was a crime to call the king a fool or predict his death, would have fit the 1918 Sedition Act comfortably into its political culture.

Over two thousand prosecutions were brought under the Espionage Act, and more than a thousand convictions were obtained, almost all for expressing criticism of the war. Prosecutions were brought under state laws as well. One man was sentenced to prison for reading the Declaration of Independence in public. A minister was sentenced to fifteen years for saying that war was un-Christian. A newspaper editor was convicted for questioning the constitutionality of the draft and charging that Wall Street had dragged the country into war. And Eugene V. Debs, twenty-four years after having been jailed during the Pullman strike, was imprisoned again for denouncing the war as a capitalist plot. Although these criticisms and opinions were harsh and were uttered with invective, they were no different in that respect from the pamphlets of the American colonists or the Republican editors in 1798 or the Democratic critics of Lincoln's policies during the Civil War.

The Sedition Act was harshly and extensively enforced, and it almost completely suffocated criticism of the war from the time it was passed in May 1918 until the end of the war that November. Prosecutions brought under the Espionage Act, which made it a crime to obstruct military recruitment or the war effort, were also aimed at pure speech, and in practice had much the same effect as seditious-libel laws. For the first time in American history, the extent to which critical speech could be punished as espionage was reviewed by the Supreme Court and measured against the First Amendment. Nine cases reached the Court, which upheld the government in all nine, categorically rejecting the argument that the First Amendment barred Congress from criminalizing mere speech. By today's standards, the Court was much too deferential to Congress and to the desire of the government to eliminate dissent during wartime. And by the standards of the Republican libertarians of the early nineteenth century, the Court cut the heart out of the freedom of expression, leaving it vulnerable to government power.

Yet despite these sorry results, the cases were significant because they were the first Supreme Court rulings on freedom of speech and marked the beginning of the development of the law protecting speech. That this process did not even start until 128 years after the Bill of Rights was adopted, and that it began by upholding the imprisonment of people for expressing their opinions, demonstrates how large a gap there was between establishing constitutional rights on paper and transforming them into actual rights. That is why, for most of our history, so many people suffered precisely the sort of punishment that the First Amendment was designed to prevent.

IS THERE A CLEAR AND PRESENT DANGER?

The very first case to reach the Supreme Court was *Schenck v. United States.* Charles Schenck was an official of the Socialist Party. He distributed a leaflet denouncing the draft. One side of the leaflet reprinted the first section of the Thirteenth Amendment, which explicitly prohibits "involuntary servitude," accompanied by rhetoric claiming that conscription was despotism. The other side of the leaflet urged people to "assert your rights," suggesting nothing but peaceful methods.

It is at least arguable that the Thirteenth Amendment prohibits a military draft. Indeed, at the time that Schenck distributed his leaflet, the Supreme Court had not yet ruled on the question. When it did so, a year later, it dismissed the Thirteenth Amendment argument with a paragraph of rhetoric no more or less colorful than Schenck's, and just as nonanalytical. Schenck's leaflet denounced the draft, but did not advocate violence or any forcible resistance or obstruction. Nonetheless, the Supreme Court unanimously upheld his conviction and dismissed his First Amendment defense.

It was in this case that Justice Oliver Wendell Holmes first announced his "clear and present danger" test. Under this test, the First Amendment was said to protect speech except when it incited an imminent lawless action. Like the "truth is a defense" rule in 1798, the "clear and present danger" test sounded good in theory but proved to be a trap in practice. One might imagine that if a lynch mob were about to storm a jail and drag the prisoner out in order to murder him, and the leader, shotgun in hand, began to run toward the jail yelling, "Charge, men, let's get him!" such yelling would not be protected by the First Amendment, because it was part and parcel of conduct that was otherwise illegal.

Had Schenck similarly led a mob to storm and destroy a government draft-board office, his cries of "Charge, men!" would not have been protected by the First Amendment. Nor would specific instructions about how to carry out the illegal act have been protected. But that is not what Schenck did. He peacefully distributed a leaflet that reprinted part of the United States Constitution and urged people peaceably to assert their rights. Justice Holmes treated this as if it were an incitement to immediate riot. He said that it was like "falsely shouting fire in a theater and causing a panic." He said that he could not see what effect such a leaflet could have except to influence people to obstruct the draft. He equated Schenck's words with the actual act of obstructing recruitment, and he upheld the conviction. Holmes never seriously considered the constitutionality of the law's being used in a way that made dissent a crime. Rather, he deferred to the government and to the notion that when a nation is at war, the government is entitled to suppress dissent if it *might* undermine the war effort.

In three other concurrent cases decided at just about the same time—all of them involving speech not much different from Schenck's—the Court continued to uphold convictions under the Espionage Act. The most famous of these cases involved Eugene V. Debs again, a leader of the Socialist Party and one of the most eloquent critics of the government's decision to enter World War I. Debs made a speech at a rally in Ohio in which he denounced the war and praised protesters who were in prison. Probably the most inflammatory thing he said was that the people of the working class "furnish the corpses, having never yet had a voice in declaring war and never yet had a voice in declaring peace," and that "you need to know that you are fit for something better than slavery and cannon fodder." Strong stuff, but hardly the equivalent of espionage, treason, or violent resistance. No riots occurred as the result of his speech. No illegal actions resulted. But Debs was charged with insubordination, disloyalty, and mutiny under the Espionage Act. He was convicted and sentenced to ten years. For his words.

The Supreme Court unanimously upheld his conviction, based on their reasoning in the *Schenck* case. Ignoring the facts and without bothering in any way to show any actual connection between Debs's speech and any criminal conduct, Justice Holmes again asserted that Debs's intent "was to encourage those present to obstruct recruiting." This case showed why the "clear and present danger" test was so dangerous: it depended not on what had actually happened, but on what a judge imagined might happen.

A few months later, even Holmes had had enough. A man named Jacob Abrams was convicted under the Espionage Act for publishing leaflets using abusive language about President Wilson and the government, for encouraging resistance to United States war policies, and for inciting people to curtail production of war materials. These charges were based on two leaflets. The first called President Wilson a coward and a hypocrite and contained rhetoric like "there is only one enemy of the workers of the world and that is CAPITALISM." It urged workers to wake up, and it was signed "Revolutionists." That was it. The second leaflet was addressed to factory workers and vaguely called for a general strike. It was signed "The Rebels."

Abrams was convicted, and when the case reached the Supreme Court, a majority upheld the conviction on the grounds that Abrams's "plain purpose" was to excite "disaffection, sedition, riots, and ... revolution." No actual conduct, other than seditious libel of the government, was shown to have occurred. For the first time, Justice Holmes dissented, joined by Justice Louis Brandeis; together they created the first crack in the Court's unanimity. It is difficult to make much sense of Holmes's opinion. He did not confess error in the previous cases; on the contrary, he asserted that those cases had been rightly decided. But in this case, he said that he didn't believe there was any proof of Abrams's criminal intent. Once Holmes found no proof of criminal intent, it was easy for him to conclude that Abrams had been convicted for his words alone. He then went on to write a ringing defense of free speech.

But there seems little to distinguish the *Abrams* case from the other cases. Abrams's words were more or less in the same vein as Schenck's and Debs's. And if no criminal conduct resulted imminently from Abrams's words, neither did any criminal conduct result from Schenck's or Debs's words. As to intent, there was no proof, other than what might be imagined from the words themselves, in *any* of the cases. So it is difficult to reconcile Holmes's dissent in the *Abrams* case from his enthusiastic support of the convictions in the other cases. Perhaps Holmes just thought Abrams too innocuous to bother convicting. In his opinion, he referred to the case as involving "a silly leaflet by an unknown man" and implied that without more evidence it was hard for him to see any immediate danger in allowing Abrams to go free. If that was the basis of Holmes's reasoning, it pointed up the problem with the Court's basic approach. Schenck's words, Debs's words, and Abrams's words were all pretty much the same. What was different was that Holmes took Abrams less seriously, and upon that subjective standard, some people would go to prison for their words while others would not. The Republican libertarians of 1798 would have had no difficulty in rejecting such a standard.

Despite the problems with Holmes's standard, the concluding paragraph of his dissent in the *Abrams* case became a rallying point for libertarian thinkers. But it would take another fifty years before the Supreme Court finally ruled that the First Amendment protected all advocacy, including advocacy of the use of force, unless the advocacy was directed *explicitly* to producing, and was likely to produce, *imminent* lawless action. This 1969 decision rejected Holmes's speculative standard and provided the most expansive ruling by the Supreme Court on what the First Amendment protects. (The law struck down in 1969 by this decision dated from 1919, the year the Court decided the *Schenck, Debs,* and *Abrams* cases.)

Today the First Amendment protects speech in pretty much the way the Republican libertarians of 1798 had suggested it should. Seditious libel is a dead concept, and mere advocacy, no matter how harsh, is protected by the First Amendment. What Thomas Jefferson had suggested in 1786 about religious speech now applies to political speech as well: "It is time enough for the rightful purposes of civil government for its officers to interfere when principles break out into overt acts against peace and good order." But between 1919 and 1969, a lot of people suffered for their words, for their beliefs, and for their political associations. The 1918 Sedition Act itself was repealed in 1921 and was never reenacted, although the rest of the Espionage Act remains on the books.

THE FIRST AMENDMENT REACHES STATE LAWS

Meanwhile, state laws continued to punish dissent. And the Supreme Court refused to apply the First Amendment to state laws.

In 1925, though, the Court suddenly and rather casually assumed that the Fourteenth Amendment did, after all, apply the First Amendment to the states, forbidding state and local governments from depriving their citizens of the right to freedom of expression. Benjamin Gitlow had published a tract entitled *The Left Wing Manifesto*, in which he argued that moderate Socialism would never work and that economic justice required a "Communist revolution." There was no explicit call for specific criminal actions, nor was there any evidence of any criminal conduct resulting from the manifesto. Gitlow was convicted anyway, under a New York law that made it a crime to advocate violent overthrow of the government. By 1921, thirty-three states had passed similar laws, although New York's, passed in 1902, was the first.

The Court upheld Gitlow's conviction, holding that abstract advocacy of the doctrine of revolution, even without any connection to actual criminal acts, was punishable; the state did not have to wait, as Jefferson had proposed, for abstract principles to break out into overt acts. Gitlow went to jail. Nonetheless, his case advanced the cause of freedom of expression, since in it the First Amendment was finally ruled applicable to state and local governments. It didn't help Gitlow, but it was the beginning of the development of First Amendment rights that Americans take for granted today.

Holmes and Brandeis continued to dissent, as they had in the *Abrams* case, and each time they did, they fleshed out the libertarian theory of free speech a little more. In *Gitlow*, Holmes wrote,

Every idea is an incitement. It offers itself for belief and if believed it is acted on unless some other belief outweighs it.... If in the long run the beliefs expressed ... are destined to be accepted by the dominant forces of the community, the only meaning of free speech is that they should be given their chance and have their way.

In this dissenting opinion, Holmes continued to draw a sharper line than he had in the *Schenck* and *Debs* cases between general advocacy and the direct incitement of specific and imminent unlawful action. Holmes's dissent also suggested the faith in democracy that had been reflected in the Republican libertarian movement after 1798. If an opinion could carry the day with the public, so be it. Faith in democracy implied a willingness to allow beliefs and opinions to contend with each other for the public's support. It was decidedly undemocratic to allow government to decide in advance which opinions were right, and to prohibit all others. But Holmes and Brandeis did not gain any other adherents on the Court, and people continued to go to jail for their beliefs and associations.

Two years after Gitlow's conviction was upheld, Anita Whitney, a niece of former Supreme Court justice Stephen Field, was convicted in California under a similar law. Her offense was even more tenuously connected to violence than Gitlow's had been. She was a member of the Oakland branch of the Socialist Workers' Party. During a dispute, the party split into two factions, one of which believed that parliamentary methods would never work and urged "revolutionary class struggle" instead. Whitney joined this faction, but actively opposed adoption of the part of their program that urged revolutionary methods. She was never involved with anything violent or criminal, and repeatedly rejected such methods. Nonetheless, she was convicted of belonging to a party that advocated violence and terrorism. In 1927, the Supreme Court again ruled that the First Amendment applied to the state of California, but it didn't protect Whitney's right to belong to that organization, despite her disavowal of violence. Her conviction was upheld.

The *Whitney* case provided Justice Brandeis with yet another opportunity to define the libertarian view of free speech. Fear of some possible violence in an imagined future is not enough to justify punishing speech or, as in Whitney's case, association with others. "Men feared witches and burnt women," Brandeis wrote, reminding us of the history of heresy. "No danger flowing from speech can be deemed clear and present," he continued, "unless the incidence of the evil apprehended is so imminent that it may befall before there is opportunity for full discussion. If there be time … to avert the evil by the process of education, the remedy to be applied is more speech, not enforced silence."

Despite the eloquent defense of free speech by Holmes and Brandeis in these cases, conviction after conviction was upheld. Benjamin Gitlow and a number of his colleagues served three years in prison before Governor Alfred E. Smith of New York pardoned them. Anita Whitney was pardoned by Governor Clement C. Young of California, and never went to prison. But until 1969, the law established in their cases prevailed, and exposed people who advocated unpopular political ideas to punishment and ruin.

THE SMITH ACT AND THE RED SCARE

In 1940, on the eve of World War II, Congress passed the Smith Act, which was modeled after the New York law under which Benjamin Gitlow had been convicted. The Smith Act made it a crime to advocate, teach, or advise the desirability or necessity of overthrowing any government in the United States by force or violence, or to belong to any organization that advocated such beliefs. In these respects, the Smith Act merely federalized the various state laws that had been around since the early twentieth century, so it didn't attract much attention when it was passed. Nor was it used very often at first.

But after World War II, it was to became a major weapon in the government's wave of repression against Communist Party leaders in the United States. The first case involved Eugene Dennis, an official of the Communist Party. Dennis was convicted in 1949 of violating the Smith Act by conspiring to advocate overthrow of the government by force and violence. No specific conspiracy was even alleged. No plan to commit any crime was uncovered. The conspiracy was entirely inferred from membership in and leadership of the Communist Party. It was true that the Communist Party generally advocated revolution, as had Gitlow, and as had Whitney's Socialist Workers' Party faction, but the government never presented any evidence that there was a clear and present danger of such a revolution occurring, or of any significant number of Americans being persuaded to foment one.

In 1949, though, fear of the Soviet Union ran rampant in America. Only a year before, the Soviet Union had blockaded Berlin and overthrown the parliamentary government of Czechoslovakia. The United States was locked in a growing struggle with its former World War II ally, and the Cold War was underway. Fear of war with France in 1798 had led to repression of free speech at home; now fear of the Soviet Union led to the same result a century and a half later. Although no evidence of criminal conduct was ever presented, Dennis and his colleagues were convicted. By the time the case reached the Supreme Court on appeal, it was 1951, and America was in the midst of a nearly paranoid preoccupation with anyone who might be sympathetic toward the Soviet Union, or toward any political belief tending even remotely to be socialistic or even egalitarian.

The Supreme Court upheld Dennis's conviction with only two dissents. The Court's majority seemed to think that because the Soviet Union itself was a clear and present danger, any member of the American Communist Party was, by virtue of membership alone, also a clear and present danger. The notion that speech and political association should be protected by the First Amendment unless it directly advocated imminent criminal conduct was therefore swept aside. Instead, the Court held that because the threat posed by the Soviet Union was so grave, Dennis's association with the Communist Party could be punished even though any actual danger he or the party immediately presented to the United States was vanishingly small. This meant in effect that the government could punish virtually any association with Communism or Communist beliefs, no matter how remote or attenuated.

The opinion in *Dennis* went much further than any previous Supreme Court opinion had in undermining First Amendment protections for unpopular speech. Whereas the Court should have been stepping in to curb majoritarian hysteria and protect individual rights, instead it reflected and encouraged that hysteria. The dissenting justices, Hugo Black and William O. Douglas, said this in no uncertain terms. Black wrote:

These petitioners were not charged with an attempt to overthrow the Government. They were not charged with overt acts of any kind designed to overthrow the Government. They were not even charged with saying anything or with writing anything designed to overthrow the Government…. The indictment is that they conspired to organize the Communist Party and to use speech or newspapers and other publications in the future to teach and advocate the forcible overthrow of the Government. No matter how it is worded, this is a virulent form of prior censor-ship of speech and press, which I believe the First Amendment forbids.

Justice Douglas picked up Black's theme: If the petitioners

were teaching the techniques of sabotage, the assassination of the President, the filching of documents from public files, the planting of bombs, the art of street warfare,… I would have no doubts…. [But] what petitioners did was to organize people to teach … Marxist-Leninist doctrine, contained chiefly in four books…. The opinion of the Court does not outlaw these texts nor condemn them to the fire, as the Communists do literature offensive to their creed. But if the books themselves are not outlawed, if they can lawfully remain on library shelves, by what reasoning does their use in a classroom become a crime?

Douglas went on to confront the Court's view that the doctrine of Communism itself presented a clear and immediate danger in America. If it is the threat of Communism in America that we fear, said Douglas, then we must conclude that "as a political party they are of little consequence."

Communists in this country have never made a respectable or serious showing in any election. I would doubt that there is a village, let alone a city or county or state, which the Communists could carry…. How it can be said that there is a clear and present danger that this advocacy will succeed is, therefore, a mystery.

Douglas in fact was doing more than expressing doubt about the Court's assumption of danger. He was expressing a faith in democracy. So long as they were plotting to throw not bombs, but only words, let them talk, Douglas said. That is the strength of a democracy. Why should we be afraid that we will be convinced by ideas that most Americans hate? What we should be afraid of instead, he implied, is allowing the government to gain the power to decide which political ideas should be permitted and which should not. For a government that today could decide to put Eugene Dennis in jail for his political ideas could decide tomorrow to put any of us in jail for our political ideas. After all, that is precisely what happened to the Republican editors in 1798, to the Democratic opponents of Lincoln during the Civil War, to Eugene V. Debs and Benjamin Gitlow and Anita Whitney early in this century.

But Black and Douglas did not prevail, just as Holmes and Brandeis had not prevailed, and Eugene Dennis and his colleagues went to prison. Other than their association with the doctrine of Communism, they had never committed any crime.

Six years later, after the Cold War hysteria had substantially subsided and many of its prominent leaders, like Senator Joseph McCarthy, had been discredited, the Supreme Court narrowed the *Dennis* ruling. After *Dennis*, conspiracy prosecutions had been brought under the Smith Act against many Communist Party officials, and between 1951 and 1956, convictions were obtained in every case. Then, in 1957, the Supreme Court reversed fourteen convictions in one case. The Court would not admit to having made a mistake in the *Dennis* case, though it did say that the *Dennis* decision had been "misunderstood." The Smith Act prohibited not advocacy of an abstract doctrine of violent overthrow, the Court now said, but only advocacy that urged the audience to take some *specific action*, and not merely to *believe* in some general doctrine. By thus correcting the "misunderstanding," the Court changed the *Dennis* ruling without openly conceding its error. And by reinterpreting what the Smith Act meant, the Court avoided having to declare it unconstitutional.

The 1957 decision effectively ended the use of the Smith Act to suppress unpopular political beliefs and associations. Of the 141 people indicted under the Smith Act, 29 went to prison. All but one had been convicted before the 1957 decision. The last person to be convicted and imprisoned was Junius Scales. He was sentenced to six years in prison in 1961. In 1963, he was pardoned by President John F. Kennedy. This too followed a familiar pattern. Jefferson pardoned those convicted under the Sedition Act of 1798; Harding pardoned Debs; Smith pardoned Gitlow; Young pardoned Whitney; and Kennedy pardoned Scales. In all these cases, Americans were convicted and sent to prison during a time of hysteria, for nothing more than their general beliefs and their insistence on expressing them. When these citizens were attacked by their government, the First Amendment should have protected them, but it did not. The courts, whose role in our system is to curb such suppressions, instead became an accomplice of them and deferred to government power, and the constitutional barrier that was supposed to limit such power and protect freedom of expression was swept aside.

What the American colonists called the propulsive, voracious tendency of power to consume liberty triumphed. Each time there was a struggle between liberty and power, liberty lost. But each loss also drew liberty closer to victory. After the convictions under the Sedition Act of 1798, the folly of depending on truth as a defense became obvious and the concept of seditious libel itself came under attack. After the initial convictions during World War I under the Espionage Act, at least a few Supreme Court justices began to see the necessity of distinguishing between advocacy and overt criminal acts, and of protecting advocacy unless it closely and immediately led to violence. After many convictions for unpopular speech under state laws, the Supreme Court began belatedly to apply the First Amendment to the states. And after the initial Smith Act decision swept too broadly, it was cut back as well.

By 1969, the Supreme Court had ruled that the First Amendment protected all advocacy, even the general advocacy of violence or the use of force, unless it is directed explicitly to producing a specific criminal act. In so doing, the Court applied that ruling fully to the states as well as to the federal government, striking down an Ohio law and reversing the rulings that had convicted Gitlow, Whitney, Debs, and Dennis. Yet the Espionage Act of 1917 was never repealed, nor was the Smith Act of 1940.

The path to freedom of political expression was long and arduous. It took nearly two hundred years for the First Amendment finally to establish firm constitutional limits upon the government's power to outlaw seditious libel and punish subversive advocacy. Many people suffered along the way because they chose to exercise their rights despite the risks; perhaps even more than those who wrote the First Amendment, they are the heroes of the struggle to secure the right to freedom of expression for us all. If we wake up each morning with the right to freedom of political speech, we have Eugene V. Debs and Benjamin Gitlow and Anita Whitney and Eugene Dennis to thank, every bit as much as James Madison and Thomas Jefferson. Their suffering established our rights.

BURNING THE FLAG: HERESY OR FREE SPEECH?

But if the concepts of seditious libel and subversive advocacy today are all but dead, many other threats to freedom of expression still exist and often provide excuses for those in power to restrict speech they do not like.

In 1969, a black man named Sidney Street burned an American flag on a streetcorner in Harlem after James Meredith had been shot in Mississippi. Meredith, the first black student to attend the University of Mississippi, had been persistently threatened and harassed prior to the shooting. While burning the flag, Street said angrily: "We don't need no damn flag.... If they let that happen to Meredith, we don't need an American flag." Had Street uttered those words without burning the flag, he surely would have been protected from punishment by the First Amendment. But by accompanying his words with the dramatic act of burning the flag—no different in concept from burning a losing football coach in effigy—Street exposed himself to risk. By itself his statement probably wouldn't have attracted much attention. Very likely, many Americans expressed similar thoughts that day. But by burning the flag, Street attracted the media's attention and greatly widened the audience for his views. He also attracted the attention of the police, and was soon arrested and convicted for violating a New York law that made it a crime to "cast contempt" upon the American flag.

Street appealed, and when the case reached the Supreme Court, his conviction was reversed. In so doing, the Court upheld Street's First Amendment right to expression against the government's desire to compel respect for a national emblem. The case recalled the Jehovah's Witness case in 1943, when the Supreme Court had upheld the right of children not to salute the flag in public school. In *Street,* the Court ruled that the flag stands in part for the right to heap contempt upon it, even to the extent of burning it. Street's words as he burned the flag made the nature of his act clear. He was expressing a political opinion. What the flag represents, the Court seemed to say, was the Constitution, including the Bill of Rights. The flag stands for the right to free speech, for the right to express one's anger at the government and at the country by destroying its symbol. As such, the *Street* case also involved a form of seditious libel. Seditious-libel laws had always made it a crime to cast contempt upon the king, or, in America, the president, the Congress, or the government in general. New York's law made it a crime to cast contempt upon the symbol of the nation. Such a law was not all that different from the fifteenth-century English law that made it a crime to call the king a fool, and the Supreme Court threw it out.

During the early 1970s, a number of similar cases arose when local law-enforcement officials tried to prosecute people who were opposed to the war in Vietnam and who had affixed decals to their automobile windows or bumpers. The decals displayed an American flag with a peace symbol, often a white dove, superimposed on it. Prosecutions were brought against such people under laws making it a crime to "desecrate" an American flag. The use of the word "desecrate," which means "defile what is sacred," was especially telling; it showed that the root of many of these laws lay in the old idea of blasphemy and in ancient prohibitions against criticizing the church as well as the king.

These cases, of course, did not involve even a flag, but rather a picture of a flag. Prosecutors said that any symbol superimposed on a flag, or on a picture of the flag, was clearly a "desecration." But it was even more clear that the prosecutions were brought because of the defendants' opposition to the war and not because of their way of expressing it. As defense lawyers pointed out in case after case, for more than a hundred years politicians running for office had distributed buttons and other campaign materials with their faces superimposed on an American flag. There was no record of any of them ever having been prosecuted. All of these flag-decal arrests and convictions were eventually thrown out.

By the mid-1970s, the right to use the flag to express political views seemed settled. Then, in 1984, outside the hall where the Republican National Convention was being held in Dallas, a young man named Joey Johnson burned an American flag to protest against the Republican Party platform and other issues. He was arrested under a Texas law similar to the ones that had been struck down years before in other states, and convicted. When the case reached the Supreme Court in 1989, the Court declared the law unconstitutional and ruled that Johnson had a First Amendment right to burn the flag.

The decision sparked a great political furor and a substantial constitutional debate. George Bush, the newly elected president, was outraged by the Court's decision and tried to amend the Bill of Rights. He became the first American president in two hundred years to propose a constitutional amendment to create an exception to the First Amendment. That exception would have allowed Congress and state legislatures to make it a crime to "desecrate" the flag. Cooler heads, wishing to avoid a constitutional crisis, prevailed in Congress, and no amendment was passed. But Congress did pass a new law that made it a crime to desecrate the flag. By wording this law differently from the Texas law, its backers hoped to win the Supreme Court's approval.

Within hours of President Bush's signing this bill into law, protesters burned an American flag in Washington, D.C., to initiate a test of the law's constitutionality. In 1990, the Supreme Court again struck the new law down, encouraged by an unusual coalition of liberal and conservative libertarians. This provoked a new attempt to amend the Constitution to create an exception to the First Amendment. After a spirited public debate, broadcast to the nation on television, the amendment failed to get the required two-thirds vote, and the Bill of Rights remained intact.

In 1991, several white high-school students in South Carolina were suspended for displaying and wearing Confederate flags, which was said by school officials to be so offensive to black students as to create the likelihood of disruption or even violence. But the Supreme Court rulings that protected Sidney Street and Joey Johnson were invoked to protect these students, and their right to express themselves was vindicated. Recalling Justice Louis Brandeis's view, as expressed in the case of Anita Whitney in 1927, that the remedy for evil speech is "more speech," one civil-rights advocate suggested that black students might want to burn the Confederate flag. By so doing, they would inextricably join their right to do so to the white students' right to display the flag, and perhaps even provoke a discussion not only about the underlying racial issues, but also about how the Bill of Rights binds us together. The school might have used the incident as an opportunity to *teach*, rather than act as police officers. But there is no record of that ever happening.

SHOULD HATE SPEECH BE FREE TOO?

The South Carolina case also illustrates another arguable exception to the right of free speech. Some people believe that any speech expressing hatred or prejudice toward others based on race, religion, sex, sexual orientation, or national origin should be prohibited. But general ideas and beliefs about the inferiority of certain groups are without doubt protected from punishment by the First Amendment; to say otherwise would require a court to take evidence and decide on the truth or falsity of beliefs, and would resurrect all the problems created by the "truth is a defense" rule in the 1798 Sedition Act cases. If false ideas were not protected by the First Amendment, we would be granting *government* the power to decide which ideas to protect and which to punish. Any idea that any government—federal, state, or local—found displeasing would then be vulnerable, and the freedom of expression of all Americans, particularly those who are relatively powerless, would be fatally undermined. That is why the Supreme Court in 1974 declared that "under our Constitution, there is no such thing as a false idea." What the Court meant was that truth and falsity had to contest freely for the public's loyalty and not be decided by government fiat.

Minorities of all kinds—whether defined politically, religiously, sexually, or racially—have a special stake in keeping the government out of the business of deciding which speech to permit. A strong First Amendment may indeed result in legal protections for hateful opinions that denigrate, insult, and injure the feelings of minorities. But if the First Amendment were set aside and government were given the power to decide which speech to permit and which to punish, minorities would suffer the most—because by definition their adversaries would more often be in positions of power. It is no accident that the cases we have been discussing almost always involved minorities of one kind or another. In 1798, it was the minority Republican Party that was the exclusive target of the Sedition Act. During the nineteenth century, antislavery advocates were most often the ones repressed. Eugene V. Debs, Benjamin Gitlow, Anita Whitney, Eugene Dennis, and Sidney Street all represented minorities, either racial or political. The religious-liberty cases almost always involved minority religions like the Amish or Jehovah's Witnesses. And in the South during the 1960s, government restrictions on free speech were virtually never applied—except when Martin Luther King, Jr., and his colleagues wished to exercise their rights.

Today, there is considerable controversy on many university campuses about whether students should be punished or even expelled for expressing views that denigrate or demean other people on the basis of race, religion, sex, or sexual orientation. Prejudice is indeed a distressingly persistent problem, and colleges have generally done a poor job of confronting it and finding effective ways to reduce it. But punishing the expression of prejudice and hatred requires giving university officials the power to decide which views to allow and which to forbid. Had such rules been in force on college campuses during the 1960s, ostensibly to protect black students from prejudicial speech, surely Malcolm X and Eldridge Cleaver would have been their most frequent target. None of this is surprising, because those who are in power at most universities do not represent minorities and are not, when it comes down to hard cases, primarily responsible to minorities. Like all people in power, they will often tend to be responsive to majorities: to alumni, to donors, and to the majority of students and their parents. Why relatively powerless minorities would want *their* views and opinions to be subject to the permission of those in power is difficult to fathom.

The key question when evaluating the likely consequences of any restriction on speech is: Who decides? The power to restrict speech will not often be voluntarily given if one imagines one's enemies in the position of using that power. Yet that is precisely the position in which minorities by definition find themselves. Speech is free until we say something that offends someone in power. That is when the value of the First Amendment becomes clear. Yet "freedom of speech" ought not to prevent the punishment of conduct that intimidates, harasses, or threatens a specific individual. Nor does it matter if words are used. A threatening phone call in the middle of the night is not protected by the First Amendment just because words are used. Extortion and blackmail use words, but they are still crimes. Like the law that finally developed to protect subversive advocacy, a careful distinction must be made between the expression of general views, no matter how reprehensible, and overt acts that may be punishable as crimes whether or not words are used.

CIVIL-LIBEL SUITS AS WEAPONS OF INTIMIDATION

Although seditious-libel laws that make it a crime to defame a public official are now prohibited by the First Amendment, it is still possible for a public official to bring a civil suit against a citizen for libel. Supreme Court Justice Hugo Black once wrote that civil-libel suits were intended only to settle "purely private feuds" and not "to punish discussion of matters of public concern." Yet under current Supreme Court decisions, the First Amendment continues to allow public officials and other powerful public figures to sue their critics and seek to punish them by huge libel judgments.

In 1984, for example, General William C. Westmoreland sued CBS Television for $120 million because of the network's criticism of his role as commanding officer in Vietnam. The suit claimed that CBS had damaged Westmoreland's reputation. Quite aside from the result in the case, the lawsuit cost CBS over $2 million just to defend. Maybe CBS could afford such a steep tariff, but smaller, less affluent media organizations could be put out of business by a public official stung by their criticism. In 1982, the *Nation,* a small weekly magazine operating on a shoestring budget, published an article about police brutality and intimidation of voters in the tiny town of McAllen, Texas, near the Mexican border. The *Nation* was sued for libel by the mayor of McAllen, who claimed damage to his reputation. The suit was legally preposterous, but the cost of going to Texas to defend itself in court threatened the magazine's existence.

Similarly, in 1975 a small group of civic-minded women in New York began a project of visiting state trial courts to observe judges' performances. As a result of what they saw, they filed a complaint against one judge with a judicial supervisory body whose job it was to hear and evaluate such complaints. It alleged intemperate and sometimes abusive behavior. The judge responded by suing the women for libel, seeking a $1 million award. The suit was completely frivolous, but the women had no resources even to hire a lawyer, and were frightened. They abandoned the court-watching project.

Such lawsuits seek to punish citizens who criticize public officials and they also intimidate other citizens by setting an example: Be forewarned—if you criticize public officials, you do so at your peril. Civil-libel suits by public officials therefore have much the same impact as the old seditious-libel laws. The government is no longer permitted to charge people with a crime for damaging the government's reputation, but the law permits the same public officials to achieve the same result through civil-libel suits. In both cases, it is not their private reputations that are the target of criticism, but their conduct as public officials. If the First Amendment is intended to insulate a citizen from punishment when he criticizes a public official, why aren't such civil-libel suits barred?

In 1964, the Supreme Court addressed this problem directly. The case began when Martin Luther King, Jr., was arrested in Montgomery, Alabama, in 1960. A group of his supporters formed a committee to finance his defense. As part of their effort, they purchased a full-page advertisement in the *New York Times* seeking contributions from the general public. The advertisement, headlined "Heed Their Rising Voices," listed a variety of harassments and threats to which King and his followers had been subjected, including the bombing of King's home and seven questionable arrests.

L. B. Sullivan, the chief of police in Montgomery, didn't like the advertisement. Had he been able to charge the *New York Times* with the crime of seditious libel, he might well have done so. Instead, he sued the *Times,* along with four black Alabama ministers who had signed the ad, for civil libel. The case went before a Montgomery jury from which blacks had been excluded. The law of libel at that time allowed Sullivan to win, even though the ad didn't name him, if the jury found that his professional reputation had been damaged. The defense of truth was available, just as it used to be in seditious-libel cases, but the ad had made a few factual mistakes—King had been arrested four times, not seven, for example. The jury awarded Sullivan $500,000.

The *Times* had argued for its constitutional right to publish the ad without fear of punishment. But the judge ruled that the First Amendment offered no protection in matters of civil libel. By the time the appeal reached the United States Supreme Court, civil-libel suits had already become a powerful weapon against the civil-rights movement: eleven libel suits, including Sullivan's, were pending against the *Times* in Alabama alone, with claims totaling $5.6 million. The *Times* asked the Court to rule that civil-libel suits by public officials directed at critics of their official conduct were the same as seditious-libel laws and should be prohibited by the First Amendment.

Three judges agreed, but the majority rejected the *Times's* argument. On the other hand, the Court did recognize that civil-libel laws in cases like this interfered with the right to criticize public officials. The Court therefore permitted such suits but made it more difficult for public officials to win them. While libel suits between private citizens involving nothing more than private feuds could continue normally, libel suits brought by public officials would now be required to meet a higher standard. Public officials could not win unless they could clearly and convincingly prove that the criticism was published with malice. Malice was defined as "knowledge that [the statement] was false or [publishing the statement] with reckless disregard of whether it was false." Applying that standard, Sullivan's suit was thrown out and the judgment against the *Times* and the four ministers nullified.

The Court's decision finally and almost incidentally declared all criminal-sedition laws unconstitutional. It specifically discussed the old 1798 Sedition Act, which it found unambiguously "inconsistent with the First Amendment." And even though civil-libel suits by public officials were not totally barred, the Court's decision was widely viewed as a victory for freedom of expression because it made the suits more difficult for public officials to win.

This victory, however, turned out to be more hollow than at first appeared. By declining to bar such civil suits entirely, the Court allowed public officials to use them to punish their critics. Even under the higher "malice" standard, public officials could try people for their words. This turned out to create a problem very much like the one posed by the old "truth is a defense" rule. People critical of public officials would still have to bear the expense and the risk of defending themselves against libel suits, even if the libel suits were ultimately unsuccessful. For those who could not afford to defend themselves, the price of criticism became prohibitive.

In the *Times* case, Justice Hugo Black recognized this immediately. He predicted that the decision, though it appeared to be a victory for freedom of expression, would provide only "an evanescent protection." As the *Nation* and the court-watchers found out years later, Black was right. Although the *Times* case and subsequent cases provided some degree of protection for criticism, civil-libel suits by public officials and public figures became a common way of punishing people who had criticized them and intimidating others who might. Today, the law remains essentially where *Times v. Sullivan* left it.

THE "NATIONAL SECURITY" EXCEPTION

Aside from the risk of civil-libel suits, however, the press is today largely free of any legal restrictions upon its right to publish anything, no matter how critical, concerning governmental operations or public policy. A major exception to that general rule is in the area of "national security." It is an exception fraught with difficulty.

The "national security" exception has been increasingly invoked by the government during the past twenty years to bar publication of certain information it would like kept secret. The legal basis for this exception began with a Minnesota case in 1931. In that case, a newspaper accusing public officials of graft and corruption had been ordered by a court to stop, on the basis of a state law authorizing prior censorship of "malicious, scandalous, and defamatory" publications. When the case reached the Supreme Court, the law was struck down. For the very first time, the First Amendment had been used to nullify a state law on free-speech grounds. The Court also made it clear that prior restraint of speech generally was prohibited by the First Amendment. But it left a loophole.

In striking down the prior censorship of the Minnesota newspaper, the Court commented, almost as an aside, that under certain circumstances prior restraints might be allowed, and it listed a few examples. One example was "obscenity." Another was "military secrets." Neither category was defined with any precision or in any detail.

One might imagine the legitimacy of restricting information revealing troop movements, for example, in advance of a military initiative. But that is the sort of information that would normally be passed along to an enemy by a spy, not published in a periodical of general circulation. In fact, the government has badly overused the concept of national security, classifying as secret a great deal of information that has nothing to do with military operations, but which the government would rather the public didn't know. Sometimes this is because the information would embarrass a government official by revealing mistakes, incompetence, or corruption; sometimes it is because the government does not wish to encourage public debate over its policies.

A classic confrontation involving these issues occurred in 1971, when the *New York Times*, soon followed by the *Washington Post, Los Angeles Times, Detroit Free Press, Philadelphia Inquirer*, and *Miami Herald*, began to publish a set of documents called the Pentagon Papers, a forty-seven-volume history of the United States government's decision-making process relating to our policy on Vietnam. The entire history was classified as secret by the government, and therefore was not available to inform the public debate over the war in Vietnam, which by 1971 had become intensely and widely controversial.

Despite the secrecy imposed on the Pentagon Papers, Daniel Ellsberg, a former Defense Department official, provided them to the *Times*. (He was later charged with violating the Espionage Act of 1917, but the case was dismissed because of government misconduct, which included wiretapping Ellsberg's former colleagues and breaking into his psychiatrist's office to steal his records.) As soon as the *Times* began publishing excerpts, the government went into court seeking an order barring further publication on the grounds that it would damage national security and endanger the lives of American troops. The judge issued a temporary order blocking publication sufficient to allow him time to examine the papers in private, but in the presence of lawyers for both sides. He later rejected the government's argument that "publication of these historical documents would seriously breach the national security."

The government appealed, and at the same time it brought an identical suit against the *Washington Post* in the District of Columbia. Both cases reached the United States Supreme Court only two weeks after publication had first begun. The Court, by a 6–3 majority, upheld the newspapers' right to publish the articles.

At the very least, the case stood for the proposition that no censorship of the press was constitutionally permissible unless the government could prove that any harm to the nation would be "direct, immediate, and irreparable." Perhaps even more importantly, the case stood for the proposition that government claims of national security should be independently reviewed by the courts before allowing censorship. The *Pentagon Papers* case sharply limited the government's power to block publication of information already in the possession of the press or individual citizens. Increasingly, therefore, the government has sought to block information from reaching the public by refusing to make it available in the first place. In the years since the *Pentagon Papers* case, the government has repeatedly relied upon claims of national security to justify withholding information, and the courts have increasingly accepted those claims, often without serious scrutiny.

The government has also used its power over employees, including former employees, to control information and ideas, and to suppress criticism. In 1980, for example, the Court upheld a substantial restraint upon the right of a former government official to publish his memoirs. Frank Snepp had worked for the CIA, which required its employees to sign a contract agreeing not to publish any classified information, and also agreeing not to publish anything, whether classified or not, without the prior approval of the CIA. In practice, this part of the agreement reinstated the old English rule of prior restraint and gave the CIA the ability to censor criticism even if such criticism revealed no intelligence secrets.

Snepp published a book about CIA activities in South Vietnam, without clearing it in advance with the CIA. The government sued, arguing that Snepp had breached his contract. Snepp argued that as long as he didn't reveal any classified information, he could not be required to obtain the CIA's permission to publish, and that such a contractual requirement violated the First Amendment. The Supreme Court upheld the government by a 6–3 vote, barely even commenting on the First Amendment question in a footnote. Instead, the Court treated the case as a simple contract case, deferred entirely to the government, and allowed the CIA to seize all the proceeds from the book's sales, thereby effectively imposing a prior censorship on any books of this nature that might be published in the future. In this and other cases, the Court stepped back from its skeptical approach in the *Pentagon Papers* case and increasingly accepted the government's claim of national security as a justification of censorship. As a result, the right to publish information that the government wants to keep secret remains at best uncertain.

STILLING THE CRITICS BY CONTROLLING INFORMATION

During the Reagan administration, government controls on the flow of information tightened significantly. Prepublication review and approval, even for former public officials, was extended beyond the intelligence agencies. Attempts were made, some of them successful, to subject hundreds of thousands of government officials to lifetime censorship agreements. Several amendments were introduced in Congress to give the government greater power to deny citizens' requests for information under the Freedom of Information Act, but none of them passed. In 1982, President Reagan issued an executive order vastly expanding the categories of information that could be classified as secret, and removing the requirement that some identifiable harm to national security first had to be demonstrated. In 1983, Reagan issued yet another order, further expanding requirements for prepublication review and approval.

Virtually every attempt to restrict the flow of public information was justified by vague and ill-defined claims of "national security," and the courts often proved to be less than vigorous in scrutinizing those claims or measuring them against the First Amendment. In effect, the government had discovered that there were two ways to curb public criticism: the first was to punish people directly for voicing their criticisms; the second was to withhold information that might substantiate such criticism.

From the beginning of our nation's history, the right to criticize the government and openly debate its policies has come under attack from those government officials who would rather exercise power without justifying it to the citizens they represent. Until relatively recently, most legal attacks on First Amendment rights were directed at the critics themselves: sedition laws that made it a crime to criticize the government; subversive-advocacy laws that prohibited rhetorical calls to action; and laws that punished people for distributing leaflets, making speeches, holding meetings, or organizing demonstrations. Government attempts to restrict these rights are relatively rare now, and when they occur, lawyers can usually obtain remedies swiftly and effectively. But where once the primary means of suppressing robust debate and criticism was to muzzle the critics, the government's efforts today focus more on controlling important information. The rights to speak, publish, hear, and read are relatively intact. But *what* we are permitted to speak about, to publish, to hear, and to read is increasingly limited to what the government wants us to know.

Nothing brought this home more clearly than a case decided by the Supreme Court on May 23, 1991. The case involved a federal law providing federal funds to family-planning clinics. As a result of intense opposition to abortion, clinics accepting such funds were not permitted to perform abortions. But in 1988, the Reagan administration went beyond what the law required and issued regulations forbidding doctors who work at such clinics to even discuss abortion with their patients, except to tell them that abortion was "inappropriate." No other information about abortion could be provided, even if the woman requested it or the doctor thought it was medically necessary. Nor could referrals be made.

Dr. Irving Rust, a physician working at a Planned Parenthood clinic in New York, challenged these regulations. He claimed that the regulations amounted to enforced malpractice, interfered with his responsibility to his patients, and suppressed his right to free speech. The Court rejected these arguments, and by a 5–4 vote ruled that since this was a government-funded program, the government could control what doctors said to their patients.

Since this was not the first time the government had tried to use the power of the purse to compel censorship as a condition of accepting government support, the Court's decision was greeted with great alarm. Because many essential activities now depend upon government support, many questions remain to be answered. If Congress someday enacts a national health-insurance system, could it prohibit any discussion between doctors and their patients about abortion, or even contraceptives? Could government support of public broadcasting bar television programs that discuss forbidden subjects? Might those who conduct scientific research on reproduction be barred from discussing or publishing articles about RV-486, the "morning-after" contraceptive pill developed in France? Could legal-services lawyers be barred from providing certain legal advice to their dependent clients? Could art and theater and music supported by federal grants be censored?

Although the *Rust* ruling did not answer any of these questions, it certainly increased the likelihood that the government would try to circumvent constitutional bans on censorship by imposing limitations on speech as a condition of federal grants, thus limiting citizens to government-approved information. The ability of the government to avoid the restrictions of the First Amendment in a world increasingly dependent upon government funds thus looms as a major threat to freedom of expression in the years ahead.

Not every attempt to restrict the public's right to information has been successful. But the public's *right to know* is a concept only partially protected by the First Amendment. The right to publish means less if basic information is strictly controlled by the government. During the Persian Gulf War in 1991, for example, unprecedented restrictions were placed on where reporters could go, what they could see, and who they could interview, far beyond anything that had been deemed necessary to protect military security during World War II or during the Vietnam War. If the public's right to know how the Gulf War was going was important, that right depended not on the independent views of reporters, but on government press releases. There was good reason to believe that these unprecedented restrictions were designed not to protect military security, but to manipulate public opinion.

The question of whether the public has a right to information free from government control remains unsettled. In 1980, the Supreme Court ruled that reporters could not be excluded from criminal trials; on the other hand, lower federal courts rejected requests by the media for greater access to the theater of war in the Persian Gulf. It is still unclear where the Supreme Court draws the line between information the government is required to disclose and information it may keep secret, between access it is obliged to grant and access it may deny.

THE "OBSCENITY" EXCEPTION

An entirely different exception to the First Amendment's protection of freedom of expression is the so-called "obscenity" exception. No one knows exactly what obscenity is, or precisely how to define it. Like "false speech," obscenity often lies in the eye of the beholder. Somewhat curiously, the definition of obscenity has been limited to words and images relating to matters of *sex* and *bodily functions*. Images of violence, for example, have not suffered nearly as many restrictions as images of sex have; some have wondered why the image of two people making love tenderly is considered obscene, although the image of one person slaughtering another is not.

In any case, obscenity laws have been used solely to restrict expression considered too explicitly sexual. Thus, such laws have more frequently impinged on the freedom of artistic expression—literature, plays, films, photographs, music—than on conventional political expression, although attempts to censor artistic expression are nearly always deeply political.

Leaving aside the question of public displays, one would think that the freedom to publish a book or produce a film no one was forced to read or see would be well within the zone of personal sovereignty that the Bill of Rights was meant to protect from government intrusion. Yet in its first major consideration of this important issue, the Supreme Court took hardly any notice of this fundamental question.

Interestingly, this occurred relatively recently in our history, in 1957. The Court was asked to review two criminal convictions, one federal, the other from the state of California. Neither the federal nor the state statute defined obscenity, so on that basis alone the Court might have struck them down: if the crime was not defined, how would anyone know whether or not they were committing it? But the Court ignored this problem. Neither did the Court examine the materials that had provoked the prosecutions, so no review of the discretion of local prosecutions or of the juries was possible. How then was the Court to decide?

Perhaps the Court should have thought of this case as involving the Ninth Amendment: so long as no one was forced to read these books, why was it the government's business to intervene at all, and punish people who in the privacy of their own homes wished to read books that others found objectionable? And if one had a right to read such a book according to one's own taste, then why should the government punish someone else for supplying it?

These were difficult questions to answer, made more so because the Court never even saw the books in question. Indeed, the Court never made a serious attempt even to inquire whether personal taste was any of the government's business, or whether the Constitution permitted the majority, using the criminal law, to impose its tastes on people who did not share them. Two justices— William O. Douglas and Hugo Black—said that obscenity was just a label for expression the majority didn't like and that, like all expression, it was protected by the First Amendment. But they were outvoted, 7–2.

The person convicted of violating the federal obscenity law, Samuel Roth, argued that, as with political speech, the "clear and present danger" rule should apply. That is, unless the book he sold could be shown to have led directly and imminently to criminal conduct, why should he be sent to prison for selling it? Why should lustful thoughts themselves, in the absence of criminal conduct, be a crime? No criminal conduct of any kind was shown to have resulted in this case, and it was in this respect no different from the conviction of Benjamin Gitlow or Charles Schenck for distributing political leaflets that the government thought *might* incite a crime, but which had not.

The Court didn't see it that way. Instead, it decided that obscenity, however defined, was so "utterly without redeeming social importance" that it was a category of speech not protected at all by the First Amendment. Questions of personal autonomy in the absence of any otherwise criminal conduct were never even raised. The convictions were upheld, and the Court started down the long and difficult path of trying to define obscenity.

OBSCENITY LIES IN THE EYE OF THE BEHOLDER

Once obscenity was removed from constitutional protection, without requiring state laws even to define it, prosecutors gained the authority to prosecute anything they wished. Soon the courts were flooded with obscenity prosecutions, many involving art, books, or plays that today are recognized as having substantial artistic or literary merit. Some were recognized even then as having great artistic merit. But so long as thousands of public officials had the power to define obscenity as they pleased and then to try and send people to jail for it, the criminal law was certain to reach many works of artistic merit and impose a regime of censorship and punishment driven either by a local majority's taste or by an ambitious prosecutor. Just as the 1798 Sedition Act made it impossible to protect truth as long as it empowered the government to prosecute error, so obscenity laws made it impossible to protect freedom of artistic expression as long as they empowered the government to prosecute whatever a local prosecutor thought was "dirty." As more such cases reached the Supreme Court, the Court was forced to do what it had largely avoided in the *Roth* case: attempt to define obscenity with more precision. It was forced to do this because many books and films were being prosecuted that the Court didn't think were obscene and hadn't meant to remove from the protection of the First Amendment.

Thus a great guessing game ensued. No one could define obscenity in advance; prosecutors tried to guess what the Supreme Court might think, and the Court would tell them only later, often in confused and conflicting opinions. All of this required the Court to examine each item thought to be obscene in every case that came before them. In fact, in 1964, the Court reversed an obscenity conviction because, after reviewing the movie in question, they decided it was not obscene. This transformed the Court into a board of censorship-review: in the 1964 case, the Court actually *required* itself to review independently all material alleged to be obscene.

None of this made it any easier to define exactly what obscenity was. One Supreme Court justice seemed untroubled by this problem. "I know it when I see it," he said. This standard, of course, was no standard at all, and meant simply that figuring out whether or not sexually explicit expression was criminal would continue to be a guessing game.

Then, in 1969, the Supreme Court decided a case called *Stanley v. Georgia*, in what seemed at first to be a breakthrough from all the muddled attempts to define obscenity. For the first time, clear constitutional principles were articulated. Robert Stanley was a man suspected of illegal gambling. The police obtained a search warrant and entered his home looking for evidence. While rummaging through a desk drawer, they found three reels of eight-millimeter film. Using Stanley's own projector and screen, they watched the films and decided they were obscene. Stanley was then arrested for possessing obscene material, indicted, and convicted. Despite its previous decision in the *Roth* case, the Supreme Court threw out Stanley's conviction and declared Georgia's law unconstitutional. Although the Court continued to say that the state could "regulate obscenity" by, for example, enacting laws designed to prohibit obscene material from falling into the hands of children, or from intruding upon people's sensibilities in public places, it ruled that the possession of obscene material in the home—however that material might be defined—could not be made into a crime.

In the *Stanley* case, the Court focused on the very principle it had avoided in *Roth:* the government would not be permitted "to control the moral content of a person's thoughts." The Court said, "Our whole constitutional heritage rebels at the thought of giving government the power to control men's minds." It seemed as though the Supreme Court had at last announced a clear rule: so long as reasonable precautions were taken not to impose "obscene" material on children or on unwilling bystanders, the Constitution would forbid the government from restricting the content of books and films.

Almost immediately, however, the Court undercut the scope of its ruling in the *Stanley* case. Two years later, the Court decided two cases at once. One involved a man who was indicted for sending obscene materials by mail to an adult who had responded to his advertisement. The ad required anyone who responded to state that he or she was over twenty-one. The second case involved a man who was carrying photographs in his luggage, which were seized by customs officials as he was returning from a trip abroad. Relying on the *Stanley* case, lower federal courts had declared both the indictment in the first case and the customs seizure in the second to be unconstitutional, since under *Stanley* a person had a right to receive and possess obscene material privately; in neither case were such materials directed at children or an unwilling public.

But the Supreme Court reversed both decisions. By a 6–3 vote, it ruled that the right to possess obscene materials in the privacy of one's own home did not mean that it was permissible to use the mails for such materials or to import them. Justice Hugo Black, joined by Justice William O. Douglas, scathingly noted in dissent that the *Stanley* case would probably in the future protect only someone who "writes salacious books in his attic, prints them in his basement, and reads them in his living room."

If anything remained of the *Stanley* ruling after these two cases, it shrank some more two year later, by which time several new appointments to the Supreme Court had been made. In 1973, the Court ruled that the state could prosecute a movie theater for showing an "obscene" film, *even if minors were excluded.* This decision further eroded the force of the *Stanley* ruling, because it meant that obscene films could not be shown in private places even among consenting adults. Presumably, the same rule applied to books.

This ruling reinforced the need for a clear definition of obscenity, and in a companion case decided at the same time, the Court took another crack at it: a film or book could be rendered criminal if "the average person" would find that the work *taken as a whole* appealed to his or her prurient interest and if the work *taken as a whole* lacked serious literary, artistic, political, or scientific value. In addition, the sexual conduct depicted or described had to be "patently offensive" and specifically defined in the state's law.

This definition was designed to insulate from prosecution books, films, photographs, dances, and plays that contained erotic passages but, taken as a whole, had serious social value. And indeed it did substantially reduce the number of obscenity prosecutions. Nonetheless, it still left lingering definitional dilemmas: Just who was "the average person"? What was "prurient interest"? Who would decide what was "patently offensive"? How would the Court measure "serious social value"?

Four justices, including Justice William Brennan, who had written the original decision in the *Roth* case, thought the entire attempt futile. They believed it was impossible to define obscenity without permitting local governments to restrict expression clearly protected by the First Amendment. Moreover, the inability of the Court to define obscenity in advance with any precision created intolerable problems of fairness. People could be sent to jail for producing or displaying books and films without knowing in advance whether or not they were legal. Brennan in particular argued for a return to the standard that seemed originally to have been implied in the *Stanley* case: "In the absence of distribution to juveniles or obtrusive exposure to unconsenting adults," he said, the First Amendment barred the government from attempting to criminalize sexually explicit subject matter. Douglas went further. Repeating the views he had articulated in obscenity cases since 1957, he argued that the First Amendment contained no exception for "obscenity" that allowed the Court to treat freedom of expression differently because of its sexual content. But the Court rejected these arguments by a 5–4 vote. Thus, although the Court tried to narrow the definition of what thoughts and images the government could control, it still permitted the government to decide who to send to prison because of the sexual content of their words or images.

THE NEW RIGHT VERSUS ARTISTIC RIGHTS

Despite the Court's decisions, or perhaps because the Court's new definitions made it harder to obtain convictions, the number of obscenity prosecutions declined after 1973 and the availability of sexually explicit material increased. In 1988, Senator Jesse Helms of North Carolina began a campaign to restrict the availability of such material. He first introduced a bill in Congress to prohibit the National Endowment for the Arts from providing grants to any artist whose work was offensive. The bill banned expression that was not even arguably obscene, and was not enacted. Helms next offered a bill that purported to incorporate the Supreme Court's obscenity definitions, but which actually went further. That bill passed, and it required the NEA to apply the Supreme Court's vague standards, make unavoidably subjective judgments about individual works, and withhold grants from art it considered obscene. The requirement provoked a storm of protest from the artistic community, and was not reenacted after it expired.

But Helms's initiative encouraged a new wave of obscenity prosecutions at the local level. In Florida, a rap group called 2 Live Crew was prosecuted for using obscene lyrics in its songs. In Alabama and Florida, record-store owners were prosecuted for selling the rap group's records. In Cincinnati, the curator of a major museum was indicted because he had authorized an exhibit of photographs by a widely respected photographer, Robert Mapplethorpe, which in part depicted homoerotic images. Most of these prosecutions resulted in acquittals by juries, indicating a change in public attitudes. The law still permits such prosecutions, however, and it is difficult to say what would have happened on appeal had the juries convicted in these cases. Moreover, another bill has passed Congress authorizing the NEA to recover grants it has made to artists if their work is later found to be obscene. Without doubt, freedom of artistic expression is much more extensively practiced today than it used to be. But freedom of political expression was also much more widely practiced in the late eighteenth century than the letter of the law allowed, and it ultimately proved to be vulnerable to sedition laws. Today, freedom of artistic expression remains similarly vulnerable to self-appointed moral guardians like Jesse Helms or those in Florida, Alabama, and Ohio who put people on trial for their words or images.

In June 1991, the Supreme Court encouraged this trend when it upheld a ban on nude dancing in an Indiana nightclub. It was agreed that the dancing, while erotic, was not obscene. Under prior Supreme Court decisions, therefore, the first Amendment should have protected such expressive conduct. But by a 5–4 vote, the Supreme Court upheld the ban, although no more than three justices could agree why. Those three said the ban was justified because of the state's interest in preventing "public nudity." They said this even though there was nothing at all public about the nudity: it took place in a private nightclub, from which minors were excluded. Yet Chief Justice William Rehnquist treated the case as if it involved the state's attempt to ban nudity on a public street.

Justice Byron White, in dissent, conceded that the performance at issue was not "high art," but if it wasn't obscene, he failed to see why the first Amendment didn't protect it or how this case would in the future be distinguished from high art that included nudity. He called the Court's reasoning "transparently erroneous" and wondered if the Court would in the future be required to assess the artistic merits of various works of art. The decisive vote was cast by the newest justice, David M. Souter, who conceded that the Court's ruling could not possibly apply to such plays as *Hair* or *Equus*. Souter said he upheld the ban not because of the nudity itself, but because of its "secondary effects," such as "prostitution," "sexual assault," and "associated crimes." He said this even though no such crimes had occurred as the result of the performance, nor had evidence even been offered by the state on the point. Just as the Court had once upheld convictions for political rhetoric based on the revolutionary impact they imagined such rhetoric might have, so now Justice Souter upheld a ban on erotic dancing based on effects he imagined might occur. There is little doubt that this decision will lead to more prosecutions of constitutionally protected artistic expression.

A great deal of political expression may be worthless or offensive; the same is true of much artistic expression. But the key question remains: Who decides? The First Amendment stands for the proposition that individuals themselves should decide and that it is always dangerous to grant government the power to make expression a crime. Certainly, history proves that when government is given such power, it will use it in ways never intended, to target expression, whether political or artistic, that it does not like or finds threatening, or that a momentary majority finds offensive. The beast of censorship, once unleashed, is impossible to control.

FUNDAMENTAL
FAIRNESS

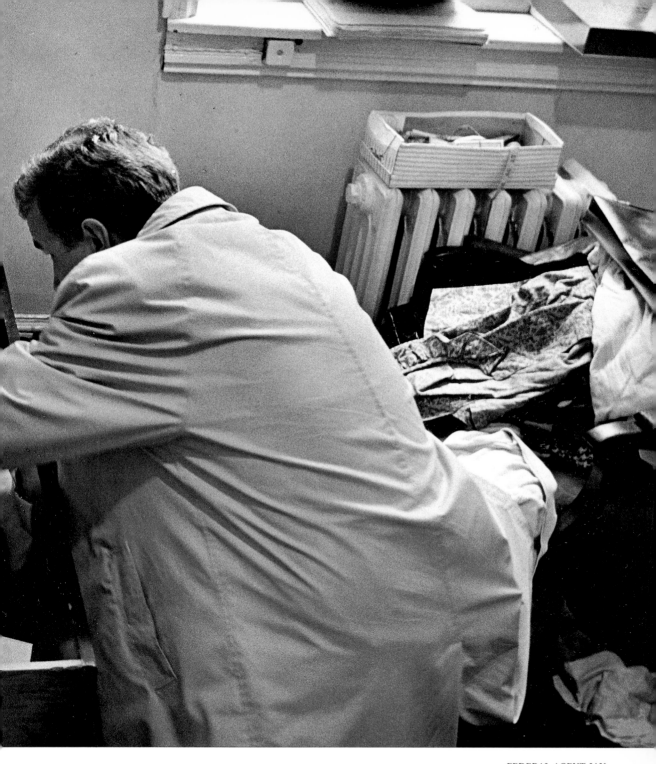

FEDERAL AGENT JAN
LARSEN SEARCHES
BEDROOM DURING
RAID ON ILLEGAL
NARCOTICS
LABORATORY. NEW
YORK CITY, 1968.

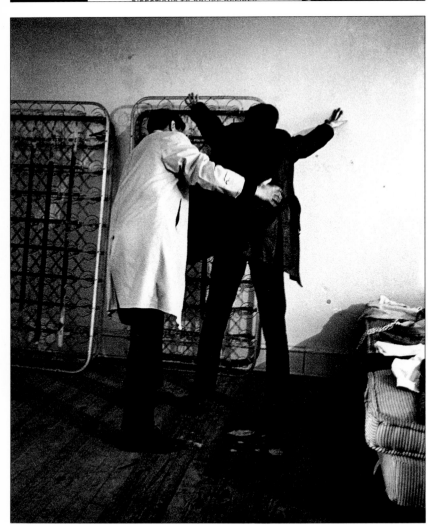

TOP: "MIRANDA
WARNING"
CHECKLIST
CARRIED BY
ALL NEW YORK
CITY POLICE
OFFICERS. 1991.

Search Warrant

FAR LEFT: NARCOTICS AGENT LARSEN "QUICK-FRISKS" CHEMIST IN LABORATORY RAID. NEW YORK CITY. 1968.

ABOVE: LARSEN INVENTORIES EVIDENCE OBTAINED UNDER AUTHORIZED SEARCH WARRANT (LEFT). NEW YORK CITY, 1968.

PICTURE COLLECTION, THE BRANCH LIBRARIES, THE NEW YORK PUBLIC LIBRARY

Coll John Lilborne.

THE MANSELL COLLECTION, LONDON

ABOVE:
COUNTY JAIL.
SUMTER,
SOUTH
CAROLINA,
1967.

FACING PAGE:
IN POLICE
CUSTODY.
MEMPHIS,
TENNESSEE,
1982.

17TH-CENTURY ENGLISH ACTIVIST JOHN LILBURNE SPENT MUCH OF HIS LIFE BEHIND BARS FOR CRITICIZING RELIGIOUS AND POLITICAL LEADERS, BUT HIS ARGUMENTS FOR FAIR TRIAL PROCEDURES WON HIM SEVERAL RELEASES, SET PRECEDENTS, AND MADE HIM A SYMBOL OF INDIVIDUAL RIGHTS. THE STAR CHAMBER IN LONDON, FOR MORE THAN 300 YEARS THE SITE OF A SPECIAL COURT FAMOUS FOR ITS ABSOLUTE POWER, BRUTAL SENTENCES, AND TOTAL LACK OF PROCEDURES TO GIVE ACCUSED PERSONS A FAIR CHANCE TO DEFEND THEMSELVES.

FUNDAMENTAL FAIRNESS

4

FREEDOM OF EXPRESSION AND RELIGIOUS LIBERTY ARE EXAMPLES OF SUBSTAN-
tive rights: they describe activities that the government may not outlaw. Other
activities, of course, may be made crimes, such as assault, embezzlement, rape,
or homicide. And the government has the legitimate authority to investigate
such crimes and try to convict those it suspects of committing them.

But when the government suspects an individual of committing a crime,
what procedures may it use to gather evidence? How much evidence is necessary before someone can be formally accused? And when the government
does accuse an individual of a crime, what procedures should be used to
determine guilt? How should society's interest in finding and punishing the
guilty party be balanced against the danger of convicting and punishing an
innocent person? And what are the risks of allowing the government too
much power in this area? These questions point to the need for *procedural*
rights: legal limits on the power of the government to investigate and prosecute crime. Such legal limits are important in order to guarantee fairness.

Obviously, if the police or other government officers had unlimited power
to decide for themselves who was guilty, then, human nature being what it is,
arrests and convictions might often be arbitrary and reflect prejudices of one
kind or another. People could be imprisoned, not because of what they did,
but because of who they were or what they represented. Racial prejudice
could become a primary determinant of guilt or punishment, as it often was in
the American South until fairly recently, or as it was in 1942, when tens of
thousands of American citizens were interned, purely because they were of
Japanese descent. Political animosity might determine guilt, as it did in 1798
and again in 1918, when laws barring sedition and espionage were selectively
enforced against opposing political parties or people with radical ideologies.
Without a legal guarantee of fair procedures, race, religion, national origin, or
political belief could become a substitute for evidence, and mere accusations
might unfairly be transformed into guilt.

Fair procedures are intended to inhibit such results, and to make sure that people who are accused of a crime have a decent opportunity to defend themselves. Fair procedures are also intended to require the government to prove its case with tangible evidence, fairly gathered and fairly presented, not only to inhibit prejudice, but also to avoid mistakes. Everyone has an interest in procedures that make it highly probable that the person convicted of a crime is the person who really committed it. Public safety is not enhanced when innocent people are convicted.

Sometimes it is argued that giving the government broad latitude to convict people will make it more likely that the guilty will be punished. But in societies where governments have had the power to imprison people without a fair trial, it hasn't worked out that way. Some guilty people may indeed be punished, but only at the price of punishing many innocent people as well. "If you hang 'em all, you'll get the guilty," goes the refrain of an old folk song, but providing any government with that sort of power would not be comforting to most of us. Fairness requires a more targeted approach, based on demonstrable evidence and some system for impartial decision-making.

THE DUE PROCESS OF LAW

The legal phrase that today refers to the concept of fair procedures is "due process of law." It has a long history, going back as long ago as 1354, when the British Parliament passed a law prohibiting the government from imprisoning anyone "without being brought in answer by due process of law." Yet from the start, it has not always been clear what is meant by due process. Everyone might agree that fair procedures should be used, but not everyone would agree on what procedures were required in order to be fair.

To a large extent, the Anglo-American system of procedural fairness is the result of a long struggle between an *accusatory* system of criminal law and an *inquisitorial* system. Up until the very end of the sixteenth century in England, for example, all criminal courts required people accused or even suspected of crime to testify against themselves. This was a key feature of the inquisitorial system, derived from ancient Roman codes, under which the government could charge a person with a crime on the basis of little more than rumor. Vague suspicions were enough to bring someone before a secret tribunal, where he would be made to tell "the truth." The methods of extracting "the truth" included torture, as well as lesser coercions. The person charged had no right to be presented with the evidence against him, or to have a fair opportunity to reply; often there wasn't any specific evidence. And the tribunal that charged him also judged him: the roles of prosecutor, judge, and jury were combined into one. Against such tribunals, an accused person stood little chance.

This inquisitorial process was widely used by ecclesiastical courts in England to prosecute heresy, or "incorrect" belief. Torture as a method of extracting the truth was eventually replaced by a procedure that required people hauled before these courts to take an oath swearing to answer truthfully all questions put to them. The questions sought to establish their guilt of certain crimes, but they were never told what those crimes were. Victims of such a process were in a terrible position: they could be punished for refusing to take the oath; if they took the oath and answered truthfully, they could be punished for crimes they didn't even know they had committed (often involving religious or political beliefs); and if they tried to respond to this predicament by lying, they could be punished for perjury.

SELF-INCRIMINATION AND THE FIFTH AMENDMENT

In 1637, a Puritan activist named John Lilburne imported and distributed various political tracts and was brought before the Star Chamber. Lilburne refused to be examined under oath, claiming that it violated "the law of the land" and invoking the Magna Carta. Condemning the oath as a procedure that was fundamentally unfair, Lilburne said he would not take it even "though I be pulled to pieces by wild horses." He very nearly was. Lilburne was held in contempt of court, publicly whipped, fined, and jailed in solitary confinement. He wasn't released until 1641. But his crusade for fair procedures and his willingness to absorb severe punishment rather than forsake principle inflamed the public — on both sides of the Atlantic — and Lilburne became a great symbol. He suffered, but not without effect: In 1641, Parliament abolished the Star Chamber and prohibited ecclesiastical courts from administering oaths requiring people to accuse themselves. In 1645, Parliament set aside the judgment against Lilburne, finding that it had indeed violated "the law of the land and Magna Carta." And in 1648, he was granted damages for his unjust imprisonment.

But that was not the end of Lilburne's travails. He remained an agitator for justice and a thorn in the side of the government. He led a group called the Levelers, an egalitarian-minded faction of reformers, and constantly provoked the government's wrath. He was arrested again and again, almost always because of his political views, and he repeatedly refused to cooperate with procedures he thought unfair, even though they were common at the time. He stood trial for his life four times, and at his very last trial he won the right — then unprecedented — to receive a copy of the charges against him and to be represented by a lawyer.

Although he died in prison at the age of forty-three, having spent much of his adult life behind bars, Lilburne was probably as responsible as any other single person for some of the rights we depend on, rights that help guarantee fundamental fairness when a person is accused of a crime. Certainly, Lilburne persuaded much of England that the inquisitorial system was corrosively unfair and that people accused of a crime should not be forced to testify against themselves. Before the end of the seventeenth century, this right had become fairly broadly established in England, and in the eighteenth century it was unquestioned. Lilburne's fight for fairness was also carried to America by his Puritan colleagues, who throughout the seventeenth century resisted similar inquisitorial methods by the king's colonial agents. The right not to be forced to testify against oneself gradually became established in the colonies and was finally codified by Madison in what became part of the Fifth Amendment: "No person ... shall be compelled in any criminal case to be a witness against himself." That language, and the right it protected, was the final vindication of John Lilburne's struggles.

Today, the Fifth Amendment right not to testify against oneself is seen by many as a dodge, as little more than a refuge for the guilty. In part, that is because the right is today seen in isolation from other procedural rights. Originally the right not to be forced to be a witness against oneself was part of a cluster of rights designed to ensure fairness at a time when criminal procedures were pervasively unfair. As Leonard Levy has pointed out, this right was closely related to the belief that torture and other forms of coercing confessions were fundamentally unfair, and to the idea that a person accused of a crime should be able to confront witnesses against him, have the right to produce witnesses in his favor, and have the right to be assisted by a lawyer. It was an integral part of the whole idea—radical during the mid-seventeenth century, but accepted without question by the time the Bill of Rights was adopted—that anyone accused of a crime remained innocent until the government proved him guilty, and that the government was required to do that without the help of the accused.

In effect, the right to stand mute and force the government to try to prove its case was simply one element of a new system of criminal procedure designed to replace the old inquisitorial system and to ensure fairness. People came to understand that forcing an accused person to confess, or to testify against himself, was not only unfair, but also not very reliable: the evidence it produced was not trustworthy, not a good way of determining guilt or innocence. From the beginning, therefore, the Fifth Amendment right not to be a witness against oneself was deeply respected by the courts. But, as with all the other rights guaranteed by the Bill of Rights, it did not at first apply to the states. Not until 1964 did the Supreme Court rule that the Fourteenth Amendment applied the Fifth Amendment right against self-incrimination to the states. Since then, the ancient right has applied to all criminal proceedings, state and federal. In the same year, reversing an earlier decision, the

Court ruled that an individual could not be compelled to testify against himself in a noncriminal proceeding if what he said might expose him to criminal prosecution.

IMMUNITY, WHOLE AND PARTIAL

An early question that arose was whether the government could force some-one to provide self-incriminating testimony if it first granted the person im-munity from prosecution. The idea was that if the right not to testify against oneself was intended to protect an individual from unfair prosecution, a grant of immunity from prosecution would provide that protection, and thus en-title the government to the witness's testimony, which it might find useful, for instance to prosecute someone else. Could the government do that? The answer to this question was yes: colonial history had supported the idea that a grant of absolute immunity from prosecution fulfilled the purposes embod-ied in the Fifth Amendment, and this was reaffirmed by the Supreme Court in the late nineteenth century and again in 1956.

In 1970, however, the Nixon administration introduced a bill in Congress that sought to dilute this rule and the Fifth Amendment as well. Under the Nixon law, known as the Organized Crime Control Act, a witness could be compelled to testify against himself as long as the government didn't use the testimony to prosecute him. Under the old rule, the government was required to grant absolute immunity from prosecution; under this new law, it could still prosecute the witness even after it compelled him to testify against him-self, provided it didn't use the testimony directly as evidence.

Two years later, a dentist named Charles Joseph Kastigar was charged with contempt for refusing to answer questions about whether he had provided dental services that helped people evade the military draft. He claimed the right, under the Fifth Amendment, not to be forced to be a witness against himself. The federal government, citing the 1970 law, said it would promise not to use his testimony against him in case it prosecuted him, but it would not grant him immunity from prosecution. Kastigar refused.

The Supreme Court ruled that the 1970 law satisfied the Fifth Amendment's requirements. Kastigar had argued that even if his testimony was not used *directly,* it could easily be used *indirectly* by providing the government with leads and information to mount a case against him. If the Fifth Amendment meant anything, he argued, it meant that he was not required to assist the government to prosecute him. Justice Lewis Powell, writing for the Court's majority, said that the state had to prove that any evidence it used to prosecute Kastigar was derived independently from a source other than his own testi-mony. But as Justice Thurgood Marshall wrote in dissent, how could anyone ever be sure that leads provided by Kastigar himself were not linked to evidence subsequently gathered against him?

The *Kastigar* case substantially eroded the Fifth Amendment and allowed the government to force precisely what the amendment was intended to prevent. In 1637, John Lilburne had protested being compelled to testify against himself, thereby facing punishment whether he testified falsely, confessed, or held his silence. The Supreme Court's decision in the *Kastigar* case left targets of government investigations in nearly the same position. Now they would be forced to testify despite the Fifth Amendment, and without a grant of full immunity from prosecution. If they refused, they could be cited for contempt. If they testified falsely, they could be punished for perjury. And if they answered all questions truthfully, their answers might be used, in ways they could never prove or discover, to help unearth other evidence that might convict them.

In 1986, Lieutenant Colonel Oliver North, a former aide in the Reagan administration, was dismissed for alleged conduct that clearly exposed him to the likelihood of criminal prosecution. Because the case involved a major political scandal in which the executive branch had quite possibly violated explicit congressional restrictions on its covert operations abroad, Congress held extensive public hearings and compelled Colonel North to testify. North refused, unless he was granted immunity. But under the 1970 law, the government was only required to promise him that it would not use his testimony directly to prosecute him. North testified, and was later prosecuted and convicted. On appeal, he argued that his Fifth Amendment right had been violated because his congressional testimony had indirectly strengthened the case against him and contributed to his conviction. The appellate court agreed, and reversed North's conviction. In May 1991, the Supreme Court refused to review the appellate court's ruling, thus letting it stand. The *North* case provides a good example of why the "use immunity" defeats the purpose of the Fifth Amendment. John Lilburne would have understood the problem.

POLICE INTERROGATION AND THE FIFTH AMENDMENT

Perhaps the greatest modern controversy involving the Fifth Amendment is whether and to what extent it extends to the police station. Certainly, the spirit and intent of the Fifth Amendment means that no one should be required, by his own words, to supply evidence that would help the government prosecute him. There is very little doubt that an individual has the right not to answer during a police interrogation. At the same time, the police traditionally were under no obligation to inform someone in their custody of his right to remain silent or, indeed, of his right to a lawyer. Although some defendants would be sufficiently aware of their rights to exercise them, many — perhaps most—would not, especially those who were poor, uneducated, and likely to be intimidated, or at least feel intimidated, in the back room of a police station. What would be the use of guaranteeing the right against self-incrimination at trial, if that right were taken away by an inquisitorial system at the police station, before ever reaching trial?

In 1966, the Supreme Court ruled in the *Miranda* case that police-station interrogations were unavoidably coercive and inquisitorial, a modern version of the old English tribunals. In order to ensure that any evidence or confessions provided were truly voluntary, and because the majority believed that it was unfair to penalize individuals less aware of their constitutional rights than others might be, the Court required the police to inform people at the earliest stage of arrest of their right to remain silent, of the fact that anything they said could be used against them, and of their right to a lawyer.

The *Miranda* decision provoked bitter dissent from four of the nine Supreme Court justices and led to a storm of public controversy that lasted for a quarter-century. The facts of the case further inflamed at least the immediate reaction, because Ernesto Miranda, the defendant in the case, had been convicted of kidnapping and rape, and was certainly no John Lilburne.

Justice Byron White was especially angry, and predicted that criminals would be returned to the streets in droves and that crime prevention would be crippled. Chief Justice Earl Warren, himself a former prosecutor, seemed surprised by the ferocity of the dissent. He pointed out that the *Miranda* decision would only require the states to use procedures that the FBI already used during its custodial interrogations. He doubted that there would be much adverse effect on crime or the conviction rate, and thought instead that the deeply intimidating, inquisitorial atmosphere of the police-station interrogation was fundamentally unfair and was likely to be ameliorated by the new requirements without much, if any, negative impact on law enforcement.

History has proven Warren substantially correct, and White's fears at best exaggerated. Perhaps immediately after the *Miranda* decision, when many police were unfamiliar with the new rules, mistakes were made that led to some reversals of convictions. Today, although many individual police officers may still resent the *Miranda* rules, that resentment is mostly symbolic, and many if not most police chiefs and administrators think the rules have professionalized police procedures and enhanced fairness. During the mid-eighties, United States Attorney-General Edwin Meese made a campaign to reverse the *Miranda* rules the centerpiece of his anticrime efforts. Nonetheless, a 1988 American Bar Association survey of law-enforcement officials nationwide showed that most did not find the *Miranda* rules a significant impediment to law enforcement.

Today the Fifth Amendment provides broad protection for all persons accused of crimes, and has expanded from its origins as a procedural right invoked primarily to protect people accused of political or religious crimes such as heresy, nonconformity, seditious libel, and the like. It has become, as it was meant to be, an integral component of a larger system designed to ensure fairness for the accused as well as justice for the community, to minimize the possibility of convicting the innocent, and to prevent abuses of the awesome power to prosecute. Although it is often claimed that such fairness significantly reduces public safety, shackles effective law enforcement, or increases the crime rate, there is little evidence to support such claims. And if many of us sometimes grow impatient with the cluster of rights that ensure fairness to those accused of crimes, perhaps it is because most of us have not yet been accused ourselves. Being accused, or seeing someone we care for accused, has a way of making us appreciate procedural rights.

FREEDOM FROM GENERAL SEARCHES

The Fifth Amendment, of course, was only one of many procedural rights designed to ensure fairness and prevent the sort of government abuses of power that had once been common. Another such major procedural right guaranteed by the Bill of Rights is the right not to be searched or arrested without good and sufficient reason. This right also exists today because the American people insisted on it in 1787. Before the Revolution, British soldiers and customs agents entered homes and offices at will and searched any person or place they wanted, often without any more reason than political animosity. The colonists came to believe that liberty could not be sustained unless the government was prevented from enjoying the unlimited authority to search.

The early Americans certainly recognized the need for the government to protect their safety and security, and to prosecute those whose behavior threatened public order. The colonists were neither soft nor naïve, and they understood the need for police to search for evidence of criminal behavior. But what they hated, and later resolved to prohibit, was the practice of government officers searching at their own unbridled discretion. Their passion for privacy was perhaps best expressed by William Pitt in Parliament in 1763, when he opposed a bill authorizing general searches:

The poorest man may, in his cottage, bid defiance to all the forces of the Crown. It may be frail; its roof may shake; the wind may blow through it; the storm may enter; the rain may enter; but the King of England may not enter.

For all its eloquence, Pitt's speech did not persuade his colleagues. The bill passed, and the authority to search at will prevailed. Such searches were common in colonial America, and feelings on this issue ran high. On the eve of the Declaration of Independence, Samuel Adams said that he regarded the unrest over general searches as "the Commencement of the Controversy between Great Britain and America." After the Revolution, there was a strong public demand to prohibit such searches forever, and this demand later found expression in the Fourth Amendment.

The Fourth Amendment was designed to permit reasonable searches and prohibit unreasonable ones. Everyone recognized that one could not leave the power to decide what was "reasonable" in the hands of the police; indeed, that was the problem: in colonial America a reasonable search was whatever the searching officer thought it was. So, from the beginning, the framers decided that the Constitution had to define what was reasonable, in order to remove that discretion from the police.

The first requirement was that before a search could be made, the police officer had to have some evidence that a crime had occurred and good reason to believe that the specific person or place he wanted to search contained evidence of that crime. Moreover, whether the officer's reason to search was sufficient could not be decided by him or his superior officer. Rather, it had to be decided by an *impartial magistrate*, who, if he was satisfied by the evidence, would authorize the search. This authorization was called a *search warrant*, and the degree of evidence required before a search warrant could be issued became known as *probable cause*. Taken together, these limitations on the power to search protect the right to privacy:

The right of the people to be secure in their persons, houses, papers, and effects, against unreasonable searches and seizures, shall not be violated, and no warrants shall issue, but upon probable cause, supported by oath or affirmation, and particularly describing the place to be searched, and the persons or things to be seized.

The Fourth Amendment revolutionized the law of search and seizure; it represented a complete repudiation of traditional English law and created a presumptive right of privacy against government intrusion. But several problems remained.

For one thing, the Fourth Amendment, like the entire Bill of Rights, applied only to the federal government. It did not restrict state or local police, who posed the major day-to-day threat to citizens' privacy. Not until the 1960s—very nearly two hundred years later—did the Supreme Court fully apply the Fourth Amendment to state and local governments.

Second, definitional problems remained. What exactly did "unreasonable" mean? What precisely constituted "probable cause"? Under what circumstances, if any, could a search or seizure be carried out without a warrant? And did these terms apply differently to the power to arrest or momentarily seize than they did to the power to search? After two hundred years, and thousands of court decisions, these questions still have not been definitively answered.

Third, if a government officer violates the Fourth Amendment, what is the remedy?

CAN ILLEGALLY SEIZED EVIDENCE BE USED?

This last question is crucial, because if a citizen has no remedy when a constitutional right is violated, then that right does not really exist. In 1914, the Supreme Court ruled that evidence seized illegally by the police, in violation of the Fourth Amendment, could not be used against a defendant in a federal criminal trial. This came to be called the *exclusionary rule*, because it excluded evidence illegally seized. Before that decision, the Fourth Amendment had little real force—the police could violate it at will, and suffer no penalty: the evidence could still be used and the individual officer would not, as a practical matter, be punished.

But the 1914 decision, though sweeping in its potential, had no effect on state or local police. Only in 1961 did the Supreme Court apply the exclusionary rule to them as well. Although by that time half the states had adopted the exclusionary rule on their own, the decision provoked a storm of controversy that continues to this day. The Court decided to impose the rule in part because a majority of justices believed it would remove the incentive of the police to ignore the Fourth Amendment. If illegally seized evidence was useless, the Court reasoned, the police would be sure to obtain warrants or otherwise make certain that Fourth Amendment restrictions governed their searches. Critics of the decision say that it doesn't achieve its purpose; it merely causes police officers to lie when they apply for a warrant or describe to a judge the circumstances of a search. Even worse, say the critics, competent evidence is excluded and guilty defendants go free.

But after years of such criticism, it is now fairly clear that very few suspects go free as the result of the exclusionary rule. A number of studies have shown that only about one-half of one percent of all cases are dismissed because of it, and three-quarters of those are in petty drug-possession cases. The exclusionary rule plays virtually no role in serious crimes of violence. Were the rule abolished tomorrow, conviction rates would not change noticeably, and crime rates would change even less. Out of thirty-six million crimes of violence committed each year in the United States, only about three million result in arrests. Most violent crimes never even enter the criminal-justice system, and of those that do, a truly negligible number involve the exclusionary rule.

For all these reasons, the claim that the exclusionary rule hinders law enforcement or significantly compromises public safety is, at best, grossly exaggerated. A 1984 study by the National Center for State Courts, for example, concluded that a constitutional search-warrant procedure did not impede law-enforcement efforts. And in 1988, a study by an American Bar Association task force revealed that a substantial majority of top law-enforcement officials nationwide agreed that constitutional rights, including the exclusionary rule, were not a significant impediment to effective law enforcement. Many of these same officials also believed that the exclusionary rule and other constitutional rights led to better-trained police and a more professional police department. They pointed out that when the police observed the Fourth Amendment, the exclusionary rule never came into play. Some thought these rights actually *enhanced* law enforcement, by discouraging illegal shortcuts and reinforcing the importance of proper investigative techniques.

None of these conclusions is perfectly demonstrable, nor have they entirely quieted the debate. However, it now seems clear that the furor over the exclusionary rule has been mostly symbolic. The number of criminals going free because of it is vanishingly small. Far more alarming, say most top law-enforcement officials, is the rate of violent crime in the first place, crime that law enforcement has only a limited capacity to reduce. The effect of the exclusionary rule on public safety is almost certainly insignificant.

The primary effect of the exclusionary rule, and one of its major purposes, is the protection of *innocent* people against illegal searches caused by malice, sloppiness, or an excess of zeal. Those who oppose the exclusionary rule suggest that when such illegal searches occur, lawsuits against the police to recover civil damages would be a better alternative. But the likelihood of such lawsuits being brought, much less being brought successfully, is exceedingly low. Most people who are illegally searched haven't got the resources to bring lawsuits, or even to hire lawyers. That is why in 1961 the Supreme Court rejected the idea of such suits as an effective remedy, and applied the exclusionary rule instead, in an effort to deter the illegal search from taking place in the first place. Even if the exclusionary rule is an imperfect remedy, no other more effective remedy exists, and it would be intolerable to have none at all.

Beyond all these practical reasons, however, a predominant justification for the exclusionary rule has to do with the integrity of the criminal-justice system. "Nothing can destroy a government more quickly than its failure to observe its own laws," said Justice Tom Clark in the 1961 case. The police should not be allowed to violate the law in order to enforce the law, and the government should not benefit from such violations. Nor should the courts, by accepting illegally seized evidence, become accomplices to illegal activities. In the end, that is one of the most persuasive arguments for the exclusionary rule.

WHEN IS A SEARCH REASONABLE?

The exclusionary rule is designed to deter illegal searches. The more fundamental question is: When and under what circumstances can a search be legally made? The Fourth Amendment prohibits "unreasonable" searches. But what makes a search unreasonable? One view is that the answer is to be found in the second half of the Fourth Amendment, which describes what is required to obtain a search warrant: probable cause to believe that particularly described items of evidence are likely to be found if the police are permitted to search a particular place or person. This, after all, is what the early Americans wanted—to replace the general search at will with a more narrowly targeted approach, where the police would have to have a good idea about what specifically they were looking for and prove to a judge why they thought they would probably find it in the particular place they wished to search. According to this view, a reasonable search is one conducted under a properly issued warrant; an unreasonable search is one that is not. With some key exceptions, Supreme Court decisions reflect this view.

One major exception involves a search that takes place incidental to an arrest. The arrest itself, called a *seizure* under the terms of the Fourth Amendment, cannot be legally made without probable cause to believe that a crime has been committed and that the person arrested probably committed it. The definition of *probable cause* itself is imprecise, though it certainly means something more than mere suspicion unsupported by concrete evidence. There must be *some* evidence, or we would be back to the at-will searches that the Fourth Amendment was meant to prohibit. The degree of evidence required to justify an arrest (or a search) is less than that required to find a person guilty at trial. It is impossible to define precisely how much evidence that is; as a practical matter, it ultimately depends on the opinion of the judge reviewing the circumstances of the case.

But although probable cause is required before an arrest can be made, the Supreme Court has ruled that a prior *arrest warrant* issued in advance by a court is not normally necessary, at least not for serious crimes, because it may often be impractical in an emergency. If an arrest has been made without a warrant, though, the arrested person is entitled to have a judge promptly review whether there was enough evidence to make the arrest. This review usually occurs at a special hearing called an *arraignment,* where the arrested person is present. Such procedures give actual meaning to the principle of liberty, because nothing interrupts an individual's liberty more directly than an arrest.

In 1991, only months before the two-hundredth anniversary of the Fourth Amendment, the Supreme Court significantly relaxed the requirement of a prompt judicial review of a warrantless arrest. In a case from California, the Court ruled, 5–4, that the police could keep someone in jail for up to forty-eight hours before having to demonstrate the legality of the arrest to a court. Justice Sandra Day O'Connor, writing for the majority, found the administrative burdens of police departments a sufficient reason to dilute individual rights. Justice Antonin Scalia, writing in dissent, traced the history of arrests without warrant under English law and at the time the Fourth Amendment was adopted, and charged his colleagues with repudiating one of the core purposes of the Fourth Amendment, which was to prevent the presumptively innocent from being kept in jail.

Given that most arrests are carried out without a warrant, the authority of the police to search during an arrest is important—especially because most searches take place during an arrest. Supreme Court decisions touching on this question are somewhat conflicting. The basic rule is that under most circumstances, the police power to conduct a warrantless search incident to an arrest is limited to the person arrested and his immediate surroundings. That allows the police to search for weapons that might place them in immediate danger or for evidence that might be destroyed, but not to conduct a comprehensive search of the entire house without a further warrant. Even this rule has its exceptions, however. For example, if there is strong reason to believe that the person arrested has friends who are involved in the crime and hiding somewhere on the premises, the police may look into rooms and closets where a person might be hiding, in order to minimize the danger to themselves. But they may not conduct a comprehensive search of the premises without a warrant. Thus, once the person arrested is under police control, and there is no reason to believe there are confederates on the scene, the authority to conduct any further search without a warrant is sharply limited.

Other exceptions to the warrant requirement have also been approved by the Supreme Court. For example, if a person is arrested while driving a car, the police may search the car and its contents, even after the person is removed from the car. A moving vehicle may be stopped and searched if there is probable cause to believe that it contains stolen goods; an automobile driver may have his blood tested for evidence of alcohol (legally, a type of search) if there is probable cause to believe he was driving while intoxicated; and a person may be stopped on the street and frisked, even without probable cause, if there is good reason to believe he is armed and dangerous.

All these exceptions are difficult to define in practice and, though they sometimes seem reasonable in principle, leave room for abuse. Police face difficult situations on the street, and sometimes overreact. An unlawful search conducted under one of these exceptions can be very difficult to prove later, when the case comes before a judge, who has to decide whether to exclude evidence seized in such a search. Often there are no witnesses other than the police officer and the suspect, and in such cases, few judges are inclined to disbelieve the police.

In any case, the general legal standard is relatively clear: before an arrest can be made or a search conducted, some degree of evidence is required to support the police officer's belief that probable cause exists. Thus, the erratic path of an automobile weaving all over the road may be evidence enough to stop the car and conduct a Breathalyzer test for alcohol; but it is unreasonable, and it violates the Fourth Amendment, to stop some cars but not others, in order to check the alcohol level of the drivers, without any observable reason to believe that the cars stopped are being driven by people who are intoxicated. On the other hand, in 1990 the Supreme Court upheld the practice in Michigan of setting up roadblocks and stopping *all* cars routinely for brief checks as a way of deterring drunken driving.

The roadblock program had been challenged by citizens who believed that it was unconstitutional to stop people whose behavior provided no evidence of intoxication. And indeed, all but 2 of the 126 people stopped were not intoxicated, and were allowed to drive on. The Michigan Court of Appeals agreed, struck down the roadblocks, and said they violated the Fourth Amendment. If the police wanted to stop any particular car, ruled the Michigan court, there had to be an observable reason to do so.

The Supreme Court reversed the Michigan court and said the roadblocks were permitted by the Fourth Amendment, even though there was no observable reason to stop any of the cars. The intrusion of a brief stop is slight, said the Court, and since every car was being stopped, no one was being singled out in a discriminatory fashion. Under these circumstances, ruled the Court, the roadblock searches were reasonable, which is all the Fourth Amendment requires. Because the Court abandoned any requirement of individualized cause, the police were permitted to search not only the 2 percent who were guilty, but also the 98 percent who were innocent. This was not only unfair to the overwhelming number of people who were stopped; it also was monumentally inefficient, leading one local sheriffs' association to call the program a waste of time and to say the public would be better protected if the police were allowed to focus on suspicious behavior.

In June 1991, the Court again expanded the power of government officials to search without focusing on specific evidence. Federal agents had boarded a bus and asked people if they would allow their belongings to be searched, without telling them that they could refuse, or were free to leave if they wished. People felt intimidated, and some "consented" to be searched. One man had illegal drugs in his suitcase, and was subsequently arrested and convicted. On appeal, the Supreme Court said that the evidence did not have to be excluded because although the search would have been illegal if it had been involuntary, the victim had been free to leave and had not had to consent, even though he had not known that. Once again, the Court ignored how obviously coercive the situation was, and allowed the police to accomplish through deviousness what they would not be permitted to do directly. People not educated enough to know their rights, or strong enough to assert them, were deemed by the Court to have waived them. Another chunk was chipped away from the Fourth Amendment's protective barrier.

SKIRTING THE FOURTH AMENDMENT: ROUTINE AND UNDERCOVER SEARCHES

When there is no question of criminal behavior, the Court has long permitted routine administrative inspections, even though such inspections have all the characteristics of a search. Thus the Court has allowed public officials to enter a person's home to check for violations of fire, health, or housing codes, without any reason to believe that the individual dwelling harbors any violation, provided that there is sufficient reason to inspect the entire building periodically. Since there was no question of criminal liability, the Court relaxed the individualized probable-cause standard. In the Michigan case, which did involve criminal liability, the Court went further, and dropped the requirement of individualized cause entirely. The problem with permitting such blanket roadblocks, of course, is that once a car is stopped, the police may widen their search by claiming they saw something "suspicious"—a little like allowing the police to enter your home without a warrant to collect evidence they can then use to get a warrant. This procedure would seem to turn the meaning of the Fourth Amendment on its head.

Something very much like that happens when undercover agents enter a suspect's home or place of business. The courts have never required the police to obtain a warrant in order to place an undercover agent in a private home or business. It is difficult to see why. If a policeman in uniform comes to your house or place of business and wants to search, you can turn him away unless he has a warrant. But if he takes off his uniform and comes in disguise—if, for example, he takes a job as your gardener or chauffeur or secretary—then he may gain entrance and search at will. In effect, undercover agents allow the police to trick the target and accomplish precisely what the Fourth Amendment prohibits if they were to do it openly.

Ironically, undercover agents are far more intrusive and their searches far more comprehensive because, unlike a uniformed officer making a limited search for a limited time, undercover agents are there surreptitiously and for a longer time. The privacy rights of innocent people—the target's family, for example—can be pervasively violated. Yet no warrant is required.

Police departments have resisted any requirement for undercover-agent warrants on two grounds: first, that they have internal mechanisms to ensure that only "reasonable" infiltrations are authorized; and second, that they need undercover agents in order to get evidence not otherwise obtainable. Both arguments fly in the face of basic Fourth Amendment principles, one of the chief purposes of which is to remove the decision about when a search is justified from the police themselves. The argument that the police have internal mechanisms to ensure that undercover agents are authorized only under proper circumstances violates that purpose and swallows one of the Fourth Amendment's basic safeguards.

As to the argument that undercover agents are necessary to obtain evidence — that, of course, is what the British colonial agents claimed when they conducted their at-will searches. The key question is not whether the police think the intrusion necessary, but whether they have enough evidence against a particular person to justify it. And that decision, under Fourth Amendment principles, cannot be left to them but rather must be made by an independent magistrate.

The courts have never ruled that the Fourth Amendment restricts the power of the police to place undercover agents in people's homes or business, so the practice continues, unrestrained by law. How much of it goes on, and how much of it goes on improperly, is not known; abuses of this discretionary power only occasionally, and usually accidentally, come to light.

ELECTRONIC SEARCHES: WIRETAPPING AND EAVESDROPPING

A closely related issue involves wiretapping and electronic eavesdropping. Somewhat like the use of undercover agents, wiretapping or electronic surveillance of a person's premises sweeps everything up, like a vacuum cleaner. It overhears and records (and may also photograph or videotape) everything and everyone, indiscriminately. A tap on the phone of one member of a family, for example, necessarily captures the conversations of all family members, and of everyone who speaks with them by telephone. Wiretapping and electronic eavesdropping were techniques not known or anticipated in 1791, so at first the Supreme Court had some difficulty coming to grips with them in constitutional terms.

The issue surfaced first during the days of alcohol prohibition. Roy Olmstead was a suspected bootlegger whom the government wished to search. Utilizing the brand-new techniques, it placed taps in the basement of his office building and on wires in the streets near his home. No physical entry into his office or home took place. Olmstead was convicted entirely on the basis of evidence from the wiretaps. In his appeal to the Supreme Court, Olmstead argued that the taps were a search conducted without a warrant and without probable cause, and that the evidence against him should have been excluded because it was illegally gathered. He also argued that his Fifth Amendment right not to be a witness against himself had been violated.

By a 5–4 vote, the Court rejected his arguments and upheld the government's power to wiretap without limit and without any Fourth Amendment restrictions, on the grounds that no actual physical intrusion of the premises had taken place. Olmstead's Fifth Amendment claim was also dismissed on the grounds that he had not been compelled to talk on the telephone, but had done so voluntarily. Thus the Court upheld the government's power to do by trickery and surreptitious means what it was not permitted to do honestly and openly. One wonders what John Lilburne might have thought about self-incrimination through hidden listening devices planted by the government. Nonetheless, the Court's ruling that the Fifth Amendment was not violated by wiretaps stood, and to this day remains the law.

The Court's ruling that exempted wiretapping from Fourth Amendment restrictions was eventually reversed, however. The case against the *Olmstead* decision was most eloquently argued in dissent at the time by Justice Louis D. Brandeis. He said that the Fourth Amendment was designed to protect privacy and warned that the "progress of science in furnishing the Government with means of espionage" would make this problem worse: such electronic methods would render Fourth Amendment rights meaningless unless the Court ruled that they were not immune from Fourth Amendment restrictions.

Brandeis went beyond requiring a warrant. He thought that because wire-taps indiscriminately picked up every conversation within their reach, they constituted the kind of general search prohibited outright by the Fourth Amendment. Referring to colonial history, he said that the old British "general warrants are but puny instruments of tyranny and oppression when compared with wiretapping." Brandeis also rejected the government's argument that the enforcement of alcohol prohibition was a sufficient moral reason to invalidate constitutional rights. In a burst of eloquence, he warned against government claims of benevolent purposes and reaffirmed the principle that the government must not break one law in order to enforce another:

Experience should teach us to be most on our guard to protect liberty when the government's purposes are beneficent. ... The greatest dangers to liberty lurk in insidious encroachment by men of zeal, well-meaning but without understanding. ... Our government is the potent, the omnipresent teacher. For good or for ill, it teaches the whole people by its example.

Brandeis did not prevail, and for forty years the Court's decision in *Olmstead* exempted wiretapping and electronic spying from any constitutional restriction. Then, in 1967, in a similar case involving gambling, the Court overruled the *Olmstead* decision by an 8–1 margin and recognized that the Fourth Amendment applied to wiretapping and electronic surveillance.

Even then, Brandeis was only partially vindicated. The Court did rule that warrants were required before wiretaps could be authorized, and that warrants could be issued only if there was evidence sufficient to satisfy the Fourth Amendment's requirement of probable cause. However, Brandeis's view that wiretapping was necessarily a general search because it inevitably recorded many innocent conversations, and should therefore be entirely prohibited, was rejected. By that time, wiretapping and electronic surveillance had been institutionalized in America for forty years, at both the federal and state level, and had become too habitual to stop. Brandeis's more fundamental objection was not seriously considered, nor has it been since, even though the government's technological capacity to spy on citizens has grown even more powerful and sophisticated.

Interestingly, these cases arose in the context of crimes like bootlegging and gambling. That pattern continues. During the past twenty years, the great bulk of wiretapping and electronic eavesdropping by both state and federal officials (aside from national-security taps, which are governed by a separate court and a separate warrant requirement) has been in cases involving drug-dealing and gambling. Serious crimes of violence, such as homicide, assault, rape, robbery, and burglary, are rarely the target of electronic eavesdropping, which is not normally a useful tool in such cases.

From the beginning, when wiretapping was virtually invented to enforce laws prohibiting the sale of alcohol, to the late 1960s, when gambling was a major target, to the present, when the use and sale of drugs other than alcohol are the main target, those intrusive devices have been used mostly to enforce laws aimed at punishing and proscribing personal conduct that society believes to be immoral. Because such conduct essentially involves private activities among consenting adults who are all likely to want to keep the activities secret, they are harder to investigate and prosecute than crimes like robbery or burglary, in which an unwilling victim will probably aid any investigation.

Many argue that criminal law is always an inappropriate means of deterring personal moral choices, and that trying to do so causes more harm than good. The nineteenth-century English philosopher John Stuart Mill put it this way:

The sole end for which mankind are warranted ... in interfering with the liberty or action of any of their number, is self-protection.... The only purpose for which power can be rightfully exercised over any member of a civilized community, against his will, is to prevent harm to others. His own good, either physical or moral, is not a sufficient warrant. He cannot be compelled to do or forbear because it will be better for him to do so, because it will make him happier, because, in the opinions of others, to do so would be wise, or even right. These are good reasons for remonstrating with him, or reasoning with him, or persuading him, or entreating him, but not for compelling him, or visiting him with any evil in case he do otherwise. To justify that, the conduct from which it is desired to deter him, must be calculated to produce evil to someone else.... Over himself, over his own body and mind, the individual is sovereign.

Mill argued that all laws prohibiting such behavior such as gambling or drinking were inappropriate. Eventually, Americans agreed, at least with respect to drinking, and repealed alcohol prohibition. And many states have now effectively legalized gambling by taking over the numbers game from private entrepreneurs and institutionalizing state lotteries. But the same principle has not been applied to the use of drugs other than alcohol and nicotine, and the invasions of privacy inherent in wiretapping and electronic eavesdropping remain with us as part of the legacy of our attempts to criminalize conduct like gambling and drinking.

The other major use of electronic eavesdropping has been to punish political dissent. For decades, former FBI director J. Edgar Hoover used wiretaps and other electronic devices to spy on political figures and citizens not even suspected of committing a crime, and built vast dossiers on their political activities and personal lives. Special units of local police called "Red squads" did the same. In 1968, most of this was ostensibly outlawed by Congress, which prohibited warrantless wiretaps and required specific evidence of criminal behavior before a wiretapping warrant could be issued. However, an exception to this warrant requirement was permitted in cases involving "national security," and for a number of years, "national security" was defined so broadly that political wiretapping and electronic eavesdropping continued with alarming frequency. In 1978, a new law—the Foreign Intelligence Surveillance Act—was passed, requiring warrants even for national-security cases, but special judges were designated to issue such warrants in secret proceedings, and it has been difficult to tell how well this law has worked. Outside the national-security area, electronic surveillance has been used mainly in campaigns against gambling and drugs.

Mill's argument therefore remains relevant and has strong advocates today among those who think that criminal prohibition of drugs causes more harm than good. Whatever the merits and demerits of that argument, it is unarguable that the very considerable loss of privacy that has resulted over the years from the use of wiretapping and electronic surveillance has been a major cost of our attempt to use the criminal law to prohibit conduct like gambling, drinking, and using other drugs.

RANDOM URINE TESTS: ANOTHER FORM OF GENERAL SEARCH

Nor has electronic surveillance been the only source of our loss of privacy. The widespread use of urine-testing in employment to see whether people may have been using certain illegal substances violates the rights of many innocent people. Urine-testing programs are not usually restricted to those who show evidence of impaired job performance that may be due to the use of drugs.

These tests are normally administered randomly, or, like roadblocks, to everyone without any specific reason—any probable cause—to suspect the individual being tested. As a result, the primary victims are innocent people subjected to humiliating invasions of privacy by their employers.

Many of these random tests have been struck down by the courts, where the government is the employer. But some have been upheld, provoking Supreme Court Justice Antonin Scalia to denounce them as "an immolation of privacy and human dignity in symbolic opposition to drug use."

The war on drugs has led to other enforcement techniques that violate Fourth Amendment principles: helicopter searches with long-range cameras flying over people's backyards; seizures of people at airports on the basis not of tangible evidence but of how they look (often this means, among other things, that they are black—Hall of Fame baseball player Joe Morgan was victimized in 1990 by such a seizure); and raids on garden-supply stores in search of the names of people who had bought equipment that could be used to grow marijuana (or tomatoes) indoors. Many of these practices have been upheld out of the same zeal that led the majority in the *Olmstead* case in 1928 to first uphold wiretapping. Some commentators have begun to speak sardonically of an apparent "drug exception" to the Fourth Amendment.

THE EXPECTATION OF PRIVACY: WHEN ARE PRIVATE RECORDS NOT PRIVATE?

More and more, the Court has relied on a concept called "expectation of privacy" to justify government searches and surveillance. According to that theory, the Fourth Amendment applies most strongly where there is an expectation of privacy (in one's home, for example), but less strongly where there is less of an expectation of privacy. The problem with that theory, as Anthony Amsterdam has pointed out, is that it permits the government to violate our privacy by first diminishing our expectations. "The government could diminish each person's subjective expectation of privacy," said Amsterdam, "merely by announcing half-hourly on television … that we were all forthwith being placed under comprehensive electronic surveillance." And while that imagined scenario has not happened, something very nearly like it has.

In a series of decisions the courts have upheld the power of the government to wiretap phones, infiltrate undercover agents, conduct camera surveillance by helicopter, search people's trash cans, obtain their bank records, stop and search their automobiles, stop and seize people in public on the basis of "drug-courier profiles" rather than on tangible evidence, test the urine of people not suspected of using drugs, and gain access to telephone-company records that register every phone number one dials. In all these cases, the courts have ruled either that the Fourth Amendment didn't restrict such searches and seizures or that it provided a reduced level of protection. The

Court has often justified its decisions by arguing that in these cases the individual had no expectation, only a limited expectation, of privacy, thereby requiring less Fourth Amendment protection. But each such decision further reduces the public's general expectation of privacy, thus becoming a self-fulfilling prophecy. As Justice Thurgood Marshall noted in his dissent in one case, "Unless a person is prepared to forgo use of what for many has become a personal or professional necessity, he cannot help but accept the risk of surveillance."

The Court's unwillingness to provide constitutional protection for personal information that is in someone else's custody is especially disturbing because of the way the modern world is organized. A great deal of personal information is now in the hands of third parties: banks have copies of all our canceled checks; credit-card companies have copies of all our transactions; telephone companies have copies of all our phone calls; insurance companies have copies of our medical histories; video stores have lists of what films we rent; and, of course, the Internal Revenue Service has details of our finances.

The sum total of these records provides a great deal of personal information, the kind of information that in 1791 would have been considered private. Had any such information existed then, it would normally have been kept at home or at a place of business. Today, virtually all such information is kept by someone else. The Supreme Court has ruled that, because it is not in our custody, such personal information is not protected; therefore, the government doesn't need a search warrant or probable cause when it wants to look.

The early Americans would have considered this outrageous. Government officers rummaging around in their personal desk and bureau drawers without a warrant was precisely what they intended the Fourth Amendment to prevent. But under current Supreme Court rulings, while the Fourth Amendment still protects our homes and places of business, the private information we used to store there is now elsewhere. And the Court has declined to protect that information, regardless of where it is kept, against unwarranted government search. So privacy rights in this area have recently depended more on federal statutes and on state laws than on the Bill of Rights.

PROCEDURE AND FREEDOM

The Fourth and Fifth Amendments establish major procedural rights and provide vivid illustrations of the relationship between fair procedures and liberty. Other specific procedural rights guaranteed by the Bill of Rights when a person is accused of a crime include the right not to be tried twice for the same offense (although state and federal governments may separately charge a person with separate violations of state and federal law based on the same conduct); to be tried speedily and in public; to have a trial by jury; to have written notice of the specific charges; to have an opportunity to confront and cross-examine witnesses; to subpoena favorable witnesses; to have the assistance of a lawyer (even if the accused is too poor to afford one); and not to be subject to excessive bail. All told, the Constitution includes twenty-two separate provisions about how a criminal trial must be conducted.

Most of these rights, taken together, were designed to ensure that people accused of crimes would have a fair opportunity to respond, and that the government would bear the burden of proving its case beyond any reasonable doubt to an impartial jury. The idea behind this system was fairness, and the early Americans who insisted upon it believed that the most important feature of a system of criminal procedures was its ability to prevent innocent people from being punished. At the same time, they believed that this system was better than any other at distinguishing between guilt and innocence.

No system is perfect, and over its two hundred years ours has resulted in convicting some innocent people and setting some guilty people free. Nor have Supreme Court decisions always been faithful to the underlying purposes of the procedural principles in the Bill of Rights. By and large, though, the system has worked better than any other yet devised on the planet, both to protect the innocent and to convict the guilty. As Justice Felix Frankfurter wrote in a slightly different context: "No better instrument has been devised for arriving at truth than to give a person in jeopardy of serious loss notice of the case against him and an opportunity to meet it. Nor has a better way been found for generating the feeling, so important to a popular government, that justice has been done."

Imperfections remain; precise definitions still elude us; questions arise every day that those who wrote the Constitution never anticipated; and the system and its basic principles continue to evolve. Public debate about procedural rights often seems technical and remote from the daily routines of our lives. What interests us more is discussion about what the substance of our rights is, not about the process by which those rights may be gained or lost.

But process *is* important. As Justice Frankfurter once said, "The history of American freedom is, in no small measure, the history of procedure." And Justice William O. Douglas, who often disagreed with Frankfurter, agreed on this point. "It is procedure," he said, "that spells much of the difference between rule by law and rule by whim and caprice."

The centuries-old fight to restrain power and to establish rights is, at bottom, a fight to establish the rule of law. The barons at Runnymede knew that, and so did John Lilburne. But the rules must be fair. Process matters, because the substance of our rights can be quickly eroded if the rules of the game are unfair.

RACIAL EQUALITY

POLICE USE   THEIR
FIRE HOSES   SUPPORTERS
TO DISPERSE   IN KELLY
CIVIL-RIGHTS   INGRAM PARK.
DEMONSTRA-   BIRMINGHAM,
TORS AND   ALABAMA, 1963.

WILLIAM LLOYD
GARRISON,
ABOLITIONIST
EDITOR OF THE
LIBERATOR,
PUBLISHED IN
BOSTON FROM
1831 TO 1865.

PICTURE COLLECTION, THE BRANCH LIBRARIES, THE NEW YORK PUBLIC LIBRARY

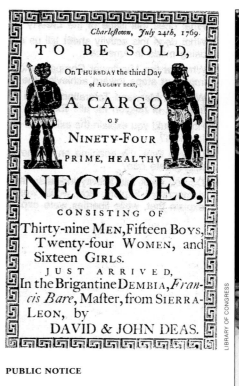

Charlestown, July 24th, 1769.

TO BE SOLD,

On THURSDAY the third Day
of AUGUST next,

A CARGO
OF
NINETY-FOUR
PRIME, HEALTHY
NEGROES,
CONSISTING OF
Thirty-nine MEN, Fifteen BOYS,
Twenty-four WOMEN, and
Sixteen GIRLS.
JUST ARRIVED,
In the Brigantine DEMBIA, Fran-
cis Bare, Mafter, from SIERRA-
LEON, by
DAVID & JOHN DEAS.

PUBLIC NOTICE

LIBRARY OF CONGRESS

FREDERICK
DOUGLASS,
FREEDOM,
WRITER,
ORATOR,
LOBBYIST FOR
ABOLITION
OF SLAVERY
AND FOR CIVIL
RIGHTS.

PICTURE COLLECTION, THE BRANCH LIBRARIES, THE NEW YORK PUBLIC LIBRARY

DRED SCOTT,
PHOTOGRAPHED
IN 1858, THE
YEAR AFTER
THE SUPREME
COURT RULED
THAT HE COULD
NOT BE A
CITIZEN AND
ORDERED HIS
RETURN TO
SLAVERY.

COURTESY OF THE MISSOURI
HISTORICAL SOCIETY, ST. LOUIS

PICTURE COLLECTION, THE BRANCH LIBRARIES, THE NEW YORK PUBLIC LIBRARY

A 1796
ENGRAVING
SHOWS
PUNISHMENT
OF A "MUTI-
NOUS SLAVE."

THE NEW YORK PUBLIC LIBRARY

UPI / BETTMANN NEWSPHOTOS

ABOVE: CHARGED WITH MURDER AND ASSAULT, ABRAM SMITH, 19, AND THOMAS SHIPP, 18, WERE TAKEN BY A MOB FROM COUNTY JAIL AND LYNCHED IN THE PUBLIC SQUARE. MARION, INDIANA, 1930.

RIGHT: PHOTOGRAPH OF A SLAVE AFTER BEING WHIPPED BY HIS MASTER ON A COTTON PLANTATION. LOUISIANA, 1863.

PUNISHMENT COMBINED WITH PREVENTION.

THE BETTMANN ARCHIVE

LEFT: PICKET-
ING THE WHITE
HOUSE FOR
DESEGREGA-
TION OF PUBLIC
ACCOMMODA-
TIONS. 1962.

RIGHT:
REVEREND
MARTIN
LUTHER KING,
JR.: "I HAVE
A DREAM,"
MARCH ON
WASHINGTON,
1963.

HIGH-SCHOOL
STUDENTS
MARCH TO
DEMAND
INTEGRATION
OF DOWNTOWN
STORES.
BIRMINGHAM,
ALABAMA, 1963.

"SITTING IN"
AT A SEGREGATED
RESTAURANT.
BALTIMORE, 1962.

LINDA AND
TERRY LYNN
BROWN, 10
AND 6, OUTSIDE
THEIR ALL-
BLACK SCHOOL
FOLLOWING
THE 1954
SUPREME COURT
DECISION IN
BROWN V.
BOARD OF
EDUCATION OF
TOPEKA,
KANSAS, WHICH
DECLARED
SEGREGATED
PUBLIC
SCHOOLS
UNCONSTITU-
TIONAL. LINDA
BROWN'S
DAUGHTER IS
SUING THE SAME
TOPEKA SCHOOL
DISTRICT FOR
CONTINUED
SEGREGATION 37
YEARS LATER.

FACING PAGE:
COUNTY COURT-
HOUSE. CLINTON,
LOUISIANA, 1964.

JACKIE
ROBINSON, WHO
BROKE THE
COLOR LINE IN
BASEBALL IN
1947, STEALING
HOME FOR
BROOKLYN
DODGERS, 1955
WORLD SERIES.

RALPH MORSE, LIFE MAGAZINE. © TIME WARNER, INC.

"I AM A REGIS-
TERED VOTER"
BUTTON PINNED
ON MAN WHO
HAS PASSED
COMPLEX WRIT-
TEN TEST ON
CONSTITUTION.
SUMTER, SOUTH
CAROLINA, 1962.

DEMONSTRA-
TORS WITH
PLACARDS OF
MURDERED
CIVIL-RIGHTS
WORKERS
DEMAND
SEATING OF
BLACK DEL-

EGATES FROM
MISSISSIPPI AT
DEMOCRATIC
NATIONAL
CONVENTION.
ATLANTIC CITY,
NEW JERSEY,
1964.

ABOVE: STREET
SCENE, "THE
BOX" NEIGHBOR-
HOOD, BEDFORD-
STUYVESANT
AREA. BROOKLYN,
NEW YORK, 1963.

RIGHT: CHILD
PLAYING IN
VACANT LOT.
"THE BOX"
NEIGHBOR-
HOOD, 1963.

RACIAL EQUALITY

5

THE IDEA OF NATURAL RIGHTS THAT BECAME CONTAGIOUS IN COLONIAL AMERICA implied *constitutional equality* in a way few people fully understood at the time. If every human being was born with fundamental rights that no government could legitimately alter or take away, then every human being must be entitled *by law* to have his—or her—rights respected and protected. How then could women be denied the right to vote—unless they were less than human? How could Indians be treated so brutally and denied the rights of citizenship—unless they were less than human? And how could slavery be accepted—unless Africans and their descendants were less than human?

"THE RACE EXCEPTION" TO THE CONSTITUTION

Many early Americans were not blind to these contradictions, particularly with respect to slavery, and more than a few wrote and spoke passionately about it on the eve of the American Revolution and afterward. But the contradictions were left unresolved, and the inhuman denials of liberty based on skin color were tolerated and became more deeply embedded in American culture. The Constitution, including the Bill of Rights, hardly seemed to take notice of this. The word "race" appeared nowhere in the original documents; neither did the word "slavery." The Bill of Rights itself seemed to be written in broad language that excluded no one. But it was well understood that in fact there was a "race exception" to the Constitution, and it endured for most of the two hundred years that followed.

It was not just that African slaves and their descendants were denied the rights of free speech, freedom of religion, trial by jury, and other rights established by the Bill of Rights. Nor was their condition merely one of peonage or bonded economic servitude. That would come later, and be seen by some as progress. No; the bondage in which blacks found themselves in the American South was, in fact, dehumanizing. If all human beings were born with rights that no government could legitimately take away, then American slavery could be legitimized only by regarding the slaves as subhuman. And in fact dominant white culture systematically denied the humanity of blacks. Under the "slave codes" that controlled every aspect of their lives, slaves had no access to the rule of law: they could not go to court, nor make contracts, nor own any property—not even highly personal items. A slave could not strike a white person, even in self-defense. Rape was common, and the rape of an enslaved woman by someone other than her owner was considered trespassing upon a white man's property, rather than a criminal assault upon a human being.

No notion of fairness or due process of law diluted the harshness of these codes, which were mercilessly enforced by slave tribunals whose procedures made the old English Star Chamber seem a model of fairness. And the tribunals were not the only means of enforcement: terrorist night patrols; public ceremonies of humiliation and torture, such as whipping, branding, and even boiling in oil; imprisonment without trial under conditions even more painful than slavery itself; and death by hanging—all were pervasive features of life in the American South. Hundreds of desperate rebellions took place, undoubtedly many more than history has recorded, but few of those who participated survived.

Against all this, the Bill of Rights offered no shelter. Politics and racism became reified in the American culture, and from the beginning overcame law and right.

ABOLITIONISTS AND THE DRED SCOTT CASE

Not everyone was swept along by the majoritarian tolerance of racism and brutality. Even at the time of the Revolution, some Americans spoke out strongly and passionately against slavery. Throughout the first half of the nineteenth century, those who advocated the abolition of slavery, though unsuccessful, kept the beacon of liberty shining through the long night of slavery that darkened the American landscape.

William Lloyd Garrison was perhaps the nation's leading and most uncompromising white abolitionist. While still in his twenties, he founded a Boston newspaper called the *Liberator*, and published it continuously from 1831 until 1865. From its pages, and in fiery speeches at public meetings, Garrison denounced slavery in the most apocalyptic terms, calling for imprisonment in solitary confinement of slave-traders and urging the North to separate from the South under the slogan "No Union with Slaveholders." Once, anticipating Sidney Street's actions on a Harlem streetcorner in 1968, Garrison burned a copy of the United States Constitution. Invoking the ancient Hebrew prophet Isaiah, Garrison declared the Constitution to be "a covenant with death and an agreement with Hell." As the law of the land went up in smoke, he cried, "So perish all compromises with tyranny!"

His passion did not go unnoticed: he was sued for libel, convicted, fined, and imprisoned; his meetings were violently disrupted; his newspaper was banned; his place of business was attacked. And he was abandoned by more moderate abolitionists, who found his rhetoric and his tactics too extreme. But Garrison would neither relent nor apologize: "Slavery will not be overthrown," he said, "without excitement, a most tremendous excitement." At the time Garrison seemed to be overstating the need for such "excitement," yet history would show that, if anything, he had understated the case, a lesson other agitators for liberty before and since have taught us as well.

In 1857, at the peak of Garrison's activities, the Supreme Court decided the *Dred Scott* case, striking down as unconstitutional a federal law that prohibited slavery in American territories outside the South. The case inflamed abolitionists everywhere, and confirmed Garrison's view of the Constitution. For if the Supreme Court was right, then the Constitution prohibited Congress from abolishing slavery not only where it existed, but where it did not yet exist. Even worse than the decision itself, however, was the language of Chief Justice Roger B. Taney, who wrote it: Blacks, he said, were "subordinate and inferior beings, who had been subjugated by the dominant race, and, whether emancipated or not, yet remained subject to their authority."

Taney's opinion was breathtaking in its scope, because it included not only slaves, but all blacks, even those who had been emancipated and were living in the North. The Constitution not only provided no relief, according to Taney, it permanently excluded blacks from national citizenship and established them legally as less than human, as "subordinate and inferior beings." Blacks, Taney went on, "had no rights which the white man was bound to respect." If that was what the Constitution meant, could Garrison's characterization of it be considered extreme?

Frederick Douglass, the most famous black abolitionist of the time, saw the *Dred Scott* decision in more political terms:

The Supreme Court is not the only power in this world. We, the abolitionists and colored people, should meet this decision, unlooked for and monstrous as it appears, in a cheerful spirit. This very attempt to blot out forever the hopes of an enslaved people may be one necessary link in the chain of events preparatory to the complete overthrow of the whole slave system.

Four years later, the Civil War erupted.

"NEITHER SLAVERY NOR INVOLUNTARY SERVITUDE"

Six months after the Civil War ended, on December 6, 1865, the Thirteenth Amendment became part of the Constitution. Chief Justice Roger Taney was no longer alive to see it, having died in office a year earlier, but William Lloyd Garrison and Frederick Douglass were. The Thirteenth Amendment finally resolved the contradictions that the original Constitution had ignored—that there could be no liberty in a land that harbored slavery. About this, the Thirteenth Amendment was crystal clear:

Neither slavery nor involuntary servitude, except as a punishment for crime whereof the party shall have been duly convicted, shall exist within the United States, or any place subject to their jurisdiction.

And because Congress understood that such a prohibition would not be self-enforcing, a second section was added:

Congress shall have the power to enforce this article by appropriate legislation.

This was the first time any amendment designed to protect liberty had explicitly granted unlimited authority to Congress to enforce the protection through additional legislation.

Congress had anticipated resistance from the Southern states, and did not have to wait very long. Almost immediately, the former slave states, seeking to maintain their subjugation of blacks, passed a series of statutes that came to be known as the "black codes."

These codes literally resurrected many of the elements of the old slave codes. Blacks were not allowed to testify in court, for example, except in cases involving other blacks. Blacks were also prohibited by law from holding certain jobs or occupations. In one state they were prohibited from becoming shopkeepers or mechanics; in another, they couldn't start any business without first getting a license, which could be arbitrarily denied, and often was. Thus excluded from the right to pursue economic opportunities, many blacks came to depend for their living on jobs performed under conditions little different from slavery. Laws making it a crime to be unemployed were passed, and blacks could be arrested and jailed for quitting a job: the acceptance of peonage became a condition of "liberty."

The right to meet or otherwise assemble peacefully was denied; residence in certain areas was prohibited; South Carolina barred blacks from entering and living in the state entirely unless they posted a $1,000 bond. All this was enforced by internal passport systems. Blacks were legally excluded from juries, from public office, and from voting. Racial intermarriage was a crime for which offenders could be sentenced to life imprisonment. The death penalty was provided for black men accused of raping white women; no similar punishment was imposed on whites who raped blacks. Social deference to whites was enforced by law: blacks were prohibited from insulting whites, or even from looking at them in the wrong way. Some codes also required separation of the races in public transportation and in schools. Most codes authorized whipping and the public pillory as punishments for violations of any of the codes, not to mention the more informal and often more brutal private punishments that terrorized the lives of black people.

All this was put in place within a year of the adoption of the Thirteenth Amendment.

But Congress was dominated by antislavery Republicans, and they moved swiftly to counter the Southern resistance and to dismantle the vestiges of slavery. In March 1866, under its new Thirteenth Amendment authority, Congress passed its first Civil Rights Act by an overwhelming majority. The 1866 act overturned the *Dred Scott* decision by establishing national citizenship for blacks. (American Indians remained excluded from citizenship, however, which showed the infinite capacity of people to avoid general principles implied by their particular cause.) The act guaranteed equal legal rights to all citizens; prohibited criminal laws that treated people differently on the basis of race or former slave status; authorized legal cases to be removed from state courts to federal courts where state courts were prejudicial; and empowered federal officials, including the military, to enforce the law. In effect, the 1866 act invalidated the black codes.

President Andrew Johnson, later to be the first president to be impeached, vetoed the bill, but Congress overrode the veto and it became law. In the same year, Congress passed the Fourteenth Amendment to the Constitution, thus going beyond the mere prohibition of slavery. The Fourteenth Amendment prohibited the states from abridging any of the privileges or immunities of United States citizens, from denying any citizen life, liberty, or property without due process of law, and from excluding any person from the equal protection of the laws. The Fourteenth Amendment, like the Thirteenth, contained a section authorizing Congress to enforce the rights guaranteed by additional legislation. Indeed, many historians believe the Fourteenth Amendment was passed quickly after the Civil Rights Act of 1866 to ensure the act's constitutionality, because up to that time no similar congressional interference with the authority of states to make laws had ever been attempted.

On July 9, 1868, the Fourteenth Amendment was ratified by the required number of states, and became part of the Constitution. This was followed by still another constitutional amendment, the Fifteenth, which guaranteed the right to vote, and prohibited the states from denying or abridging that right "on account of race, color, or previous condition of servitude." These three amendments became known as the Civil War Amendments, and have become, by practice, part of the Bill of Rights, although, of course, they were not among the original ten.

Armed with these new constitutional powers, Congress passed a series of additional laws: the Civil Rights Act of 1870, which reenacted parts of the 1866 act; the Civil Rights Act of 1875, which outlawed racial discrimination in public transportation, hotels, inns, theaters, and parks; and a number of other acts, such as the Peonage Act, which made it a federal crime to hold any person in a condition of peonage or to arrest anyone for that purpose. These were the first antidiscrimination laws ever passed by Congress, and the last for nearly a hundred years. They represented a vigorous attempt by the antislavery forces to dismantle the structure of Southern racism in the wake of the Civil War. This attempt was not limited to passing laws. Congress also established the Freedmen's Bureau, providing emergency relief for those impoverished by war, both black and white; set up special courts to arbitrate disputes between blacks and whites; and facilitated a massive voter-registration campaign: by 1867 there were 735,000 blacks and 635,000 whites enrolled to vote in the ten states of the Old South. And all this was enforced by a strong federal military presence throughout the South.

RECONSTRUCTION AND REVERSION

At first, it looked as if a political transformation had taken place that might over time radically reconstruct the entire region even without federal enforcement. State constitutional conventions were convened throughout the South. Dominated by antislavery Republicans and newly freed slaves now empowered to vote, the conventions wrote new state constitutions that not only guaranteed equal rights, but also obligated the states to care for the poor, the sick, and the mentally ill; barred debtors' prisons; eliminated property qualifications for voting and holding office; called for universal public education; and called for universal voting rights (although not for women).

But it was not to be. White-supremacist groups, willing to use terror and murder to achieve their ends, sprang up everywhere. Their immediate targets were the newly reconstructed state governments. Voters, especially black voters, were intimidated and even murdered. Blacks were run out of public office. Life itself became the price of political participation. All this occurred at the local level, in small towns and remote rural areas, far from where federal forces were stationed. So enforcing the law usually fell to local sheriffs, who more often than not were in league with the gangs of terrorists.

In 1874, during state and local elections, white violence against blacks intensified. Blacks who showed up at polling places to vote were surrounded by white mobs and beaten. A black senator from Mississippi was murdered by nightriders. By 1876, only three states—Louisiana, South Carolina, and Florida—still retained governments controlled by Republicans; the rest were now controlled by Democrats committed to the subjugation of blacks.

Meanwhile, the rest of the country was fast losing its egalitarian resolve. President Johnson had never supported the attempt to reconstruct the South, having even vetoed the very first Civil Rights Act in 1866. President Ulysses S. Grant, who followed him, wasn't much better. White resistance in the South encouraged this phenomenon, as did white racism in the North.

The congressional elections of 1874 proved to be a turning point. In the House of Representatives, the Republicans had enjoyed a 110-vote majority. After the 1874 elections, the Democrats held a 60-vote majority, an astonishing reversal. Many Republicans read the handwriting on the wall, and began to back away. Speaking at the 1876 Republican National Convention, a disheartened and angry Frederick Douglass asked:

What does it all amount to if the black man, after having been made free by the letter of your law, is to be subject to the slaveholder's shotgun? The real question is whether you mean to make good to us the promises of your Constitution.

Douglass's cry was to be echoed nearly a hundred years later when Martin Luther King, Jr., said, in a speech the night before he was murdered, "All we say to America is, 'Be true to what you said on paper!'" In 1876, the Republican Party was not prepared to do that. It nominated as its candidate for president Rutherford B. Hayes, who had campaigned for "home rule" for the South, a euphemism that meant the withdrawal of federal troops and the abandonment of black citizens to their tormentors.

As the Republican leadership's commitment to racial justice collapsed, the Democratic Party nationally continued to ascend, increasingly supported by Southern Democrats determined to restore white supremacy. In the presidential election of 1876, Democrat Samuel J. Tilden won a majority of the popular vote. But the electoral-college vote narrowly eluded him: 185 votes were necessary to win, and Tilden had 184. Hayes had 166. The remaining 19—from the only three Southern states still under Republican control—were contested. A bipartisan commission was appointed by the two political parties to count the votes and, voting along party lines, gave all the contested votes to Hayes, electing him 185–184.

The outcome was eventually thrown into the House of Representatives, which under the Constitution was empowered to decide. Tilden seemed to have the advantage because the Democrats were now in the majority; still, there might have been enough Northern Democrats who would have voted for Hayes to assure his election. Seeking to stop that, Southern Democrats threatened to filibuster and in the end extracted a deal: they would vote for Hayes if the Republicans would renounce the use of federal force to defend the rights of Southern blacks. The deal stuck; Hayes became president; federal troops in the few states where they still sustained Republican rule were promptly removed; and federal force was never used again to support the constitutional rights of blacks in the South until 1957, when President Dwight D. Eisenhower sent troops to Little Rock, Arkansas, to protect black children going to newly desegregated schools. Blacks were abandoned, their liberties once more prey to the power the Constitution was supposed to control.

THE SUPREME COURT EVISCERATES THE FOURTEENTH AMENDMENT

The Supreme Court was not much help during this sorry period. Designed to restrain political power, the Court instead reflected it. In 1873, as we have seen, in the first case in which it ever interpreted the Fourteenth Amendment, the Court had already ruled that the amendment did not mean what it said. Although the amendment appeared to prohibit the states from passing or enforcing any law that abridged the rights of United States citizens, the Court interpreted this to mean only *national* rights, such as the right to travel, or to go to Washington to petition the *national* government. The Court did hold that the Fourteenth Amendment required states to make and enforce their laws without racial discrimination, but beyond that, it left the states with the discretion to decide what rights its residents should have and the extent to which these rights would be enforced. This decision occurred just as the national political commitment to the rights of Southern blacks was waning; it robbed the Fourteenth Amendment of most of its force, setting the stage for the resurrection of white-racist hegemony in the South. Indeed, it is no exaggeration to say that it paved the way for the Ku Klux Klan's long reign of terror. Once the definition and enforcement of civil rights were left to state and local governments, blacks were again at the mercy of their oppressors.

The crushing impact of the Supreme Court's evisceration of the Fourteenth Amendment was not long in coming. In the very same year, several hundred armed white nightriders stormed a courthouse in Louisiana where hundreds of blacks were peaceably assembled at a meeting. They burned the courthouse to the ground and murdered a hundred people. The federal government moved in swiftly and prosecuted several of the attackers under an 1870 federal law that made it a crime for two or more people to conspire to injure or intimidate any citizen exercising his constitutional rights. Certainly, assembling peaceably was one such right, explicitly guaranteed by the First Amendment. Three people were convicted, and they appealed.

In 1876, the Supreme Court unanimously reversed their convictions. Basing its ruling on the prior 1873 decision, the Court said that the right to assemble in Louisiana was exclusively subject to the jurisdiction of that state, not the federal government. The Fourteenth Amendment conferred no authority on the federal government to define, protect, or enforce such a right. Thus violence against black citizens could not be remedied by Congress, and the convictions were overturned. No similar federal prosecution would be sustained for another eighty years. Mob violence against blacks exercising their constitutional rights was left entirely to state and local governments to control. Most of the time, the latter approved of such violence, either tacitly or with quiet enthusiasm.

The Supreme Court might have interpreted the Fourteenth Amendment as conferring upon the states an obligation to protect black citizens' rights, as an alternative to locating that authority with the federal government. But the Court did not do that, either. Private violence thus joined with police inaction in a suffocating system of oppression that the Fourteenth Amendment was entirely powerless to modify. The constitutional provisions that had been designed to establish the long-denied rights of black citizens instead became, through these Supreme Court decisions, yet another instrument of their oppression.

It soon became clear that only the narrowest and most obvious denial of fundamental rights by state governments would be struck down by the Supreme Court. For example, in 1880, the Court nullified a state law that explicitly prohibited blacks from serving on juries. Yet on the same day, it ruled against two black defendants accused of murdering a white man. They had sued to get their case removed from state court to federal court, contending that their right to a fair trial by jury would be denied in state court, because both the grand jury that had accused them and the trial jury empaneled to try them were drawn from jury lists composed entirely of whites. The Supreme Court denied their claim because in this case there was no state law requiring whites-only juries and because they had not been able to prove any intent to discriminate, despite the fact that no blacks had *ever* served on any jury in the county where they were to be tried. In the absence of any explicit and deliberate exclusion of blacks, all-white juries, said the Court, were not racially discriminatory.

This reasoning prevailed for nearly a hundred more years, and substantially destroyed any chance for fairness in criminal cases where blacks were the defendants. After this decision, blacks disappeared from jury rolls all over the South. If a black citizen accused of a crime was lucky enough to avoid mob violence and even make it to a jury trial, he would be judged only by whites.

IF EVERYTHING IS PRIVATE, NOTHING IS ILLEGAL

Three years later, in 1883, the Supreme Court issued yet another decision that helped unravel constitutional protections for black citizens. The decision encompassed five cases; each involved a black citizen who had been denied accommodations that white citizens enjoyed—either in a hotel, at a theater, or on a railroad. Discrimination of this kind was then explicitly prohibited by the federal Civil Rights Act of 1875, and the act had been enforced against the owners of these facilities. They appealed, and the Court took their cases.

In these five cases, federal civil-rights law collided with the culture of racism that was fast reemerging in the South. In a decision that demolished efforts to establish basic equality of rights for black citizens and delayed equal justice for the better part of another century, the Court again ruled that Congress had no authority, under either the Thirteenth or Fourteenth Amendments, to pass the Civil Rights Act of 1875 in the first place, or to outlaw racial discrimination in privately owned public facilities. The act was struck down, and the enforcement clause of the Fourteenth Amendment was eviscerated. The strength of the Thirteenth Amendment was also severely restricted, and for all practical purposes nullified, not to be revived for another eighty-five years.

To do all this, the Court first had to create the doctrine of "state action." The Court had already ruled that only explicit and deliberate acts by state governments — such as laws excluding blacks from juries — could be prohibited by the Fourteenth Amendment. And the Court had also had held, in the Louisiana mob-violence case, that mayhem committed by white citizens against black citizens to deny them their constitutional rights could not be prohibited by the Fourteenth Amendment either. In the public-accommodations cases, the Court expanded this disingenuous approach into a full-blown legal doctrine. The Fourteenth Amendment didn't authorize Congress to outlaw racial discrimination on railroads and in hotels and theaters, said the Court, because the Fourteenth Amendment prohibited explicit racial discrimination only by state *governments*, not by privately owned facilities, even if such facilities were generally designed to serve the public and were licensed or otherwise supported by the state.

This was a dishonest ruling for a number of reasons.

First of all, one of the cases involved a railroad. At that time, railroads were practically creatures of government, which had given them the power to condemn and take over private property, a power justified only by its public purpose. Indeed, the only constitutional justification for allowing the taking of private property, even with just compensation, was for public use. Railroads were granted this power because the government thought their function — to transport people and goods — was an important public purpose. In addition, the railroads were heavily subsidized by public funds. They were unquestionably performing a public function and clearly doing so as an agent or partner of the government. But when it came to the question of whether these same railroads, which had exercised government powers and been nourished by government money, could discriminate against black citizens, the Supreme Court suddenly converted them into the equivalent of private carriages, pretended the government wasn't involved, and ruled that they were exempt from Fourteenth Amendment restrictions.

Moreover, the Fourteenth Amendment prohibited the states from denying to any of its citizens the "equal protection of the laws," and authorized Congress to pass laws enforcing that prohibition. Might not Congress then decide that access to public facilities such as railroads, hotels, and theaters were rights of citizenship that could not be denied on the basis of race? One justice—John Marshall Harlan—thought so, but in 1883, an 8–1 majority of the Supreme Court thought not, and ruled that the Fourteenth Amendment provided no authority for Congress to outlaw racial discrimination in privately owned public facilities.

What about the Thirteenth Amendment, which prohibited slavery by private individuals? Congress was authorized to pass legislation to enforce that prohibition as well. Might not privately owned public facilities that discriminated against blacks be deemed by Congress to be a residue of slavery, and therefore outlawed as an enforcement of the Thirteenth Amendment? Again, Justice Harlan thought so. In their heyday, slaveowners had physically branded slaves; if now blacks were everywhere relegated to inferior status in public facilities—banned from theaters and hotels and restaurants open to everyone else, banished from railroads or limited to a segregated section—was this not a mark of their former status as slaves, a mark perhaps more damaging and enduring than any physical mark they bore, a mark, moreover, that by law and custom could be passed on to their children and grandchildren, thereby forever stamping blacks as inferior? Harlan made that argument as well, but again was outvoted, 8–1.

Harlan also pointed out the cynical inconsistency of the Court's decision. He reminded his brethren that before the Civil War, when Congress had passed a law called the Fugitive Slave Act, designed to help Southern slaveowners to recapture slaves who had fled to free states, the Supreme Court had upheld the constitutionality of the act, even against the laws and courts of free states in the North. In that case, in order to vindicate slaveowners' property rights against the liberty of escaped blacks, the Court had allowed federal law to override state law and to sustain direct and punitive federal power over individuals who tried to help the runaway slaves. But now, Harlan said, the Court had grown more timid, and found reasons to prohibit federal law from reaching public accommodations. The Fugitive Slave Act, which authorized punishment of an innkeeper for hiding an escaped slave, had been upheld. But the Civil Rights Act of 1875, which authorized punishment of an innkeeper for barring black citizens, was struck down. What made both decisions consistent was their result: in both cases, the power of whites was upheld against the rights of blacks. Once again, racism had overcome law, and the Supreme Court offered no relief.

Combined with the political abandonment of blacks in 1877, this decision signaled the end of the post–Civil War attempt to extend constitutional rights to black citizens. No new civil-rights law would be passed for another eighty years.

WHITE SUPREMACY ASCENDANT

Thus immunized from constitutional limits on their power, Southern states moved quickly to reestablish white dominion. New laws, called Jim Crow laws (after the title of a minstrel song that portrayed blacks as childlike and inferior), were passed in every Southern state to enforce racial separation. A rigid caste system of segregation and discrimination was comprehensively imposed, by custom if not by law, reaching into every corner of Southern life. Blacks were not allowed at all in many places—in hotels, restaurants, barbershops, theaters, and even public restrooms—and everywhere they were allowed, they were separated from whites. In Birmingham, Alabama, it was even a crime for blacks and whites to play checkers or dominoes together. And by 1885, most Southern states had also established segregated school systems.

In 1892, the Democratic Party gained control of the presidency and both houses of Congress for the first time since the end of the Civil War. And in 1894, the Democrats repealed most of the civil-rights laws not already undermined by the Supreme Court. In particular, the Civil Rights Repeal Act of 1894 abolished laws that had provided for federal control of voting rights through the appointment of federal officials. The removal of federal supervision paved the way for new Southern efforts to deny blacks the right to vote; seventy years later, federal election officials would be brought back once again to supervise Southern elections and guarantee the right to vote.

The Supreme Court had another opportunity to ease the oppressiveness of this system in 1896. By then, most Southern states had passed laws that required separating blacks and whites in public transportation. Gone was the pretense that when railroads discriminated against blacks, it was only the action of private individuals. Now state laws commanded such separation. Like the law struck down in 1880, which banished blacks from juries, these laws explicitly required racial segregation. Was it possible that the Court would strike them down because they were examples of overt state action? The states thought not. They thought they could get around a charge of racial discrimination by creating a new fiction: separation did not mean inequality; indeed, these new laws required railroads to provide facilities that were both separate and equal. At least in railroad cars, it was possible to maintain roughly equal accommodations. But the entire purpose of state-enforced racial separation was to strengthen white supremacy and to brand blacks as inferior, barring them from white society.

In Louisiana, black citizens decided to challenge the law. Homer A. Plessy, who had one black great-great-grandparent, got on the railroad in New Orleans headed for another city in Louisiana and sat in a car reserved for whites. He was arrested and convicted; he then appealed, invoking his rights under both the Thirteenth and Fourteenth Amendments. When the case reached the Supreme Court, Justice Harlan, still on the bench thirteen years after the 1875 Civil Rights Act was struck down, again argued eloquently for the Constitution. "Our Constitution," he said, wishing it were so, "is color-blind, and neither knows nor tolerates classes among citizens." But once again, he was alone: the Court upheld the Louisiana law, 8–1. The majority's decision was revealing. While the Court conceded that the purpose of the Fourteenth Amendment was "to enforce the absolute equality of the two races before the law," it went on to say that "mere legal distinctions" based on color were not necessarily outlawed so long as the separate facilities were equal. This gave the states everything they had hoped for.

Of course, the Court's argument was an invention specifically designed to uphold the state's power against Plessy's claim of right; historically, there is little doubt that the Fourteenth Amendment was precisely intended to abolish all legal distinctions based on color. Moreover, the contemporary evidence that state-enforced racial segregation was an integral part of a comprehensive system of subjugation was unavoidable. But the Court closed its eyes to history and to reality as well as to law.

The cynicism of this decision seemed boundless. The Court argued that federal laws could not *eradicate* prejudice, yet ignored the plain fact that state laws had helped *establish* prejudice. It claimed that segregation actually enhanced the public good, because if the two races were allowed to mix freely, disorder would result. That racial discrimination itself was a disorder, and of the most pathological kind, was not considered. In what was perhaps the *Plessy* opinion's most cruel and gratuitous passage, the Court located the discriminatory nature of segregation not in segregation itself, but in the minds of blacks: If "the enforced separation of the two races stamps the colored race with a badge of inferiority," the Court scolded, "it is not by reason of anything found in this act, but solely because the colored race chooses to put that construction upon it."

Justice Harlan could hardly contain his contempt. This opinion, he said, would in time be seen as being just as pernicious as the *Dred Scott* decision. The fiction of "separate but equal" would fool no one, he said, "nor atone for the wrong this day done." But the *Plessy* decision stood undisturbed for sixty years. In 1883, the Court had denied Congress the power to prohibit segregation; now, in *Plessy,* it protected the states' power to require it. The *Plessy* decision paved the way for Southern laws to compel racial separation everywhere. No effective constitutional limits on the power of states to subjugate blacks remained. Despite the heroic efforts of Congress in the years immediately following the Civil War, the cancer of racism spread, until it overpowered the frail body of liberty.

RESTRICTING VOTING RIGHTS: LITERACY TESTS AND GRANDFATHER CLAUSES

In the years following the *Plessy* decision, the loss of basic civil liberties among black Americans was nearly total. More and more laws enforced racial separation. And as the Supreme Court closed off the possibility of legal remedies, the Southern states moved to close off the possibility of political remedies. Southern states introduced literacy tests and poll taxes that effectively denied the right to vote to those blacks not already intimidated by shotguns and nightriders. The literacy tests, if applied equally, would have disqualified large numbers of whites as well, so most of them contained special clauses, called "grandfather clauses," allowing illiterate citizens to vote if they had been eligible to vote before the Civil War, or if they were descended from someone eligible to vote at the time. Many years would pass before the Supreme Court struck down these grandfather clauses, and it would be longer still before the literacy tests themselves were abolished, not by the Court, but by Congress.

Even without grandfather clauses, literacy tests provided infinite opportunities for local officials to deny blacks the right to vote. One Alabama registrar rejected a black applicant by writing this explanation on his registration form: "Error in spilling." Other literacy tests required applicants to explain a complex provision of the Constitution, offering local authorities an unlimited assortment of reasons to refuse them. Not until 1965 were these techniques abolished. And poll taxes were not fully abolished until a year later. In the years following the *Plessy* decision, blacks practically disappeared from the political system. In Louisiana, for example, the number of registered black voters plummeted from 130,334 in 1896 to only 5,320 in 1900.

During this period, antiblack violence increased. From 1884 to 1914, there were at least 3,600 lynchings—rarely fewer than 100 a year in that period, and rarely fewer than 50 in each of the next ten years. Private violence was often intertwined with police power, so that for blacks, lynchings and beatings became the predominant form of Southern "justice." In 1898, in Wilmington, North Carolina, four hundred white men, led by a former congressman, invaded the black community, set homes and stores on fire, killed and wounded scores of people, and drove hundreds more out of town, fleeing for their lives. In the same year, groups of "white-caps" in South Carolina rode throughout Greenwood County, shooting and lynching large numbers of blacks; in Lake City, a black postmaster was burned to death in his home, and his family was gunned down as they tried to escape. No police protection was available, no legal remedy imaginable.

Blacks were thus banished from Southern politics, as they had been during slavery, their right to vote denied both by state laws and by unbridled violence, which the states permitted and the Fifteenth Amendment was powerless to restrain. Black Americans were thus exiled, in effect, from their own communities, though often imprisoned there as well. Children learned, in ways they were likely never to forget, that they were inescapably inferior, and that their horizons were sharply limited. If any dared to dream, those dreams were quickly crushed. Economic opportunity was systematically cut off, at its roots. Poverty, subjugation, and dependence were institutionalized. And at a time when men were expected to be able to provide for their families and protect them, black men were allowed to do neither. Emasculation became a condition of survival.

Meanwhile, racial discrimination had become entrenched in the North as well. A nation willing to tolerate the rebirth of racist laws in the South and the suffocating system of oppression that flourished there, despite the Constitution's plain prohibitions, was a nation not wholly free from racism anywhere. The doctrine of "state action," invented by the Court to strike down the Civil Rights Act of 1875, immunized "private" power everywhere, not only in the South. Since employment, housing, and access to goods and services were almost entirely controlled by privately owned firms and corporations, legal rights that restrained only the power of government were no barrier to discrimination.

Thus, although racial segregation was not imposed by law in the North, it nonetheless became pervasive. Blacks were excluded from many jobs and confined by custom to separate neighborhoods. Employers were free not to hire blacks, and most did not. Real-estate agents, mortgage lenders, and apartment-house owners all helped produce a system of housing segregation in the North that was often more extreme than that found in many Southern towns. And housing segregation led to school segregation because of neighborhood schools. No laws commanded any of this in the North, but no laws prohibited it, either. By the early twentieth century, blacks moving North found less relief than they had expected, and more resistance. Race riots broke out: in New York City in 1900; in Springfield, Ohio, in 1904; in Greensburg, Indiana, in 1906; in Springfield, Illinois, in 1908.

THE BIRTH OF THE NAACP

Throughout most of the first half of the twentieth century, racial discrimination, Northern and Southern, remained the greatest, most comprehensive denial of civil liberties in the country. When relief finally came, it came first not from the courts, nor from Congress, but from the victims themselves, and from those relatively few white Americans who supported them.

In June 1905, W. E. B. Du Bois, a Harvard-educated black historian and sociologist, brought together a group of young black intellectuals in Niagara Falls to discuss how to combat the rising tide of discrimination and lynchings. They called themselves the Niagara Movement, and drew up a platform for change that listed among its priorities full voting rights and the abolition of all legal distinctions based on race. These goals, of course, were identical to those reflected nearly four decades earlier in the post–Civil War constitutional amendments and the federal civil-rights laws that followed. Now it would all have to be done again.

A few years later, in 1909, the Niagara Movement joined with white re-formers and veterans of the old abolitionist movement to organize the National Association for the Advancement of Colored People (NAACP). Its program, described in its tenth annual report in 1919, became a blueprint for the movement to establish equal rights for black citizens:

1. A vote for every Negro man and woman on the same terms as for white men and women.
2. An equal chance to acquire the kind of an education that will enable the Negro everywhere wisely to use this vote.
3. A fair trial in the courts for all crimes of which he is accused, by judges in whose election he has participated without discrimination because of race.
4. A right to sit upon the jury which passes judgment upon him.
5. Defense against lynching and burning at the hands of mobs.
6. Equal service on railroad and other public carriers … at the same cost and upon the same terms as other passengers.
7. Equal right to the use of public parks, libraries, and other community services for which he is taxed.
8. An equal chance for a livelihood in public and private employment.
9. The abolition of color-hyphenation and the substitution of "straight Americanism."

The NAACP used a number of traditional organizational methods to pursue these goals, but one was not traditional. NAACP attorneys began to look systematically for cases they could bring to court that might, if carefully orchestrated, whittle away at the Jim Crow laws. Mindful of prior Supreme Court decisions, they sought to construct their cases, and the facts that gave rise to them, in ways that increased the probability of success. This technique, later to prove explosively effective, was the beginning of what today is known as public-interest law—the use of litigation as a strategy for social change.

For many years, this strategy bore very little fruit. But a number of important though limited victories foreshadowed the spectacular success that lay ahead. Probably the most important of these emerged from a 1917 case, *Buchanan v. Worley.* NAACP lawyers decided to challenge a Louisville, Kentucky, law that prohibited a black person from moving into a house on a block occupied by a majority of whites. The lawyers set up the case with great care. A black agreed to buy a house from its white owner on a block where the majority of residents was white. The contract had an escape clause: the purchase would be made only if the buyer had the legal right to live in the house. The seller then sued to fulfill the contract, and the buyer defended the suit on the grounds that the Louisville law prevented him from moving in. The local Kentucky courts upheld the buyer, as well as the law. By the time it reached the Supreme Court, the case had attracted a great deal of attention. Many others not directly involved filed legal briefs. These were called *amicus curiae* briefs, Latin for "friend of the court"; such briefs are today a common feature of Supreme Court cases involving important issues of public policy and constitutional law. For that time, however, the number of such "outside" briefs filed in the *Buchanan* case was unusually high.

In its first departure from the string of late-nineteenth-century decisions upholding laws and practices that required racial segregation, the Supreme Court unanimously struck down the Louisville law as a violation of the Fourteenth Amendment. Although the Court tried to distinguish this case from *Plessy* by pointing out that in *Plessy* the law provided for separate but *equal* accommodations, that distinction was not persuasive. After all, the buyer in this case might also have been able to find an equally acceptable sale. *Buchanan v. Worley* was seen publicly as a major civil-rights victory, and indeed it represented the Supreme Court's first attempt to impose constitutional limits on Jim Crow laws.

By 1921, the NAACP had established four hundred branches throughout the United States and become a fixture of the American civil-rights landscape. Other organizations, such as the National Urban League and the Commission on International Cooperation, arose to help. And in 1920, the American Civil Liberties Union (ACLU) was organized. In its early days, the ACLU normally referred all cases involving the rights of blacks to the NAACP, but before long the ACLU became virtually the only predominantly white national organization to champion racial justice during the 1920s. There were sometimes disagreements between the ACLU and the NAACP on matters of free-speech rights for people espousing doctrines of white supremacy; nevertheless, the two organizations worked closely together. A high-ranking NAACP official always sat on the ACLU executive committee, and the ACLU repeatedly condemned Ku Klux Klan violence. In 1931, the ACLU published *Black*

Justice, a comprehensive report on the continuing denial of equal rights to black citizens.

The public-interest movement for equal rights grew daily stronger, yet the rights themselves remained precarious. And with the exception of occasional victories like the *Buchanan* decision, the power of the Constitution to protect the rights of black citizens remained dormant. In 1927, for example, a unanimous Supreme Court — including such luminaries as Oliver Wendell Holmes, Louis D. Brandeis, and Harlan Fiske Stone — upheld a Mississippi decision that had assigned a young girl of Chinese ancestry to a black school. Once again declining to declare such practices in violation of the Fourteenth Amendment, all nine justices agreed that racial segregation in public schools "has been many times decided to be within the constitutional power of the state ... without the intervention of the ... Federal Constitution." Nor did Congress show any inclination to engage again in the kinds of civil-rights efforts that had marked the years just after the Civil War.

This situation continued essentially unchanged until after World War II. Indeed, during World War II the nation experienced — and tolerated — one of the most blatantly racist acts in our history. This act — the imprisonment in concentration camps of more than 100,000 American citizens of Japanese descent — was committed not by any Southern state, but by President Franklin D. Roosevelt, and was permitted by the Supreme Court.

JAPANESE-AMERICANS LOSE THEIR RIGHTS

On December 7, 1941, Japan attacked Pearl Harbor, provoking the United States' entrance into World War II. Though people immediately began to worry about an attack on America's West Coast, in the months that followed, according to army estimates at the time, "there was no real threat of a Japanese invasion." However, a large number of people of Japanese ancestry lived on the West Coast, in California, Oregon, and Washington. Although they never exceeded more than one percent of the West Coast population, prejudice, jealousy, and animosity toward Asians were widespread, especially in California. Spurred by a variety of private organizations like the American Legion and the Los Angeles Chamber of Commerce, and supported by a number of political leaders — including Earl Warren, then the California attorney-general — pressure began to build to "relocate" Americans of Japanese descent.

In the beginning, no one in the national government seriously suggested that anyone be moved. In Hawaii, which after all had been attacked and was closer to the Pacific war zone, one-third of the population was of Japanese ancestry. Yet no one ever proposed evacuating them. On America's West

Coast, however, the tiny Japanese-American minority came to be seen as a threat. Fear mingled with racism to produce an ugly amalgam, perhaps best expressed by John DeWitt, an American army general who, in his official report to the War Department on the West Coast situation, wrote, "The Japanese race is an enemy race." He was talking about American citizens.

Francis Biddle was the United States attorney-general at the time. He opposed the proposal to evacuate the Japanese, as did a number of his colleagues in the Justice Department. Nonetheless, President Roosevelt decided to go ahead, and on February 19, 1942, he signed an executive order authorizing the military to exclude anyone they wanted from any area in the United States if, in their judgment, it was necessary to protect against espionage and sabotage.

The executive order made no distinction between American citizens and aliens, nor did it require any evidence of espionage or sabotage against any individual. And although written broadly enough to apply to anyone, it was aimed at Japanese-Americans almost exclusively. One month after the executive order was issued, Congress passed a law—without a single dissent—making it a federal crime for any civilian to disobey a military order to "relocate." With the exception of the American Friends Service Committee, a Quaker organization, and the American Civil Liberties Union, almost no one spoke out against or challenged what followed.

The new law subjected everyone of Japanese descent to a curfew: people could not leave their homes between 8:00 P.M. and 6:00 A.M. Even during noncurfew hours, they were barred from moving outside a five-mile radius of their homes or places of work. The law also authorized excluding them from "military areas," which in effect meant the entire West Coast. Ultimately, they were forced into camps, initially called "concentration camps" in some government memoranda, but later sanitized to the more benign-sounding "relocation centers." People were given one week to leave their homes and report to "assembly centers," taking only bedding, toilet articles, eating utensils, and such clothing and other personal belongings as they could carry.

Trapped by the curfew order, and unable to leave the area, Americans of Japanese descent could only wait for the inevitable exclusion order that would force them to report to the assembly centers. Violation of these orders was a crime; faced with the threat of criminal prosecution and imprisonment, few of them resisted.

Government officials thought that the assembly centers would be a brief stopping place before those who had been forced to leave their homes could be "resettled" somewhere else. But at a meeting of the governors and other public officials from nearby states, a wave of racist opposition swept that hope away. Governor Nels Smith of Wyoming said that his constituents "dislike Orientals" and that Wyoming would not be "California's dumping ground." If Japanese-Americans attempted to buy land in Wyoming, Smith warned, "there would be Japs hanging from every pine tree" in Wyoming. Governors of other states also did not mince words. Governor Herbert Mow of Utah proposed that Japanese-Americans "be put into camps" and compelled to work as agricultural laborers. He added that the federal government seemed "much too concerned about the constitutional rights of Japanese-American citizens." And Governor Chase Clark of Idaho flatly proposed that all Japanese-Americans "be put in camps under guard" for the duration of the war. Clark's attorney-general, Bert Miller, went further: all Japanese, he said, should "be put into concentration camps" and "no attempt should be made to provide work for them." Revealing his feelings, he added, "We want to keep this a white man's country."

In the end, the idea of resettlement gave way to detention, under a harsh regime of barbed wire and armed guards that made no provision for personal or family privacy. By October 30 of that year, 112,000 people, mostly American citizens, were confined in ten camps scattered from the California desert to the swamps of Arkansas.

Although all three aspects of this program — the curfew order, the evacuation order, and the detention — were challenged in court, the Bill of Rights was not able to protect the victims against government power driven by prejudice, especially during wartime, when fear provided a cover for racial animosity.

Three Japanese-Americans challenged the program. Gordon Hirabayashi, then a college senior and now a sociology professor in Canada, challenged both the curfew and the evacuation order. Fred Korematsu, then a shipyard welder and now an industrial draftsman, challenged the order removing him from his home in San Leandro, California. Minaru Yasui, then a young lawyer in Portland, Oregon, and now a government official in Denver, defied the curfew and spent more than nine months in solitary confinement "in a stinking jail cell in Oregon."

Later, they were joined by a young woman named Mitsuye Endo, a twenty-two-year-old clerical worker for the California Department of Motor Vehicles. She had been raised as a Methodist, neither read nor spoke Japanese, had never visited Japan, and had a brother serving in the United States Army. She did not challenge either the curfew or the evacuation order. But after she was in detention, she filed a writ of habeas corpus, the ancient English writ designed to test whether one's imprisonment was lawful or not. Her lawsuit was designed to force the Supreme Court to decide whether her detention was constitutional. To avoid this result, government lawyers offered Endo her freedom, if she promised not to return to the West Coast. But she refused to abandon the legal challenge and remained behind barbed wire for another two years while her case moved through the courts. In 1944, the Supreme Court finally decided it.

Hirabayashi's case reached the Supreme Court first, though, in 1943. He had been charged with the crime of violating the curfew in his home town of Seattle and refusing to report to an assembly center. He was convicted and sentenced to three months in prison. On appeal, the Supreme Court unanimously upheld his conviction. The Court was simply not willing to look behind the government's claims during a time of war. The government said it believed the curfew and evacuation orders were a matter of military necessity, and the Court deferred to that claim without any serious scrutiny. There was no evidence that anyone in the government thought an invasion by the Japanese was likely; nor did the government introduce any evidence of espionage or sabotage against Hirabayashi or anyone else subject to the orders. The government just said "military necessity" and the Court closed its eyes.

The Court did even worse: it deferred to the government's racist assertions as well. Government lawyers had argued that the racial characteristics of Japanese-Americans "predisposed" them to commit espionage and sabotage, even though not a shred of evidence existed to show any actual crime. And the Court echoed that assertion: "Residents having ethnic affiliations with an invading enemy," said Chief Justice Harlan Fiske Stone, "may be a greater source of danger than those of a different ancestor." Moreover, the blatant racism of the program was accepted with hardly a murmur of protest: no similar program existed for Americans of German or Italian descent; indeed, suspected cases of espionage or sabotage against people of German descent had turned up, but these were investigated and dealt with on a case-by-case basis, utilizing the normal rules of evidence and criminal procedures. Why treat Americans of Japanese ancestry differently? The Court decided that the government must have had a good reason, and let the question go unanswered.

Eighteen months later, in December 1944, the Court decided Fred Korematsu's case. In the *Hirabayashi* case, the Court had simply upheld the curfew order, doing so unanimously. Now it ruled upon the evacuation order: did the Constitution permit the government to force Fred Korematsu, an American citizen, out of his home on the basis of national origin and without any evidence of a crime having been committed or even planned? By a 6–3 vote, the Court said yes.

The Court paid lip service to the Constitution's demands by declaring that restricting the civil rights of anyone on the basis of race was "immediately suspect" and must be subjected to "the most rigid scrutiny." Having announced that rule, the Court quickly abandoned it. The rule of law was perhaps established for the future, but it would not be applied here. No "rigid scrutiny" of the government's claims was undertaken; indeed, once again, the Court deferred to those claims without any scrutiny at all.

Justice Frank Murphy, writing in dissent, called the evacuation program "utterly revolting among a free people who have embraced the principles set forth in the Constitution of the United States," and he called the Court's decision what it was: "this legalization of racism."

Endo's case was decided the same day. It had been designed to force the Court to decide on the constitutionality of the detention, as distinct from the curfews or the evacuations. But the Court found a way to duck even this issue. Having already approved the government's authority to assume that all Japanese-Americans were probably disloyal, it could not help but approve their detention, at least for a brief period sufficient to determine whether in fact they were disloyal. Mitsuye Endo's loyalty had been conceded. Therefore, ruled the Court, she could no longer be held. Her writ of habeas corpus had to be granted, and she had to be released.

By ruling on her individual application, however, the Court declined to rule on the prior question: Was it legal for the government to detain citizens for a long period of time based on nothing more than their ancestry and the community's hostility? This was no academic question: at that time, only six months before the end of World War II, 70,000 American citizens still languished behind barbed wire. Justice Owen Roberts, joined by Justice Murphy, accused the Court's majority of constitutional cowardice; he thought the detentions violated the Bill of Rights, and said so. But the majority refused to decide the question, and it remains unanswered to this day. It lies there, like a land mine, waiting to explode should similar circumstances arise.

Forty years later, using the Freedom of Information Act, a historian doing research for a book on these cases discovered government documents that irrefutably proved that the government had knowingly and deliberately lied to the Supreme Court about its claim that the evacuations were militarily necessary, and had actually altered the legal briefs submitted to the Supreme Court to hide that fact. In 1983, Fred Korematsu, Gordon Hirabayashi, and Minaru Yasui filed suits in federal courts on the basis of this new information, and their convictions were overturned. In 1988, Congress confessed its error and passed a bill providing for financial reparations to the victims and their descendants. In signing that bill into law, President Ronald Reagan called the Japanese-American detention an act of "war hysteria and racism."

It was forty-five years too late. Liberty matters when liberty is denied. And when liberty was denied in 1942, the Bill of Rights provided no relief—not because it was not written clearly enough, but because those entrusted with the responsibility to enforce it did not have the courage to do so, or else believed the government's racist claims.

Only a few years after Congress and President Reagan tried to atone for what was done in 1942, it became plain that not everyone had learned the lesson. In January 1991, the United States went to war against Iraq in the Persian Gulf. Almost immediately, national origin once again became a substitute for evidence. The FBI began systematically to question American citizens of Arab descent, regardless of which Arab country they or their ancestors were from, and even though some of those countries were allied with us against Iraq. The FBI defended its practice by claiming that they wanted to find out whether Arab-Americans were experiencing any discrimination, but it also questioned them closely about terrorism and whether they had any information about sabotage that might help the FBI.

Arab-Americans reacted with fear: Why were they being singled out? Was there any specific reason the FBI was questioning them as a group? Or was this one more example of what the Supreme Court had approved in the *Hirabayashi* case—blatant racism?

After much protest, the FBI backed off, but the automatic association of ancestry with suspicion was not encouraging. And the widely publicized FBI practice seemed to encourage private discrimination against Arab-Americans. Arab-American homes and places of business were attacked, and Pan American World Airways announced that it would ban all Iraqis from its flights. Since Pan Am had no idea how to tell who was Iraqi (at least not on a domestic flight, where passports are not required), people with darker skin and Moslem names were widely harassed. Lebanese, Syrians, and Pakistanis were denied tickets or abusively searched. One American citizen of Iranian descent was pulled off an airplane, intrusively searched, and detained for several hours; when he asked why, he was told he fit the profile of a terrorist.

The Persian Gulf War was soon over, and the immediate threat to Americans at home was negligible. But if the war had been longer or more difficult and the threat to Americans more plausible, one wonders whether the lessons we learned from the events of 1942 would have prevented similar outrages from happening again. And it is disquieting to remember that the fundamental constitutional question of whether the Bill of Rights prohibits detention based on ancestry has never been answered.

CHIPPING AWAY AT JIM CROW

Ironically, some of the legal standards announced by the Supreme Court in the Japanese-American cases, though not applied in those cases themselves, helped black citizens in later cases. The *Korematsu* case established the idea that legal restrictions of the civil rights of a racial group are "immediately suspect" and must be subjected to "rigid scrutiny." This legal doctrine turned out to be helpful in civil-rights cases decided soon after World War II.

World War II changed the American landscape in other ways as well. It had been a war for survival against an explicitly racist ideology, Nazism. The rhetoric of racial equality had therefore been part of the propaganda effort at home, and now it would be harder than ever to reconcile that rhetoric with the American reality.

Black soldiers, in racially segregated military units, had fought and died by the tens of thousands, ostensibly to protect American liberty; it would be harder now for them to sit still when they were denied liberty at home. Jackie Robinson, later to become the first black player to break the color barrier in major-league baseball, was court-martialed while stationed at an army base in the South because he refused to relinquish a seat on a bus reserved for whites. He was acquitted. A. Philip Randolph, the stately and militant president of the Brotherhood of Sleeping Car Porters, had threatened to lead a massive march on Washington unless President Roosevelt banned racial discrimination in defense industries. Roosevelt issued the order

In 1945, the United Nations Charter was drafted in San Francisco. It proclaimed devotion to "the equal rights of men and women" and stated as one of the United Nation's main purposes a respect for rights "without distinction as to race, sex, or religion." At the same time, Gunnar Myrdal, an internationally respected Swedish economist and sociologist, published a major study of race relations in the United States in which he described the enormous gap between the American ideal of equal rights and the American reality of racial discrimination and subjugation. He also concluded that the subordinated status of blacks in America was the result not of any inherent inferiority, but rather of segregation and discrimination. America's black citizens, he concluded, were trapped in a "vicious circle of cumulative causation," in which their lowly status, created by discrimination, in turn became the justification for perpetuating it.

On December 5, 1946, President Harry S. Truman established a national Commission on Civil Rights to examine this problem, and in 1947 the commission issued a report, *To Secure These Rights*. The report recommended expanding the Civil Rights Section of the Department of Justice, establishing a permanent civil-rights commission, enacting federal legislation to end racial discrimination in voting, and abolishing school segregation. On July 26, 1948, President Truman issued an executive order ending racial segregation in the military. For the first time since just after the Civil War, the federal government began, very slowly, to use its power to advance equal rights.

During this same period, NAACP lawyers continued to bring cases designed to chip away at Jim Crow laws. And for the first time, the Supreme

Court showed signs that it was prepared to respond. One case involved a Virginia law requiring racial segregation of passengers on buses. A black woman, riding a bus from Virginia to Maryland, refused to move to the back of the bus. She was arrested, convicted, and fined. On appeal, the Supreme Court struck down the law with only one dissenting vote. The impact of this decision was limited, however, because it was based on the principle of *interstate* travel and on the idea that there had to be a uniform national rule for seating passengers on buses and trains. Thus, the old Louisiana law that Homer A. Plessy had challenged and that the Supreme Court had upheld in 1896 was left standing. The NAACP's lawyers relied on an old and somewhat obscure 1877 Supreme Court decision relating to the interstate travel of a Mississippi steamboat, and never even ventured to raise the question of whether the Fourteenth Amendment prohibited the Virginia law. No unnecessary risks were taken, and only small gains were made.

Still, the law was struck down, and an important public victory was won, without forcing the Court to confront a difficult constitutional question that it was probably not ready to confront in 1946, and without forcing it to reverse any of its previous decisions. Careful, strategic litigation had achieved a small victory, seeding the ground for larger victories in future cases. Constitutional law remained unchanged; but Virginia's practice of segregated busing, at least in interstate travel, was ended. People began riding at least some desegregated buses, and they began getting used to it.

Two years later, in 1948, the Supreme Court ruled that private contracts prohibiting white homeowners from selling their houses to blacks were unenforceable. The case was significant because, in effect, it got around the "state action" limitation used in 1883 by the Supreme Court to avoid applying the Fourteenth Amendment to discrimination by private parties. Now the Court ruled that the discriminatory contracts, because they were private, were not themselves unconstitutional, but that it was unconstitutional for any *court*— which was, after all, an arm of the state — to enforce such a contract. This was another important victory for the NAACP.

Then, in 1950, the first constitutional crack began to appear in the legal wall separating blacks and whites in school. Texas had established separate law schools for blacks and whites, while Oklahoma admitted blacks to its state-university graduate programs, but required them to sit in segregated alcoves and at separate tables in the library and cafeteria. Lawsuits challenging the legal doctrine of "separate but equal" were filed against both practices, at least in the context of higher education. Southern states saw exactly what was at stake: eleven of them filed briefs supporting Texas and urging the Court to reject the challenge.

In a stunning reversal of at least the result in the old *Plessy* case, the Court ruled *unanimously* that both the Texas and Oklahoma practices violated the

Fourteenth Amendment. The Court declined, however, to declare the "separate but equal" doctrine unlawful; it struck down the Texas and Oklahoma practices not because they were *separate* but because they were *unequal.* The Court said nothing about enforced separation itself being a state-imposed badge of inferiority; instead, the Court relied on the actual inequality in education that resulted from the separation. In the Texas case, for example, Chief Justice Fred M. Vinson emphasized how important faculty reputations were in legal education, how influential to one's career alumni were, and how educationally critical it was for future black lawyers to mix with whites, who would constitute the overwhelming number of judges, lawyers, witnesses, and juries that they would face.

The case illustrated the importance of litigation strategy. The "separate but equal" doctrine was not challenged frontally. Instead, it was used against itself. The doctrine of "separate but equal" was accepted, but the assumption of equal facilities was attacked. However possible it was for the Louisiana railroad in 1896 to provide roughly equal accommodations, thereby allowing the Court to take refuge behind the theory of "separate but equal," in the field of education, and especially law-school education, the argument for equal accommodations was hard to sustain, particularly to judges who themselves were intimately familiar with how careers in law develop. This incremental litigation strategy exploited the fault in the "separate but equal" doctrine, ultimately producing a constitutional earthquake that shattered it forever, and reversed the 1896 *Plessy* decision.

THE END OF "SEPARATE BUT EQUAL"

These decisions, all coming within five years after World War II, also showed the effect of politics on judicial interpretation. In 1896, the political climate had been unapologetically racist; by 1950, while racism was still everywhere in evidence, it had become somehow less acceptable. In a number of those cases, the Truman administration had filed *amicus* briefs in support of the NAACP's arguments.

In retrospect, the Texas and Oklahoma decisions made the revolutionary decision in *Brown v. Board of Education*, which followed a few years later, seem inevitable. But in fact it was anything but inevitable. It represented the culmination of a twenty-year effort by the NAACP, and it remains today the outstanding example of how litigation was used strategically to make the Bill of Rights work.

Linda Brown was a seven-year-old girl who attended an all-black school about a mile from her home in Topeka, Kansas. To get to school each day, she first trekked through railroad switching yards and rows of warehouses on streets without sidewalks, and then boarded a bus. On a sunny September day in 1950, Linda's father, Oliver Brown, took her instead to the school for white children about seven blocks from her home, and tried to register her there. He was, of course, rebuffed. Soon after, the NAACP filed suit, challenging Topeka's segregated school system. The *Brown* case was eventually joined with four others that had been filed in Virginia, the District of Columbia, Delaware, and South Carolina. All five reached the United States Supreme Court in December 1952, where they were argued by a team of lawyers headed by Thurgood Marshall — now a Supreme Court justice, but then the NAACP's chief lawyer, and for years the main architect of its litigation strategy.

The case was not immediately decided. The Court was deeply worried about the consequences of any decision it might make. At first, the justices were divided on the central *legal* question: was the system of "separate but equal" public schools a violation of the Fourteenth Amendment guarantee of equal protection of the laws? There were also *factual* questions: the Texas and Oklahoma cases had struck down separate facilities in higher education on the grounds that they were not in fact equal; could a similar case be made out in these five public school systems? Third, there were questions of *remedy:* if any or all of these systems were declared unconstitutional, what should be done to dismantle them? Lastly, the most troubling questions of all: If the Court struck down school segregation, would the South accept it? Would there be violence? Would there be political resistance? These were not speculative questions. Segregation had by now been institutionalized for eight decades, written into the laws and the culture of the Southern states, fused deeply into the blood and bones of the body politic. Could it now, after so many years, be exorcised? At what cost?

In an internal memorandum to his colleagues, Justice Felix Frankfurter expressed this concern candidly: "For me, the ultimate crucial factor ... is psychological — the adjustment of men's minds and actions to the unfamiliar and the unpleasant." All the Supreme Court justices had grown up and become politically aware during a time when white violence against black citizens in the South was common. Even now, in 1953, they seemed at least as concerned about the problems whites would have adjusting to equality as they did about the problems blacks had endured for years adjusting to inequality. So the Court decided not to decide the case right away, and instead scheduled it for reargument in the fall of 1953. During that summer, Chief Justice Fred M. Vinson — who had written the Texas and Oklahoma higher-education opinions, but who was rumored to be inclined not to extend those rulings to public schools — died suddenly of a heart attack. He was replaced by Earl Warren, then the governor of California.

On May 17, 1954, the Court unanimously struck down school segregation. The decision has undoubtedly had the broadest consequences of any Court decision of the twentieth century. It went well beyond the Texas and Oklahoma cases. It did not evaluate whether each separate school for black children was in fact unequal. Instead, it ruled that state-enforced separation was itself inherently unequal, at least in the context of education. All segregated systems were struck down at once. "To separate [children] from others of similar age and qualifications solely because of their race," wrote Chief Justice Warren, "generates a feeling of inferiority as to their status in the community that may affect their hearts and minds in a way unlikely ever to be undone."

The 1896 *Plessy* decision, which had given birth to the constitutional doctrine of "separate but equal," though it was not formally overruled, did not long survive. *Brown* unleashed the power of the Fourteenth Amendment, long dormant, to unravel the Jim Crow legal caste system in the South. Race relations in America would never be the same. The *Brown* decision delivered a jolt of electric energy to the civil-rights movement that would propel it to victory after victory during the next fifteen years.

The *Brown* decision also launched an egalitarian legal revolution that made the Bill of Rights a living document for tens of millions of people who had not previously enjoyed its protections. After *Brown,* the demand for equal rights became contagious. Women seeking an end to discrimination based on sex were the first, but they were far from the last. The movement for equality spread to all sections of society. Equal rights became a rallying cry for groups never before thought to be protected by the Bill of Rights: Asians, Hispanics, American Indians, gay people, children in school and in foster care, people with disabilities, soldiers, inmates of mental institutions, prisoners, aliens, and those too poor to protect their rights in a wide variety of legal proceedings. All began to see the Bill of Rights as a weapon that they might use, as black citizens had, to gain rights they had long been denied.

"SEGREGATION FOREVER!"—AND VIOLENT RESISTANCE

But all that would come later. In the immediate aftermath of the *Brown* decision, there was much resistance, some of it violent, nearly all of it orchestrated, encouraged, or led by elected public officials.

Within three years of the *Brown* decision, seven Southern states passed resolutions calling for defiance of the Supreme Court and threatening armed resistance. Arkansas promised to defend itself against "all illegal encroachments upon the powers reserved to the state." In 1957, Governor Orval Faubus made good on that threat. He called out the National Guard to prevent black teenagers from entering Central High School in Little Rock. They were joined by an angry, seething mob. One woman later recalled how, as a fifteen-year-old girl, she walked excitedly to school on what she thought would be a great day, only to have her way blocked by soldiers brandishing bayonets, while the crowd taunted her, calling her "nigger bitch" and yelling for her to be lynched then and there. On September 25, 1957, President Dwight D. Eisenhower, who had previously lent the *Brown* decision only lukewarm support, sent federal troops—the first time that had happened since the 1870s—and Central High School was desegregated.

Hostility and resistance were not limited to Arkansas. In 1956, nineteen Southern United States senators and eighty-two members of the House of Representatives—virtually the entire Southern delegation—signed a "Southern Manifesto," denouncing the *Brown* decision; one senator, from Mississippi, called racial integration "a radical, pro-Communist political movement." The manifesto was organized by Senator Sam Ervin of North Carolina, who years later, during the Watergate scandal, was to emerge as a constitutional hero on other issues.

Meanwhile, in Little Rock, black children were going to school, but only because of the presence of federal troops. Public hostility, encouraged by official resistance, remained at fever pitch. The school board filed suit in federal court, asking permission to postpone desegregation because of "extreme public hostility engendered by official attitudes and actions of the governor and the legislature." At stake was the issue of whether constitutional rights could be denied or "postponed" because of community hostility. In 1958, the Supreme Court said no, and denied the school board's request for delay.

The Court's decision rejected community hostility as a legal justification for denying constitutional rights, but it could not eradicate the hostility itself, which remained bitter and undiminished throughout the region. In 1956, Autherine Lucy entered the University of Alabama under a federal court order, only to be forcibly removed by state officials. In 1961, violence greeted blacks admitted to the University of Georgia. In 1962, James Meredith was attacked at the University of Mississippi when he became the first black student to enroll, provoking President John F. Kennedy to send troops to protect one man's right to attend a state-supported school. In January 1963, at his inaugural in Montgomery, Alabama, Governor George Wallace defiantly proclaimed: "Segregation now, segregation tomorrow, segregation forever!" Six months later, on a warm June night in Jackson, Mississippi, Medgar Evers, the head of the local NAACP branch, was shot and killed in his driveway after returning home late one night from a meeting. Three months after that, a black church in Birmingham, Alabama, was bombed during Sunday-morning services. Four little girls were killed; twenty-three others were injured. The next summer, three young civil-rights workers—James Chaney, a black from Mississippi, and Andrew Goodman and Michael Schwerner, two whites from New York—were abducted by a local Mississippi sheriff, murdered, and buried in an earthen dam. In March 1965, Viola Liuzzo, a white woman who had come from Detroit to work in the Southern voter-registration movement, was shot and killed in her car. During these years, the FBI, under the direction of J. Edgar Hoover, offered no relief from the terrorism that enveloped civil-rights activists. Indeed, the FBI was often part of the problem, sometimes even collaborating with local police, who themselves were frequently associated with the Ku Klux Klan.

By 1964, a decade after the Supreme Court first decided that school segregation was unlawful, seven of the eleven Southern states still had failed to achieve even one percent integration in their public schools. Five years later, only about ten percent of black children attended majority-white schools in Alabama, Georgia, Louisiana, Mississippi, and South Carolina. The Supreme Court had called for desegregation at a reasonable pace, which it characterized as "all deliberate speed." But in fact progress was unacceptably slow. Nonetheless, time was running out on the white-supremacists. Although their resistance was fierce and their willingness to resort to violence frightening, the return to segregation that had occurred in the late nineteenth century never came. Little by little, terror subsided and the rigid caste system of legalized segregation began to crumble.

The Bill of Rights was brought to the South not primarily by political leadership from Washington or by the Supreme Court, but by a remarkable movement of black people who systematically began to assert the simplest of rights and whose struggles, increasingly supported by whites, finally transformed the fight for legal equality into a moral crusade that swept the country, engaged the president, and galvanized Congress into actions it had not taken since just after the Civil War.

BOYCOTTS AND SIT-INS—NONVIOLENT INSISTENCE

The *Brown* decision provoked rage and resistance from white-supremacists. But it also filled black people with hope and emboldened them to believe that if they continued to assert their rights, the system would respond. On December 1, 1955, Rosa Parks, a black seamstress going home from work, refused to relinquish her seat to a white passenger on a city bus in Montgomery, Alabama. Like Homer A. Plessy before her, she was arrested. This time, however, the response was not a legal argument made to a court but a moral argument made to the nation.

Black citizens, assisted and eventually led by a then-unknown twenty-seven-year-old Baptist minister named Martin Luther King, Jr., organized a citywide boycott of buses. For over a year, blacks walked to work. As the months wore on and the boycotters stood fast, the attention of the nation focused on this nonviolent struggle. Although provoked repeatedly, the boycotters never responded with violence. And when the city of Montgomery finally gave in and integrated the buses, the tactic of nonviolent resistance spread throughout the South, and a movement was born.

On February 1, 1960, the first sit-in took place, in Greensboro, North Carolina. Four black college students sat down at a segregated lunch counter and requested service. They were refused and were arrested for trespassing. There was no law to protect them, because the Supreme Court had long ago held that the Fourteenth Amendment could not be used to outlaw racial discrimination by privately owned public facilities. But this was no longer only a legal struggle. They kept coming back, in larger and larger numbers, continuing to exercise their rights, and enduring arrest, imprisonment, and beatings without violent response.

Over the next few years, hundreds of such nonviolent actions took place: sit-ins at segregated restaurants, kneel-ins at segregated churches, wade-ins at segregated swimming pools, read-ins at segregated libraries. Voter-registration campaigns sprang up throughout the South, the first since just after the Civil War. Freedom rides were organized: whites and blacks rode through the South together on interstate buses, which the Supreme Court had ordered desegregated in 1946.

Many of these actions met with violence; people were beaten brutally; some were permanently injured and more than a few were killed. Southern police usually provided no protection; sometimes they perpetrated the violence themselves or quietly encouraged it. Those who were not beaten were often arrested, sometimes for walking peacefully to the courthouse to register to vote or to express their grievances. The First Amendment gave them the right to do that, but 175 years after it had been adopted, the First Amendment wasn't yet recognized in the South. Again and again, protesters had to go to court to seek protection from the Bill of Rights just to allow their protests to go on. Towns passed ordinances barring speech they found "offensive," requiring insurance bonds that could not be obtained and permits that could be denied at the whim of local officials. But this time, the Supreme Court upheld protesters' rights and ruled that the First Amendment prevented local officials from interfering with the movement's freedom of expression or their right to assemble peaceably.

On August 28, 1963, these actions reached a stirring climax when 250,000 people, of all races and religions, from all over the country, assembled in Washington. They surrounded the Reflecting Pool in front of the Lincoln Memorial, to voice their demand for congressional legislation that would at last guarantee equal opportunity in employment, equal access to public accommodations, prompt enforcement of school desegregation, and equal voting rights: in short, equal *citizenship*. It was the largest group of citizens that had ever assembled in the nation's capital to demand legislation of any kind, much less legislation designed to achieve racial justice. And there were indications that Congress and President John F. Kennedy were ready to respond.

The dream deferred since 1877 and reannounced in the NAACP's annual report of 1920 had now reached the stage of political reality. Bills were introduced in Congress by the Kennedy administration to convert into law many of the demands of the March on Washington. A few months later, Kennedy was assassinated in Dallas, Texas, but President Lyndon B. Johnson, himself a Southerner, steered the bills through Congress. In 1964, the first major federal civil-rights law since just after the Civil War was passed. It limited the use of discriminatory literacy tests as a bar to voting, authorized the United States attorney-general to file lawsuits challenging segregated public facilities and schools, outlawed racial discrimination in public accommodations such as hotels and restaurants, prohibited discrimination in any program that accepted federal funding, and forbade discrimination in employment by most private employers.

The part of the law that prohibited employment discrimination outlawed discrimination based on sex as well as race. This was not intentional. Southerners who opposed any law prohibiting race discrimination added an amendment outlawing sex discrimination, in the belief that it would generate opposition and help kill the entire bill. Their move backfired, and the bill passed with the amendment, thereby setting the stage for the second great egalitarian movement, which was shortly to follow.

The constitutionality of this law as applied to privately owned public accommodations was quickly challenged in court, as its 1875 predecessor had been. But this time the Supreme Court upheld the law as a valid exercise of congressional power under the Constitution. Interestingly, however, the Court avoided confronting the old rulings that the Fourteenth Amendment didn't authorize Congress to outlaw private-sector discrimination, relying instead on Congress's constitutional power to regulate interstate commerce. Later, the Court breathed new life into the Thirteenth Amendment, in effect overruling the result of its old 1883 decision, by ruling that the Thirteenth Amendment gave Congress broad authority to outlaw private acts of racial discrimination. In so doing, the Court revived the old Civil Rights Act of 1866, which granted blacks equal rights in the making of private contracts. This was then used successfully to prohibit racial discrimination in employment, in the sale and purchase of homes, and in the admission of children to private schools.

A year later, Congress passed the Voting Rights Act of 1965. By the time this act was passed, relatively few blacks were registered to vote in the South. In Mississippi, only 6.4 percent were registered, in Alabama, 19.4 percent, and in Louisiana, 31.8 percent (compared to 80.2 percent of whites). After nearly a hundred years of intimidation and terror, bringing the numbers of voters up to the roughly equal proportions that had been achieved right after the Civil War was a very distant goal.

The Voting Rights Act, and its subsequent amendments in 1970, 1975, and 1982, outlawed discriminatory voting tests and, for the first time since 1871, authorized federal courts to appoint registrars to supersede state officials in cases where there was widespread denial of the right to vote or register. One of the act's protections, however, was new and startling. The experience with school desegregation had taught Congress that Southern officials could be endlessly inventive in creating mechanisms to circumvent court orders and civil-rights laws. So the Voting Rights Act contained a new and especially effective device: *preclearance*. In any jurisdiction with a history of racially discriminatory tests or low voter participation by minorities, the act required that any local change in voting procedures or election law had to be approved first by the Department of Justice or by a federal court. Later amendments expanded the reach of this preclearance provision and extended its life until the year 2007.

The preclearance provision of the act turned out to be the most important voting-rights remedy. Many Southern jurisdictions responded to large increases in black voter registration by fixing election districts in order to exclude blacks from office. One device utilized was the *at-large* district. A large area being represented, say, by ten elected officials on a legislative body or school board, might be composed of neighborhoods or areas, some of which were predominantly black while others were predominantly white. If the area were divided into districts, with each district electing its own representative, the legislative body would likely include black representatives. But if all ten were elected at large — that is, by the region as a whole — then the white majority, voting along racial lines, could submerge the black vote and all ten representatives would be white.

In areas of longstanding racial hostility, this is precisely what happened, resulting in hundreds of jurisdictions across the South where not a single black candidate had ever been elected, despite rising numbers of registered black voters. Thanks to preclearance and other provisions of the Voting Rights Act, the number of elected black officials in the South has risen dramatically during the years since 1965.

But none of that was automatic or self-executing. It required the efforts of private lawyers, from the American Civil Liberties Union, the Lawyers Committee for Civil Rights Under Law, and other civil-rights groups, working systematically to identify and challenge these devices in jurisdictions throughout the South and elsewhere. When the Supreme Court suggested in a 1980 case that blacks suing under the Voting Rights Act had to prove *intentional* discrimination on the part of state election officials — a burden of proof that could not often be met—a major legislative campaign was launched by a broad coalition of civil-rights groups to persuade Congress to amend the law to make clear that a racially discriminatory *effect* was enough to trigger the law's remedies. In 1982, Congress passed such an amendment.

In 1968—only a few weeks after Martin Luther King, Jr., was murdered on a motel balcony in Memphis, Tennessee, where he had gone to support striking black sanitation workers—Congress passed the Civil Rights Act of 1968, outlawing racial discrimination in the sale, purchase, rental, financing, and advertising of housing. It was the nation's first federal fair-housing law, and it capped the second great era of civil-rights legislation. With the passage of this law, most of the basic legal principles sought by the civil-rights movement were established.

AFFIRMATIVE ACTION—TRYING TO SET THINGS RIGHT

But the residual effects of centuries of slavery and government-sanctioned discrimination supported by terror could not be so easily erased. The removal of legal barriers to equal opportunity and the inclusion of black people as full-fledged citizens proved to be only the first stage in a longer, more painful struggle that continues to this day. Racial exclusion from the benefits of society and the rights of citizenship is certainly no longer nearly total, as once it was, but it still limits the opportunities and stifles the hopes of many black Americans. In many counties of the old South, for example, blacks are still effectively excluded from the political system, even though the blunter instruments of intimidation and formal legal barriers no longer exist. In many school systems, North and South, inequality of education still reigns, as do separate racial patterns of attendance.

In most metropolitan areas, there is still a firm division of the races between city and suburb—what a presidential commission in 1968 called "two increasingly separate Americas"—that cannot be traced to any explicitly racial law, and which is worse now than it was twenty years ago. Unemployment rates for blacks remain disproportionately higher, especially for young males, than corresponding rates for whites. The availability of medical care, which is predominantly tied to employer-provided insurance coverage, is so racially stratified that in 1991 the *Journal of the American Medical Association* called it a racist system. Blacks are disproportionately arrested, disproportionately imprisoned, and disproportionately executed. In 1990, there were more young black men in prison than in college. And homicide is the leading cause of death among black males between the ages of eighteen and thirty.

It began to grow clear, at least to some, that what had been done to black citizens over centuries would not be easily remedied by removing the legal barriers to citizenship. Once, perhaps, that might have been enough. Now it was too late. The destruction that had been visited upon blacks in America was too harsh, too wounding. Like the Marshall Plan, designed to rebuild a shattered Europe after World War II, something more would be required if equal opportunity were to be achieved.

In a 1965 speech at Howard University, President Lyndon B. Johnson said:

Freedom is not enough. You do not wipe away the scars of centuries by saying, "Now, you are free to go where you want, do as you desire, and choose the leaders you please." You do not take a man who for years has been hobbled by chains, liberate him, bring him to the starting line of a race, saying, "You are free to compete with all the others," and still justly believe you have been completely fair. Thus it is not enough to open the gates of opportunity.

The idea of *compensatory opportunity* was not new to American society. After the Civil War, Congress established certain economic and educational programs for which only recently freed slaves and other blacks were eligible. The judgment was made that blacks as a group had suffered a special disadvantage—slavery—and therefore now required special advantages to restore what had been taken away. These programs were swept away in the tidal wave of reaction that reestablished legal barriers to citizenship.

But the principle seemed fair, and in nonracial settings it has been applied without controversy. The GI Bill of Rights and various other special benefits for war veterans after World War II provided special advantages—including extra points on Civil Service examinations—because they had been out of the economic mainstream for three or four years. These special programs did not require veterans to prove any personal disadvantage. Nor were nonveterans eligible for these benefits, even if they could prove they had suffered comparable disadvantages as the result of a war. Instead, society agreed that because all veterans, as a group, had been taken out of the race, all veterans as a group were entitled to various compensatory advantages to help them catch up.

The veterans' program has generally been perceived by most Americans, without controversy, as morally justified. The idea of compensatory opportunity for blacks, however, which came to be known as "affirmative action," was greeted by mounting resistance, charges of "reverse discrimination," and claims that the merit system would be undermined. While mistakes were certainly made in some affirmative-action programs, it is hard to see injustice in the basic idea. Certainly, the disadvantages suffered by blacks as a group were infinitely more severe, more longstanding, and more damaging than those suffered by war veterans.

Moreover, while choosing candidates for college or employment on the basis of merit is a laudable goal, the claim that our society functions as a meritocracy has always been overstated. Colleges have often considered geographic distribution in admitting students, and given special preference to children of alumni or to athletes. Employers have given preference not only to veterans, but also to the children of relatives, friends, and colleagues. Nor have objective standards to determine merit—tests that try to predict which employees or which students will prove successful—proved to be of much use. Such tests often cannot validly predict performance, and often reflect bias themselves. At best, such tests can perhaps be used to determine which candidates are clearly unqualified. The claim that affirmative action is necessarily at odds with prevailing standards of merit and competence has always rested more on myth than on reality.

To many civil-rights advocates, it began to seem that the sharp difference between the way affirmative-action programs were accepted for veterans but rejected for blacks was itself a reflection of racial discrimination. Similarly, the invocation of merit—long honored more in the breach than in the observance—as a reason to oppose efforts to ensure compensatory opportunities for race-disadvantaged people often seemed designed to maintain the advantages that discrimination had secured. The underlying morality of compensatory opportunity was not easy to understand, however, and it provoked what came to be called "white backlash." Racial resentment has never been difficult to arouse in America, and there was no shortage of politicians ready to pander to it for political gain.

But despite substantial opposition, the Supreme Court repeatedly approved affirmative action in principle as a necessary remedy for discrimination, even though it did not always approve every example of it. In a number of key decisions the Court endorsed the idea that in a society that had been so destructively race-conscious for so long, the road to a color-blind society required at least some transitional period during which *constructive* race-conscious remedies would be permitted and, in instances where discriminatory exclusion was persistent, even required.

Today, that idea remains under sustained attack. During the Reagan administration, opponents mounted systematic efforts to overturn the principle of affirmative action—and, indeed, to dilute the force of all the civil-rights laws. Then, in 1989, serious cracks began to appear in the Supreme Court's support of civil-rights remedies. As it did in the late nineteenth century, although to a far lesser extent, the Supreme Court, in a series of decisions, badly undermined the ability of people with claims of discrimination to obtain relief in the courts. In one case, the Court ruled that the Civil Rights Act of 1866 bars discrimination in hiring, but does not bar racial harassment by the employer once a person is hired. In another, the Court changed the rules of proof in employment-discrimination cases so that employers could more easily defend themselves against claims of discrimination, while employees were saddled with much more difficult burdens of proof. These and other decisions prompted one Supreme Court justice, Harry A. Blackmun, to say, "One wonders whether the majority still believes that discrimination is a problem in our society, or even remembers that it ever was."

These decisions suddenly reinterpreted the meaning of civil-rights laws that had stood, and been enforced, for nearly two decades. In 1990, Congress resolved to amend these laws to restore their old meaning with language so clear that the Court could not retreat from it. In October 1990, the new law was passed by both houses, but was vetoed by President George Bush, who characterized it as a "racial quota" law, even though it explicitly prohibited quotas. Congress's attempt to override his veto by a two-thirds majority failed by one vote in the Senate. In 1991, the bill was introduced again, and at this writing, in June 1991, it is still pending.

The struggle for equality of opportunity has shifted from the effort to win the legal rights of citizenship to the effort to gain fair access to society's resources, particularly to jobs, housing, and education; from the fight against crude and savage forms of racial discrimination to the fight against more subtle forms of racial subordination; from claims based solely on race to claims based on an amalgam of race and poverty; from the goal of statistical desegregation to the more elusive goal of true cultural and socioeconomic integration.

Relentless poverty and the loss of hope are not accidents in American life. They are calamities that are not distributed evenly among us; on the contrary, they exist disproportionately among blacks, and there is evidence that this disproportion is getting worse. In large part, it is a consequence of slavery and, perhaps even more, of the century of state-imposed segregation, discrimination, and terror that followed slavery. Few have wanted to admit the uniqueness of what was done to African-Americans in the United States, or to assume the obligation to heal the injuries that remain. Much has been accomplished; indeed, between 1954 and 1968, there was a legal revolution in this country that provided more impetus for the idea of equality than anything that had come before. But there is still much that remains to be done if we mean to reach a time when the color of our skin no longer determines where we work or whether we work, where we live or how well we live, where we go to school or how well we are educated, whether we are treated fairly, and whether our children wake up each morning with a stake in the future and a believable reason to hope.

Toward this end, the courts have contributed little, and have often been destructive, with the shining exception of that brief time beginning in 1954 when the Supreme Court acted as Thomas Jefferson had thought it might on that long-ago day in France when he penned his thoughts to his friend James

Madison. Nor has there been much leadership from Congress, or from the White House, with two exceptions immediately after the Civil War and during the 1960s, when sweeping federal legislation designed to ensure equal rights was passed.

The achievements of the Supreme Court and of Congress during these exceptional periods should never be minimized: they not only established long-denied principles of legal equality, but sustained and nourished the political movement for equal rights as well.

But, in the end, it was the civil-rights movement itself that was the major factor in the struggle to apply the Bill of Rights equally. What equality exists today is a testament to those who refused to give in, who risked everything and often lost everything because they would not accommodate themselves to injustice. They are the heroes of the struggle for equality and the heirs of the ideals with which this nation began and which it has so imperfectly realized: from Frederick Douglass and William Lloyd Garrison to Homer A. Plessy and Rosa Parks; from W. E. B. Du Bois and A. Philip Randolph to Martin Luther King, Jr., and the three young men who ended up in a Mississippi ditch in the summer of 1964; and all those, famous and unknown, who stood with them, who were willing to be beaten, arrested, imprisoned, and even killed until finally the Supreme Court and Congress did their duty and fulfilled their obligations under the Constitution. If there is to be further progress, it is to people like them that we must look.

INCLUDING ALL
AMERICANS

SECRETARY
AND BANK
EXECUTIVES,
DALLAS,
TEXAS, 1965.

THE BETTMANN ARCHIVE

ABOVE: MARCH-
ING FOR THE
RIGHT TO VOTE,
NEW YORK CITY,
1910.

RIGHT: FEMINIST
PARADE, NEW
YORK CITY, 1976.

ABOVE: ARMY
MEDIC BIDS
GOODBYE TO
HER BABY AND
CIVILIAN
HUSBAND
BEFORE LEAVING
FOR ACTIVE
SERVICE IN THE
PERSIAN GULF
WAR. FORT
BENNING,
GEORGIA, 1990.

RIGHT: FEMALE
CONSTRUCTION
WORKER. NEW
YORK CITY, 1989.

TOP: A MOVIE-
INDUSTRY
DELEGATION
JOINS PRO-
CHOICE
LEADERS IN
DEMONSTRA-
TION AGAINST
CUTBACKS IN
THE RIGHT TO
ABORTION.
WASHINGTON,
1989.

ABOVE: PRO-
CHOICE
ADVOCATES
ARGUES WITH
HECKLERS AT
FEMINIST
PARADE. NEW
YORK CITY,
1976.

PRO-LIFE
DEMONSTRATORS
DISPLAY GREATLY
MAGNIFIED
PHOTOGRAPH
ON THE STEPS
OF THE SUPREME
COURT BUILDING.
WASHINGTON,
1991.

(C) COPYRIGHT 1982
BABY BOY, CORONER'S CASE, #82-1901-1
CENTER FOR DOCUMENTATION OF THE AMERICAN HO
PALM SPRINGS, CA 92263

CRAIG DEAN
AND PATRICK
GILL, WHO
HAVE FILED
SUIT AGAINST
THE DISTRICT
OF COLUMBIA
FOR THE RIGHT
TO BE LEGALLY
MARRIED.
WASHINGTON,
1990.

SIGN STENCILED
ON PAVEMENT.
NEW YORK CITY,
1991.

AP / WIDEWORLD PHOTOS

**LEFT: AN AFTER-
HOURS DISCO.
NEW YORK CITY,
1978.**

**ABOVE: SELF-
STYLED DYKES
ON BIKES LEAD
THE 17TH
ANNUAL SAN
FRANCISCO
LESBIAN-GAY
FREEDOM DAY
PARADE, 1986.**

COMMON ROOM, WILLOWBROOK STATE SCHOOL. AFTER A 1972 TELEVISION EXPOSÉ REVEALED NAKED AND NEGLECTED RETARDED CHILDREN LIVING AMIDST FILTH AND DISEASE, CIVIL-LIBERTIES LAWYERS BEGAN A GROUNDBREAKING SUIT THAT LED TO UNPRECEDENTED RIGHTS FOR CHILDREN WITH DISABILITIES. STATEN ISLAND, NEW YORK, 1974.

RESIDENCE FOR
THE ELDERLY.
EVANSTON,
ILLINOIS, 1976.

TOP: ACCUSED
TESTIFIES AT
YOUTHFUL-
OFFENDER TRIAL.
MEMPHIS,
TENNESSEE, 1979.

ABOVE: IN
THE MEMPHIS
JUVENILE-
DETENTION
CENTER. 1979.

INCLUDING ALL AMERICANS

6

THE MOVEMENT FOR RACIAL EQUALITY HAD A STRONG CATALYTIC EFFECT ON other Americans whose rights had long been denied or diluted. The unprecedented application of the Bill of Rights by the Warren Court to situations where it had never been applied before encouraged such people to believe that they, too, could benefit from the Bill of Rights and be brought under its protective umbrella.

SEX DISCRIMINATION

One unexpected addition to the Civil Rights Act of 1964 — a prohibition against sex discrimination in private-sector employment — provided the first significant legal opportunity for women to assert their claims against sex distinctions in job opportunities. Before that, the Constitution certainly hadn't been any help. From the end of the Civil War to 1971, in *every case* in which a claim was made that the Fourteenth Amendment's guarantee of equal protection of the laws applied to women and prohibited legal sex distinctions, the Supreme Court rejected the claim.

The first case appeared before the Court in 1873, only five years after the Fourteenth Amendment was adopted. Myra Bradwell, a married woman, was the editor of the *Chicago Legal News* and had been certified by the Illinois state board of legal examiners as educationally qualified to be admitted to practice law. But when she applied for admission to the Illinois bar so that she could practice law, admission was denied solely because she was a woman. She challenged the denial, and became the first to argue that such a distinction violated the new constitutional guarantee of equal protection of the laws.

The Supreme Court rejected her argument, 8–1. It reaffirmed its decision earlier that year in the Louisiana *Slaughterhouse* case. The states remained free to deny legal equality to their citizens, even though the Fourteenth Amendment seemed to say otherwise.

In rejecting Myra Bradwell's claim, however, the Court also added a wave of gratuitous remarks that revealed the discriminatory attitudes that confronted women at the time, which were to remain embedded in our laws for another hundred years. The "spheres and destinies" of the two sexes were different, three justices said. Men were designed to protect women, while women were "timid" and "delicate" and as a result unfit for many occupations, including law. "The paramount destiny and mission of women," they wrote, "are to fulfill the noble and benign offices of wife and mother. This is the law of the Creator." This attitude led not only to direct restrictions of opportunity for women like Myra Bradwell, but also, ironically, to laws that appeared on their surface to provide special protection for women, but which in practice limited their opportunities and maintained their dependence.

In 1908, for example, the Supreme Court refused to strike down an Oregon law prohibiting women from working more than a specified number of hours in certain industries. The state claimed that the law was intended to protect women, who, it said, were more frail and vulnerable. In fact, such laws, under the guise of protecting women, actually limited their opportunities: men could advance themselves through long hours of work, while women could not—not because of the physical incapacity of any particular woman, but because the law prevented any woman from even trying.

The Court unanimously upheld this law, reflecting the prevailing way that women were viewed. It talked about women's physical weakness and their maternal functions, said that long hours at work would threaten their ability to produce healthy and vigorous children, and declared that this ability had to be protected and preserved by the state out of a concern for the "well-being of the race." The long history of women's dependence upon men proved their lack of self-reliance, the court concluded. Just as discrimination against blacks had produced lower levels of achievement that were then used to justify further discrimination, so the dependence of women, virtually mandated by law and custom, was used to justify laws that sustained their dependence.

This approach dominated constitutional decisions by the Supreme Court, as well as state legislation, up until about twenty years ago. Women were kept off juries, barred by law from a wide range of occupations, and "protected" from long hours, night work, and jobs thought to be too hazardous. Even the right to vote, perhaps the single most critical index of citizenship, was denied. In 1875, the Supreme Court unanimously ruled that although women were citizens, the Fourteenth Amendment, which guaranteed equal protection of the laws to all citizens, did not guarantee women the right to vote. State laws, which on their face gave some citizens (men) the right to vote and denied it to others (women), were found not to have violated the Fourteenth Amendment. From that moment on, it became clear that it would require a constitutional amendment to establish the right of women to vote.

In 1920, the Nineteenth Amendment was adopted, giving women a constitutional basis for the right to vote. This was a victory that capped more than seventy years of political struggle. During that period, women's political groups arose and organized nearly a thousand campaigns designed to win support from legislators for the right to vote. Over two million women participated. The arguments against the Nineteenth Amendment were full of imagined problems: if women could vote, socialism, anarchy, free love, and marital discord would surely follow. Like the imagined fears that would arise to defeat the Equal Rights Amendment in the early 1980s, these fears expressed little more than prejudice and discomfort with change. Such fears, if widely expressed, can often have great impact even if false, because it is impossible to prove that they are false. But in 1920, the movement for equal rights proved too strong, and the voting-rights amendment passed.

After this victory, however, the women's-rights movement lost steam, and other issues such as job discrimination, birth control, and domestic relations were neglected, except by a few. Once the right to vote had been achieved, women did not vote as a bloc, did not support women candidates, and did not for the most part agitate for women's issues in a focused, systematic way. Despite the vote, no significant ground was gained against discrimination in employment, education, credit standards, or family law for a very long time. And for another fifty years, the courts would provide no relief either.

But just as World War II had created social conditions that made it possible for black citizens to make progress toward achieving equal rights, so the war began to undermine the assumption that women belonged exclusively at home, raising children and tending to family chores. Women who had never before worked outside the home began to do so during the war. After the war, changes in the economy greatly expanded jobs in the service sector relative to those in manufacturing, which opened new lines of opportunity for women. Population control became fashionable, and contraceptives were more widely used. More and more, women's lives were not being automatically dominated by child-rearing responsibilities. These trends accelerated into the 1960s.

Then, in 1971, the Supreme Court suddenly and surprisingly departed from its unbroken tradition of upholding sex distinctions in the law. An Idaho law gave men preference over women in deciding who should be the administrator of an estate. Sally Reed challenged that law and the Supreme Court unanimously struck it down, ruling that she had been denied equal protection of the laws as guaranteed by the Fourteenth Amendment. This was the first time the Court had ever struck down a government classification based on sex. Less than two years later, the Court considered a law that discriminated on the basis of sex among people in the military. A male soldier automatically received extra housing and health-care allowances for his wife, without regard to the degree of her dependence, while a female soldier could not receive such allowances for her husband unless she could prove that he provided less than one-fourth of their combined support. The law was not based on the actual fact of dependence, regardless of sex; it assumed female dependence, and apportioned benefits accordingly. The Supreme Court struck that law down, 8–1.

In neither decision did the Court quite decide that sex, like race, was a "suspect" classification requiring the highest degree of judicial skepticism. As a result, the constitutional protection against sexual discrimination was not as strong as that against racial discrimination. In later decisions, the Court confirmed this view, gradually settling on a standard for judging sexual distinctions that was high, but not quite as high as the standard for judging racial distinctions. During the same period, advocates of equal rights for women campaigned for a new constitutional amendment, called the Equal Rights Amendment, that would unambiguously prohibit all discrimination based on sex. Congress passed such an amendment in 1972, but ten years later the deadline for ratification by the states expired without the approval required from three-fourths of them.

The ERA created a great deal of controversy about what its unintended consequences might be in a culture still characterized by a great deal of role differentiation based on sex. Some of this controversy reflected the same sort of imagined fears, driven by political animosity, as had arisen during the fight over the Nineteenth Amendment more than fifty years earlier: women were told they would lose custody of their children or be forced to work outside the home if the ERA were ratified. But some force was also taken out of the ERA movement as a result of the steady victories for equal rights through court decisions and legislative acts during this time.

THE TRAP OF "PROTECTIVE" LEGISLATION

Since the first two Supreme Court decisions in the early 1970s striking down laws reflecting sex distinctions, the Court—even without the ERA—has fairly consistently continued to prohibit laws and practices that use sex as a proxy for other traits. In 1975, the Court struck down a Utah law requiring a parent to support a son until he was twenty-one, but a daughter only until she was eighteen. In the same year, the Court invalidated laws excluding women from jury duty unless they volunteered. And in 1981, the Court rejected a Louisiana law allowing husbands unilaterally to dispose of property they owned jointly with their wives.

As these decisions multiplied, gradually using constitutional principles of equality to erase longstanding sexual distinctions that placed women at a disadvantage, a related question arose: what about laws that appeared to *favor* women? At first, the Supreme Court upheld them. For example, in 1974, it approved a state law that granted a tax benefit to widows, but not widowers. A year later, it permitted a differential "promotion or discharge" policy allowing female naval officers more years of service than males before dismissing them if they had not been promoted. These decisions, now largely discredited, appeared then to give women the best of both worlds: sex distinctions in the law would be struck down if they disadvantaged women and upheld if they benefitted them.

These decisions were soon seen as a trap, the same sort of trap that was implicit in "protective" legislation limiting the number of hours women could work. Most of the distinctions that benefitted women in the short run were based on the premise that women were weaker and necessarily dependent, and required special assistance to survive. This premise was at the root of most sexual discrimination in employment, and it sharply limited equal opportunity for women.

In 1975, the Court began to move away from this idea, began to see that using sex as an automatic substitute for evidence of need was presumptively discriminatory — and in the long run responsible for the denial of equal rights to women. The argument for special advantages, so powerful in the area of race, was more complicated with respect to sex discrimination, because of the long history of apparently benign special protections for women that had actually resulted in restricting their opportunities.

Recognition came first in a case involving the Social Security Act. The act provided money to mothers whose husbands had died, so that they could hire someone to take care of their children when they went to work. But it did not provide such benefits to fathers whose wives had died. The assumption was that a man normally was the main source of income in the family, and therefore, if his wife died, he could afford to hire a paid care-giver for the children, whereas a woman was a secondary source of income at best, and required government assistance to survive when her husband died.

Although this assumption was undoubtedly accurate for many men and women, it still substituted sex for function. Instead of providing benefits for sole surviving parents, it supplied benefits only for widowed mothers. A young man whose wife had died in childbirth, but whose child survived, brought suit to challenge this distinction. The law in the short run disadvantaged men and benefitted women. But it stood for the idea that all women in that situation needed help because they were women, while no men needed help, because they were men. Indeed, in defending the law, the government argued that it was necessary "to offset the adverse economic situation of women." Of course, that adverse economic situation was itself the product of laws and customs defining income-producing work as primarily the man's domain, and child-care as primarily the woman's. Thus did differential opportunity, enforced by law, create justifications for its own perpetuation.

The Supreme Court rejected the government's arguments, unanimously struck down that provision of the Social Security Act, and extended its benefits to men as well as women. In effect, the Court converted the widowed-mother beneficiary into a sole-surviving-parent beneficiary, thereby establishing a sex-neutral classification based on a government assumption of need for all people who found themselves in that situation.

In the wake of this case, a string of decisions confirmed that sex distinctions in all kinds of laws would not be permitted. In 1976, the Court struck down an Oklahoma law that allowed women to buy 3.2 percent beer when they turned eighteen, but prohibited men from doing so until they turned twenty-one. The state justified the law on the ground that young men between the ages of eighteen and twenty-one were more likely to drive while drunk than young women. But the Court ruled that being male was an impermissible "proxy for drinking and driving."

The Oklahoma decision turned out to be one of the most powerful weapons in the campaign to secure equal rights for women, because it established the principle that any distinction based on sex would be subjected to a high degree of scrutiny by the Court and struck down if the Court found that such distinctions were not substantially or appropriately related to an important governmental objective. In this case, the Court conceded that traffic safety was an important government objective, but said it was inappropriate to advance this objective by assuming that all young women were cautious drinkers and safe drivers because they were women, while all men were irresponsible and reckless because they were men.

This case again illustrates the point about how legal rights that protect us all get established. Here is a case that appears to be completely trivial: the right to purchase 3.2 percent beer before you are twenty-one would hardly seem to rank in importance with, say, the Magna Carta. Moreover, the case apparently benefitted men, not women. But like the Magna Carta, the legal principle established in this case extended far beyond its immediate context and beneficiary. It went on to be used by women over and over again to secure important rights for themselves that the law had not previously recognized. This often happens in constitutional litigation: cases that seem unimportant, or appear to benefit people we don't care much about or even despise, end up determining fundamental rights for all of us.

Following the Oklahoma case, the Court confirmed the legal principle it had established. In 1977, it struck down another Social Security distinction based on sex when it rejected the policy of automatically providing death benefits to widows, but not to widowers unless they could prove that their wives had provided three-quarters of their combined support. Again, the immediate beneficiaries here were men, but as Justice John Paul Stevens said, the discrimination against males in this instance was "merely the accidental byproduct of the traditional way of thinking about females." This "traditional way of thinking about females" needed to be struck down before equal rights and equal opportunity for women could become possible. Two years later, the Court invalidated a law requiring husbands, but never wives, to pay alimony; and in 1980, the Court confirmed its earlier decision when it declared unconstitutional a Missouri law that provided death benefits to all widows, but again only to those widowers who could prove they had been dependent on their wives' incomes.

All these cases involved the underlying notion that a woman's proper place was in the home, caring for children, while men went out and did the world's work. Regardless of what specific laws were struck down in these cases, and who initially benefitted from them, what was really struck down was that notion. For the first time in a hundred years, the Supreme Court seemed willing to rule that the Fourteenth Amendment sharply limited the discretion of the government to make distinctions based on sex. It came a century too late for Myra Bradwell, but she would no doubt have been pleased to know that when it did come, one of the Supreme Court justices participating in the decision, Sandra Day O'Connor, was a woman.

As with racial cases, however, the Court did not entirely rule out practices that created advantages for women, provided the government could show that such advantages were narrowly designed for compensatory purposes: to remedy a pattern of sex discrimination or to make up for the effects of past discrimination. Discriminatory laws that reflected little more than the traditional view of a woman's proper role would be struck down, even if they momentarily benefitted women, while sex-conscious measures intended to remedy the effects of discrimination might be upheld.

Sometimes conflicts between rights arose. In 1979, Helen Feeney challenged a Massachusetts law that compensated military veterans for disadvantages they had suffered while in service by giving civil-service jobs to veterans with minimal passing grades in preference to nonveterans with high, or even perfect, scores on their civil-service examinations. When such preferences have been given to blacks or women they have been controversial, although no controversy existed, then or now, about such preferences for veterans.

Helen Feeney did not challenge the propriety of preferences for veterans in general. Nor could she claim that the law intended any sex distinction. Female veterans benefitted just as male veterans did, and male nonveterans were as disadvantaged by the program as Helen Feeney. But if the law was not sex-discriminatory in its own terms, its effect certainly was. Ninety-eight percent of Massachusetts veterans were male, and this was in large part due to the fact that official government policy had excluded women and sharply restricted their military opportunities through the use of quotas and other devices. If the government had restricted women from this line of work, could it now make matters worse by providing lifetime preferences in civilian jobs to those who had benefitted from the original exclusion of women, thus compounding the discrimination?

By a 7–2 vote, the Supreme Court said yes, and rejected Helen Feeney's claim. They conceded the discrimination effect, but said it wasn't intentional, even though it could have been foreseen. And two years later, the Court cemented this sort of discriminatory effect by ruling that it did not violate the Fourteenth Amendment to draft men, but not women, into military service. In short, the Court basically deferred to the government's judgment in military matters, as it often does. The mere invocation of "military necessity" by the government has usually been enough to cause the Court to abandon scrutiny, as it did with the Japanese-American internment program during World War II.

Yet in the draft case, the Court's willingness to defer seemed strangely reflexive. For one thing, no war was imminent; indeed, no military draft was imminent. The law challenged only required young men to register, in case at some future date a draft should be required. Moreover, the president and the Joint Chiefs of Staff had urged that women be registered. It was hard to see what military judgment the Court had in mind. More likely the exclusion of women was merely another reflection of the traditional way of thinking about females, especially in the context of one of the last strongholds of male exclusivity. The Court, as it has so often done, reflected prejudice instead of curbing it as the Constitution commanded.

Fortunately, in this area, as in others, rights are not secured by courts alone. By 1991, women were participating in military actions, such as the Persian Gulf War, in unprecedented numbers, often shoulder to shoulder with their male counterparts. The sight of women prisoners of war returning home with their male colleagues after the war was over undoubtedly did more to further equal rights, at least in the military, than any court decision did.

EQUAL JOB OPPORTUNITY

Equal opportunity for women in employment, especially in the private sector, has become a major focus of both legislation and judicial attention during the past two decades. Because of the continuing vitality of the "state action" doctrine, attacks on private-sector discrimination have relied on the Civil Rights Act of 1964 and its amendments, not on the Constitution directly, although the Fourteenth Amendment authorizes Congress to pass laws like the Civil the Civil Rights Act to limit private-sector discrimination. Explicit exclusion from jobs on the basis of sex is now clearly illegal, and has been for some time. Less clear is what constitutes sex discrimination when the exclusion is not based overtly on sexual distinctions. The discriminatory effect of rules that do not explicitly mention sex—like the veterans'-preference rules that Helen Feeney challenged—has been the subject of much controversy and more than a few convoluted court decisions.

Rules relating to pregnant women, which exclude them from work or from benefits associated with work, obviously affect only women. At first the Supreme Court found such rules unfair and unconstitutional. For example, when an Ohio school board required a pregnant teacher to take maternity leave without pay five months before her child was due, without inquiring into her actual fitness to continue working beyond that date, the Court struck down the rule, 7–2. It did the same with a four-month rule imposed by a Virginia school board. The Court struck down these particular rules because they rigidly barred all pregnant women from working after a certain point, without inquiring into whether a specific woman was actually no longer able to work.

But the Court never accepted the idea that it was discriminatory to exclude women, and only women, simply because they had the ability to become pregnant. A year later, the Court similarly ruled that women who were willing and able to work, but who had been forced to leave their jobs, could not for that reason be denied unemployment benefits by the state. On the other hand, the Court ruled that a government disability-insurance program, which replaced income for employees temporarily disabled, was not required to pay benefits to women temporarily disabled by pregnancy—although it paid men temporarily disabled by, say, a vasectomy. Two years later, in the context of private-sector employment, the Court ruled that General Electric could exclude its pregnant employees from its group-disability coverage without violating the Civil Rights Act's prohibition against sex discrimination. The Court actually said that this exclusion did not discriminate against women because all "nonpregnant persons," women as well as men, were treated alike!

It was hard to make much sense out of these conflicting decisions, and they left the law in disarray. No one knew when or whether a particular rule that disadvantaged pregnant women was considered unlawful discrimination. In 1978, Congress seemed to have cleared up the confusion by amending the Civil Rights Act of 1964 to say explicitly that distinctions based on pregnancy were to be treated no differently from distinctions based on sex. Yet even that did not quite end the controversy. Now employers began to promulgate rules ostensibly designed to protect the well-being of fetuses from hazardous substances to which women might be exposed at work. Curiously, or perhaps not so curiously, these rules often excluded women from jobs they had not traditionally been allowed to hold.

For example, in the late 1970s and early 1980s, the American Cyanamid Company barred all women of childbearing age—whether or not they were pregnant or even married—from jobs manufacturing paint at a plant in West Virginia. The company claimed that fetuses could be damaged by lead and other toxic substances. Out of a professed concern for the health of children yet unconceived (and to protect against their own liability in case such children were born with defects), the company banned all women of childbearing age from these jobs *unless they could prove they were sterile.*

Several women who needed the jobs had themselves sterilized in order to meet the company's requirements. Later, along with other women, they sued the company, claiming that its policy violated the law's prohibition against sex discrimination. A long and complex pretrial investigation ensued. Studies were produced to show that men's reproductive organs were affected by toxic substances in a way that could also lead to damaged babies, but no similar rule applied to them. Expert testimony was offered to show that it was possible to provide a safer workplace where exposure to toxic substances was limited, a remedy preferable to firing women or forcing them to be sterilized. In the end, the company settled the suit and paid a large sum of money to the women to compensate them for the damage they had suffered. So the case never reached the Supreme Court.

Policies like that of American Cyanamid continued at other companies, however, potentially affecting as many as twenty million women. In 1991, a similar case finally reached the Supreme Court, this one involving a Milwaukee company, Johnson Controls, which manufactured automobile batteries. In 1982, the company had adopted a policy barring all women, regardless of age or plans to bear children, from certain manufacturing jobs unless they could show proof of sterility. The Court unanimously agreed that Johnson Controls' policy violated the Civil Rights Act of 1964, and struck it down. A majority thought that the act prohibited all so-called fetal-protection policies. Justice Harry A. Blackmun, writing for the majority, said, "Decisions about the welfare of future children must be left to the parents who conceive, bear, support, and raise them rather than to the employers who hire those parents. Women as capable of doing their jobs as their male counterparts may not be forced to choose between having a child and having a job."

PREGNANCY, PERSONAL FREEDOM, AND ABORTION RIGHTS

These decisions were important because they helped to determine whether women could in fact participate fully and equally in the nation's political and economic life, or whether their ability to bear children would result in fewer rights, less opportunity, and, in the end, second-class citizenship. In that context, the argument over whether pregnancy discrimination was a form of sexual discrimination ultimately led to the core issue of abortion, easily the most persistently intense constitutional controversy of this century.

The right to decide whether to become pregnant, and, once pregnant, whether to continue the pregnancy, has been primarily formulated as a right of personal autonomy, what John Stuart Mill called personal sovereignty. According to this formulation, an individual woman cannot be forced to do what the state wishes with respect to her reproductive decisions. She cannot be prevented from using contraceptives if she wishes to avoid pregnancy, or from having an abortion should an unwanted pregnancy occur. Nor can she be prevented by the government, as women are in some countries, from having more than a government-approved number of children. Over herself and her own body she is sovereign, and the government may not intervene.

This argument—that a woman, and she alone, should have the right to choose whether to continue an unwanted pregnancy—was no ordinary issue of personal autonomy, however. Forcing a pregnant woman to bear a child was seen as the most severe invasion of a woman's bodily integrity, often involving substantial physical burdens and sometimes irreparable harm. The intensity of feeling by proponents of the right to choose also derived from the fact that women were, and are still, expected to bear the major responsibility for child care. In this context, unwanted parenthood can sharply limit a woman's opportunities and permanently alter her personal development. Laws requiring this result were therefore seen as the most discriminatory of all laws affecting women. The right to choose thus became the nonnegotiable battle cry of a broader movement for women's equality.

These arguments immediately collided with another: perhaps people ought to be sovereign over their own bodies, but when a woman becomes pregnant, it is not only *her* body that is at stake, but an unborn child's body as well. According to this line of argument, abortion is murder, indistinguishable from infanticide. Just as it would be unthinkable to suggest that a mother might have a legal right to kill a newborn child, so it is unthinkable to suggest that a woman may choose to abort a fetus.

The clash between these two views inevitably brought theological differences to the surface. At issue is the question, When does life begin? The issue is even more complicated than that. One might concede that the fetus, or even the fertilized ovum, had "life" without conceding that such "life" was the equivalent, either morally or legally, of the sort of life we have in mind when we think of a born child. In the end, confronting these arguments honestly means conceding that the question of when human life begins is a matter more of belief than of fact, more of faith than of science: ultimately a theological question.

And in fact, different religions hold different beliefs on the subject. Some believe strongly that human life begins at the moment of conception; this religious belief causes them to think of abortion as murder, at *any* stage of pregnancy. Others believe that human life begins at the stage that used to be called "quickening" and today is called "viability"—the stage at which a fetus, if removed, could be sustained and allowed to develop into a child. This belief implies a right to abortion, but not beyond a certain stage of fetal development. Still others believe that human life begins at birth.

What few want to admit is that the struggle over the right to choose abortion is in large part a struggle over whether the religious beliefs of some should be codified into law and imposed on others who do not share those beliefs. Hundreds of years ago, it was common for religious beliefs to be transformed into laws that severely punished nonbelievers who transgressed them. That seems wrong to us now, but it didn't seem wrong to most people then— except to those who suffered. Indeed, much of the history of the struggle for religious liberty is about the effort to prevent religious doctrine from being converted into the force of law.

Of course, many secular laws *coincide* with religious commands and sometimes even derive from them. "Thou shalt not kill," one of the Ten Commandments, is reflected by and coincides with secular laws prohibiting murder. On the other hand, it would clearly be improper to enact a law making it a crime to eat pork because those religions which forbid it became powerful enough to cause such a law to be enacted. The fact that a secular law is consistent with a religious belief should not by itself invalidate it. Secular laws against murder enjoy a universal public consensus, for example. But in the absence of such a consensus or, even more, when there are deep divisions in society, including religiously based divisions, law should not be used to impose the religious beliefs of some upon others. That is why the First Amendment to our Constitution was intended to strictly separate church and state, to keep the legislature from establishing any religious belief.

For those who see the struggle over abortion in these terms, the solution is clear: if the question of when human life begins is essentially a question of religious belief, which deeply divides society, then the government must stay out of it, must pass no law nor take anyone's side in the dispute, and instead permit people to exercise their choices as their own individual beliefs command. But the Supreme Court has never seen it that way, or even seriously entertained the validity of that mode of analysis. On the few occasions when a serious effort has been made to present such an analysis—in one instance by Justice John Paul Stevens in a 1989 dissent—the Court either has failed to address the argument or has summarily and without much consideration swept it aside.

The Court has also chosen not to see the abortion issue in terms of sexual equality. Yet that is undoubtedly how many women see it. A woman's ability to decide whether to bear a child is crucially related to her ability to control and plan her life; to maximize her freedom of choice in other areas; to decide when, whom, and whether to marry; and to pursue economic, educational, or political opportunities. And much of the opposition to the right to choose abortion has come from those who would like nothing better than to keep women "in their place," and who remain as uncomfortable with the prospect of sexual equality as many white Southerners once were with racial equality.

In 1973, the Court decided two cases—*Roe v. Wade* and *Doe v. Bolton*—that for the first time attempted to determine whether the Constitution permitted the government to prohibit abortions or to restrict them. In these cases, the Court struck down a Texas law prohibiting all abortions except to save a pregnant woman's life and also invalidated parts of a Georgia law restricting the right of a woman to have an abortion. Although the Court articulated a constitutional doctrine of personal autonomy, its decision in these cases also reflected political compromise. Essentially, the Court extended its reasoning in the 1965 contraceptive case. If a man and a woman had the right to decide whether to beget a child, then a woman had the right to decide to bear it once she became pregnant. These were private decisions, not to be intruded upon by the government.

However, the Court recognized that the issue of abortion was more complex than the contraceptive case. There was the question of the woman's health and the question of the point at which the developing fetus became able to live and develop outside the womb. The Court ruled that the government had a legitimate interest in both these questions, which limited the right of the woman to choose whether to continue a pregnancy. During the first three months of pregnancy, the abortion procedure was very safe, and therefore the Court decided that no special government regulation to protect the health of the woman could justifiably limit her freedom to decide to end the pregnancy. Similarly, the fetus was unable to live and develop outside the womb during the first three months. So during this time, the government may not intrude. In the second trimester, the fetus is still incapable of living outside the womb. But the abortion procedure at this later stage of pregnancy can be more risky, and therefore the government may constitutionally impose reasonable regulations to protect the woman's health. During the third trimester, the fetus is presumed to be viable, and therefore the government has a legitimate interest in potential life at this stage and may prohibit abortion entirely except to save the women's health or life.

This schematic decision reads more like a detailed statute passed by a legislature than a statement of clear and coherent constitutional principle.

Making legal distinctions based on the viability of the fetus was not itself novel; historically, abortion was not a crime, for example, until after "quickening." But if the Court had examined the abortion issue in terms of sex discrimination, it would have had a much clearer doctrinal way to set constitutional limits on what is in part a political dispute over the proper role of women in society, and whether they should be in fact equal. And by analyzing the dispute in terms of personal autonomy without confronting and deciding the issue of religious belief, the Court has been unable to resolve the fundamental question, even on its own terms. As a result, both the Court and the right to an abortion have been buffeted by the winds of political change much more than they might have been. Today more and more questions affecting the right to reproductive autonomy, especially who has access to that right, are being fought out in dozens of state legislatures. Meanwhile, the basic question of why legislatures should be permitted *any* special authority in this field, beyond the authority they normally exercise to protect health and safety in all other medical procedures, remains unanswered.

In the end, the answer may well be provided by the political process before it is provided by the courts. And the entire problem may be altered by developing views about the importance of population control. It is even possible that in the future, reproductive freedom may assert itself as a right to bear children in the context of a government decision to limit childbirth as a means of controlling population size. This has already happened in other countries.

Finally, technology may redefine the problem. Developing neonatal techniques are not likely to significantly alter the point at which a fetus becomes viable. But once a pill is available that can prevent implantation in the uterine wall of a fertilized ovum, thereby requiring far fewer occasions when women need medical assistance to limit their own pregnancies, the government's ability to detect such activity as well as its interest in doing so may diminish sharply. Full equality for women, once they are released from the chains of unwanted and uncontrolled pregnancies, may well result more from such developments than from the resolution by the courts of questions of personal autonomy and the proper limits on government authority.

SEXUAL ORIENTATION

One of the final frontiers of the struggle for equal rights involves people who love people of the same sex. Such citizens remain subject to criminal sanctions (which, however, are rarely enforced) and pervasive discrimination in employment, housing, and a wide variety of social benefits. Although today such people are labeled homosexuals, as if they were fundamentally different from other people, in fact both the concept of homosexuality and the word itself are relatively recent, having been invented in the mid-nineteenth century. Before then, sexual activity with someone of the same sex was something a person *did*, but it did not define what or who that person *was*.

Sexual activity between men, for example, was widely believed to be immoral and illegal before 1870, but not generally more so than the same sexual practices between men and women. In 1791, when the Bill of Rights was adopted, eleven of the original thirteen states prohibited anal intercourse, but only three singled out sexual acts between men. The other eight prohibited such sexual acts between men and women as well, including men and women who were married to each other. Moreover, none of these statutes prohibited oral sex. In 1868, when the Fourteenth Amendment was adopted, no additional states had singled out same-sex sodomy for special prohibition. By that time, thirty-two of the thirty-seven states prohibited sodomy, but most outlawed sodomy between men and women as well. According to at least one legal treatise written as late as 1893, anal intercourse was considered to be a crime even if committed by a man and his wife. If the wife consented, she was considered to be an accomplice to this crime. And oral sex was still not generally believed to be included; in seven states, it was explicitly excluded from the definition of sodomy.

So until the late nineteenth century, no legal distinction had been made between homosexual sodomy and heterosexual sodomy: it was the act that was prohibited, regardless of who committed it. Homosexuals as such were not singled out and homosexuality as a thing apart was nowhere legally defined. This was generally true in ancient times as well. Sexual relations between men were widely tolerated in ancient Rome, for example, and were not outlawed anywhere in the Roman Empire until the sixth century. In the year 533, sexual acts between men were prohibited, and became punishable by death, but even then homosexuality was not singled out: adultery was also prohibited and made punishable by death. Thus, the prohibition of sexual acts between men was not special, but rather part of a larger prohibition against a wide variety of sexual behavior considered to be immoral.

This remained true until the late thirteenth century. Before then, homosexual activity was completely legal in most of Europe. And until about 1300, church law paralleled secular law, condemning homosexual activity only to the extent that it also condemned other nonmarital sexual activity and noncoital sexual activity within marriage.

The origin of most of these laws proscribing sexual activity was ecclesiastical. Sodomy, adultery, and masturbation were all condemned because the church believed that sex outside of marriage and for any purpose other than procreation was a sin. Not until 1533 did sodomy become a secular crime in England, not because the state suddenly acquired a new secular reason to prevent such sexual behavior, but because after Henry VIII broke with the Roman Catholic Church, the state had simply taken over much that had before been within ecclesiastical jurisdiction. Even then, sodomy was not defined in a way that exclusively targeted homosexual behavior. The law did not prohibit oral sex; at the same time, it prohibited "unnatural" penetration between men and women as well as between men. The laws against sodomy in sixteenth-century England thus simply reflected prevailing religious beliefs about the appropriate role of sex. Sex for pleasure among consenting adults, sex that was not intended to create children, was believed to be a sin, and this belief was transformed into laws that made it a crime for anyone to be different or act differently.

This tradition was carried over to America by the colonists. If there were any proponents of liberty who spoke out strongly against it, history has not recorded their protest. In 1655, for example, the Colony of New Haven, which generally followed the Massachusetts Bay Colony's "Body of Liberties" in establishing its laws, not only prohibited sex between men, but also made it a crime punishable by death to engage in lesbianism, heterosexual anal intercourse, or masturbation. The only known attempt during the revolutionary period to liberalize this attitude was made by Thomas Jefferson in 1777, when he wrote a Virginia bill that would have reduced the penalty for sodomy from death to castration for men and the cutting of a large hole in the noses of women. And even this "liberal" bill was not enacted.

Not until much later was oral sex explicitly prohibited. This did not happen in England until 1885, and in America about a decade later. But with very few exceptions, these changes in the law did not single out homosexual behavior either. The majoritarian view that any sexual conduct for purposes other than procreation was an "unnatural pleasure" prevailed and became embedded in our legal tradition. So in America, this tradition led not only to sodomy laws that proscribed common sexual practices between married men and women as well as between members of the same sex, but also to laws that made adultery a crime, made the sale of contraceptives a crime, and made abortion a crime. The foundation of all these laws was the belief that sex outside of marriage or sex for pleasure even within marriage was a sin, and therefore could be made a crime. When in 1965 the state of Connecticut sought to justify its prohibition of contraceptives, for example, it did so in part by claiming an interest in discouraging sex outside of marriage.

All these laws raised a fundamental constitutional question: Why is it the government's business to intrude upon such intensely personal, intimate behavior among consenting adults? For a long time no one even asked this question, at least not in court. For one thing, the subject itself was taboo and could hardly be discussed in public. Although extramarital sex, oral sex, and anal sex were widely practiced, such practices could not easily be openly admitted. For another, if anyone thought of challenging laws that criminalized such behavior by invoking the Bill of Rights, they were quickly discouraged by the fact that until the mid-twentieth century the Bill of Rights did not apply to state laws.

During the early 1960s, all this began to change. A broad change in sexual mores preceded changes in the law. Women began to move strongly toward legal equality, and that included sexual and reproductive independence. New contraceptive technologies were developed and made widely available. And people began to insist openly on the right to be let alone, on the right to make personal decisions without government interference, and on the right to decide for themselves, together with those close to them, how to live. "Personal sovereignty" became a popular idea, and increasingly the old laws prohibiting certain sexual behavior were openly violated, and fell into disuse.

The Supreme Court's 1965 decision striking down a Connecticut law that made it a crime for married couples to buy and use contraceptives both reflected and encouraged this trend. Seven years later, the Court extended this constitutional protection to unmarried people. These decisions created a zone of personal sovereignty that insulated sexual behavior among consenting adults from government intrusion.

KEEPING THE GOVERNMENT OUT OF THE BEDROOM

Nonetheless, these decisions proved to be of little help to lesbians and gay men. They were widely seen not as broad protections for personal sovereignty, but as more limited protections for sexual privacy, insulating the bedroom from government surveillance and intrusion. This was a great victory, but not for gay people. Heterosexuals strolling arm in arm in public could not automatically be targeted; even if a local district attorney were inclined to prosecute heterosexuals for engaging in forbidden sexual practices, he could not invade people's bedrooms in the dead of night to gather evidence and he could not infer such illegal behavior from public displays of affection between heterosexuals.

Public displays of affection between gay people, on the other hand, could lead to plausible, indeed highly probable, inferences about illegal behavior behind closed doors. If the Court's decisions protected only sexual privacy, then to be safe, most gays would have to hide themselves from public view. This defensive strategy worked: gay people who remained discreet in public suffered no serious likelihood of prosecution, and also escaped other social punishments. So the issue for them involved more than sexual privacy; indeed, it was the opposite of privacy, involving in some ways a First Amendment right of expression.

Imagine, for example, that Jews or Moslems—or, in eighteenth-century terms, Sectarian Baptists—were to be permitted their beliefs and practices only so long as they remained hidden from public view. Religious beliefs and practices would be permitted under this imagined regime, but public expression of such beliefs would remain a crime: no Stars of David; no Moslem clothing; no visible churches or synagogues. No American would today consider such a regime constitutionally permissible. Yet that was precisely the situation gay men and women faced, and in many places still face.

Being open about one's homosexuality also triggered other disabilities: discrimination in employment, in housing, in education, and in public accommodations. Gay people could not be open because they could not risk such discrimination, as long as no legal remedies to protect them existed. The Fourteenth Amendment, which had only just begun to realize its intended potential to end discrimination against blacks and women, was not likely soon to prevent discrimination against gays. Until very recently, all the statutes that outlawed discrimination against blacks and women failed to do so against gays. Without legal remedies, gay people feared the consequences of disclosure, which were real and often severe. The rights the rest of society took for granted had to be repressed. Expressing affection for someone you loved — even by a glance or a hug, or by holding hands — was something to avoid. What other people cherished, gay people were forced to fear. What was for others a source of joy became for gays a source of punishment.

Moreover, the law not only failed to protect gays against discrimination, but also actively imposed inequality upon them. For example, the law prohibits gay people from getting married. This is no small matter. Two gays who make the same personal commitments to each other that heterosexuals make — to believe in each other, trust in each other, defend each other, and support each other through bad times as well as good — may nonetheless not participate in the legal benefits and protections of marriage, not because there is any deficit in their personal relationship, but because the government says no.

Why should the government be allowed to do that? Is the fact that a majority of Americans don't approve of such relationships and would not themselves enter into them a sufficient warrant for the government to intrude? Serious consequences follow from the inability to marry. Medical insurance is unavailable for partners who are not spouses. Hospital visitation rights when one partner is ill may be denied. Apartment leases do not easily pass to the surviving partner when death ends a relationship. Tax benefits for joint income are denied. And loving relationships have to bear the burden of official government disapproval.

Many, perhaps most, Americans consider these questions unimportant. However, if the government can intrude into such intimate personal decisions, it can do so in a way that affects all Americans. And it has. For a long time, miscegenation laws prohibited interracial marriage. Laws have long existed, some still on the books, that make adultery a crime, that prohibit fornication, that outlaw unmarried people, including heterosexuals, from living together, or that punish children born out of wedlock. The so-called illegitimacy laws, originally designed to ensure male dominance by locating the generational transfer of wealth and status in the father, also survived because they expressed the majority's moral belief in marriage as a condition of cohabitation and childbirth. Many of the sodomy laws still on the books in nearly half the states prohibit sexual practices that are common between men and women, even when they are married.

All Americans have a stake in keeping the government out of their lives, in constitutionally prohibiting the government from intruding into intimate matters. But the general question of whether the government should have the power in the first instance to enforce the moral beliefs of the majority on people who are or want to be different remains unsettled, and threatens us all. In 1976, for example, a lawsuit was filed to challenge Virginia's sodomy law as a violation of the Fourteenth Amendment's guarantee of equal protection of the laws. The case was dismissed by the lower federal court and the dismissal was summarily affirmed, without a written opinion, by the Supreme Court. Ten years later, in *Bowers v. Hardwick,* the Court upheld Georgia's sodomy law by a 5–4 vote. The case arose in 1982, after Michael Hardwick was arrested in his own bedroom while engaged in oral sex with another man. He and his partner spent ten humiliating hours in jail, but were never prosecuted. Not relishing the prospect of another such experience, Hardwick filed suit in federal court, challenging the constitutionality of Georgia's law.

Although the law was challenged by a gay man, the law itself prohibited heterosexuals as well, including married heterosexuals, from engaging in oral sex. So the case was not only about the right of people of the same sex to make love to each other; it raised the broader question of whether *all* consenting adults had a right to engage in certain sexual activity privately without fear of criminal prosecution. As Justice John Paul Stevens pointed out in dissent, Georgia's law prohibited all adults from sexual behavior not designed to produce children. Surely, he said, the Constitution contradicts this.

In fact, the Supreme Court had said as much in a number of previous cases. The Court had already established the right of heterosexuals to use contraceptives and to decide whether to beget or bear a child. Thus, the right of heterosexuals to have sexual relations for pleasure or to express love had already been recognized by the Court. The Georgia law explicitly prohibited such relations. How could it be upheld without undermining the Court's prior decisions and the rights of all Americans as well? Justice Byron White, who wrote the majority decision, ignored this question. He also ignored the language of the statute, and pretended that the law outlawed only homosexual sodomy. In fact, Justice White said explicitly that the case was trying to establish "a fundamental right to engage in homosexual sodomy." What was really at stake, however, was the larger question of whether the government could constitutionally intrude upon the sexual intimacy of all Americans.

The answer to this question, had it been honestly confronted, would surely have been no. It is hard to believe that Georgia's law would have survived challenge had it been used to arrest a married couple engaged in oral sex in the privacy of their bedroom. In fact, the law had never been used against heterosexuals, although it could have. So it was convenient for Justice White to avoid the larger question and pretend that the law applied only to homosexuals.

In finding such a law constitutional, he had to distort history as well. First, White ruled that the Bill of Rights couldn't possibly protect what Michael Hardwick did, because at the time it was adopted, "sodomy was … forbidden by the laws of the original thirteen states." He was wrong: it was forbidden by only eleven of the states, and only three singled out homosexual sodomy; none prohibited oral sex, which was what Hardwick had been charged with. Second, White ruled that in 1868, when the Fourteenth Amendment was passed, "all but five of the thirty-seven states had criminal sodomy laws." Again, most did not single out homosexuals and none prohibited oral sex. White made the same mistake when he relied on ancient laws and traditions. Finally, White suggested that the state of Georgia specifically intended to prohibit homosexual activity. The opposite is closer to the truth: the statute applied to certain sexual conduct—whether engaged in by homosexuals or heterosexuals. If the words of the law itself were to be used as a guide, one would have to conclude that Georgia did not believe homosexual sodomy to be more immoral or illegal than heterosexual sodomy.

White's reliance on history to support the majority's ruling was, at best, shaky. One commentator called it "one of the most transparently unprincipled exercises of judicial power in recent years." And Justice Stevens said that if Georgia had selectively enforced its law only against homosexuals, for no discernible reason other than prejudice, then it should be struck down as a denial of equal protection of the laws, as guaranteed by the Fourteenth Amendment. Indeed, the Court's 5–4 decision seemed itself to reflect little more than prejudice, or at least a willingness to defer to prejudice. The *Bowers* decision, of course, was only the latest example of the Court's tendency to reflect conventional majoritarian moral beliefs instead of developing coherent constitutional principles to protect people who are different.

One need only recall the racial prejudice that pervasively infected the Court's language in the *Dred Scott* and *Plessy* cases or the prejudicial view of women reflected in the *Bradwell* case to conclude that what the Court did in *Bowers* was both typical and, it is to be hoped, temporary. But the word "temporary" ought to comfort no one; it took a hundred years before changing public mores and different judicial decisions finally provided relief to the victims of prejudice based on race and sex. No one expects the current Supreme Court to reverse itself and strike down sodomy laws anytime soon, but it is significant that Justice Lewis F. Powell, Jr., now retired, has stated that he thought he made a mistake when he cast the deciding vote in the 5–4 *Bowers* decision.

Today, despite the Supreme Court, there is wider public tolerance of gay people. Yet tolerance is not the same as a legal right. Tolerance depends on the goodwill of the majority, while a legal right limits the majority by law. Tolerance can be present in some places and absent in others; law seeks a uniform standard. Tolerance by some is no remedy for discrimination — or even violence — from others; law seeks to establish rights by providing enforceable remedies wherever discrimination occurs. Beneath discrimination and intolerance lie fear and fantasy. As Justice Louis D. Brandeis said long ago and in another context, "Men feared witches and burned women." Much racial violence, and certainly most violence against homosexuals, has been the result of the deeply held personal fears and insecurities of those who engage in such violence — fears about their future, about their status, about their own sexuality. It is the function of law to protect minorities — whether religious, political, racial, or sexual — against such fears when they break out into overt acts of discrimination or violence.

The struggle for equal rights has always taken place on the frontier of the legal wilderness where liberty meets power. Liberty has claimed much of that wilderness now, but the frontier always lies ahead of us. Constitutional principles may remain invariant, but the process of extending them moves much too slowly. The frontier of liberty may have expanded far beyond where it began. But for those without rights, it always seems somehow on the horizon, just beyond their reach.

TRADITIONAL RIGHTS IN UNTRADITIONAL SETTINGS

In eighteenth-century America, the government consisted of the political institutions of the state; the individuals whose liberty needed protection against those institutions were citizens. Two hundred years later, the government has grown to include the social institutions of caring: public schools, mental hospitals, public-housing authorities, developmental centers for the retarded, foster-care agencies for children, nursing homes for the aged, and welfare agencies for the poor.

A common phrase, "social services," arose to describe these institutions, and they came to be widely perceived, especially by political liberals, as entirely humanitarian and benevolent, as an undifferentiated and untroublesome so-

social extension of humanity's best individual instincts. If it was natural—indeed imperative—for individuals to love and provide care for their infant children or for those members of their family who had become helpless through age or other natural calamity, then it was just as natural, and nearly as uncomplicated, for society to love and provide care for those who needed it and could not otherwise get it.

This undifferentiated view of social services tended to blind people, often including those who generally supported civil liberties, to certain unintended consequences of their good works. Because their motives were benevolent, their ends good, and their purpose caring, they often assumed the posture of parents toward the recipients of their largesse. They failed utterly to resist the impulse toward paternalism, and expanded their power to establish *dominion* over people's lives. Dominion became legitimate: those who managed social services came to enjoy a degree of discretionary power over their clients that normally only parents are allowed over their children. As a result, they infantilized those they intended to help, and denied them their rights.

Until the clients of social-service institutions rebelled in the 1960s, no one looked with skepticism at these good works. No legal restraints were built into the delivery systems of social services. The system of law constructed to protect citizens' rights by restraining the power of public officials did not apply in the context of social services. The fiction arose, often advanced by social-service professionals themselves, that the interests of clients were identical to the interests of the agencies. The view that the early Americans brought to their understanding of government—that power and liberty were antagonists—played no part in our understanding of social services. Vast discretionary powers thus came to be vested in an army of civil servants, appointed by examination and organized into huge service bureaucracies, which began quietly but surely to trespass upon the private lives and rights of millions of citizens. If any of those citizens complained about such trespassing, for a long time no one listened.

Many people, though decidedly not children, came routinely to depend, as if they were children, upon social services provided by the state for their daily sustenance, and sometimes for survival itself. From a direction wholly unanticipated by the early Americans, government power thus came to touch millions of people, and in ways that clearly violated the Bill of Rights. Sometimes the violations were substantial and the intrusions nearly total. During the 1970s, for example, there was much public debate about nursing homes, increasingly used as residences for elderly people in a society that no longer harbored them within extended families. Much of the debate concentrated upon the quality of care provided, or upon fiscal fraud. What few people noticed, however, was the impact on the residents of institutional pressures inherent even in "good" nursing homes.

Nursing homes had an interest—a legitimate interest—in getting paid for the services they provided. That also should have disqualified them from acting as impartial protectors of aged people's assets. Nonetheless, nursing homes often controlled the financial assets of their patients, manipulating those assets to their own ends and to the detriment of their patients'. Similarly, a competent elderly resident might desire the freedom to come and go, to socialize, to have visitors and activities, to have privacy, while the home's interests might run more to administrative convenience and order. When such conflicts of interest arose, the nearly parental powers of the nursing home frequently suffocated the basic rights of individual residents.

As a result, many nursing-home patients found themselves in a desperate position, stripped of power and desolate of dignity. They were, most of them, competent in the eyes of the law. They had not been convicted of any crime, or adjudged insane or a danger to themselves or others. They were not children. They were adults. Yet despite their legal status as free citizens, nursing-home residents came to share much with children, mental patients, and even prisoners. The control over individual life in nursing homes was often total. The elderly person was dependent upon the institution for food, clothing, medical care, recreation, companionship—in short, for all the physical and emotional elements of survival. The home often exercised great discretionary power over the aged person. It decided whether the patient was capable of receiving mail, or of handling and spending money, or of going for a walk in the neighborhood. It decided who would be allowed to visit the patient and when. And it decided whether the patient could stay or leave. The discretionary power faced by the aged in nursing homes had a corrosive effect upon the personal rights that residents had taken for granted all of their lives. And the situation they faced was also faced by residents of other service institutions, such as mental hospitals and foster-care institutions. Dependence created a context in which rights were exchanged for services.

In a strange and probably unintended way, the residents of such institutions came to resemble soldiers in the army and convicts in prison. In Erving Goffman's classic description of institutional life, every detail of an inmate's life is potentially open to scrutiny and inspection. It often begins with the very process of admission, with

taking a life history, photographing, weighing, fingerprinting, assigning numbers, searching, listing personal possessions for storage, undressing, bathing, disinfecting, hair-cutting, issuing institutional clothing, instructing as to rules, and assigning to quarters.

The new arrival is thus "shaped and coded into an object that can be fed into the administrative machinery of the establishment, to be worked on smoothly by routine operations." Afterward there are various other "abasements, degradations, humiliations, and profanations of self": meaningless make-work, denial of sexual activity, forced deference, penalties for self-expression, unfair procedures.

The reach of the institution extends to the most personal aspects of one's life, and significantly to aspects that are meaningless to anyone else—to dress, style, personal appearance, and deportment. In the military, the function of such dominion is undisputed: if you can control the personal details of someone's life, if you can impose your institutional will even upon personal appearance, then you can control everything—how the individual he thinks, acts, and responds to orders. However appropriate such control may be in the military, it is hard to justify within caring institutions. Yet inmates of such institutions were often subjected to very similar controls. In the end, as Goffman puts it, "The inmate cannot easily escape from the press of judgmental officials and from the enveloping tissue of constraint."

Nor was this "tissue of constraint" limited to residential service institutions, such as nursing homes or mental hospitals. Similar intrusions were also to be found, though to lesser degrees, in the administration of public schools, housing, and welfare. For a long while, no one thought of questioning such intrusions or of limiting the discretionary powers of public servants providing social services to the needy. Violations of individual rights that would have created an instantaneous political and legal furor had they been perpetrated by the police went unrecognized when they were perpetrated by social-service professionals. Because such professionals were presumed to be acting in "the best interests" of their "clients," no one questioned the excesses of their power. They were not police.

In fact, they were more like parents. How could a parent, looking through a child's belongings, be accused of an illegal search? How could a parent, demanding deference, determining a child's bedtime, telling him what clothes to wear, punishing him for "talking back," or even hitting him, be accused of violating constitutional rights? In some institutions, social-service professionals actually and explicitly claimed the legal powers of surrogate parents— a legal doctrine called *in loco parentis*, Latin for "in the place of the parent." According to this doctrine, parents, just by sending their children to school, delegate their powers to school officials, who are then permitted to act in the place of the parents. Child-care agencies literally and legally assumed complete parental powers over their wards. Under certain conditions, so did mental hospitals and nursing homes. Other services, like public housing, often treated their clients like children, even without claiming the legal power of surrogate parents.

And so a tradition grew up. The Bill of Rights existed, but it did not apply to social-service institutions. For people who needed shelter, the government provided public housing. But admission could be denied for such reasons as poor housekeeping, an irregular work history, frequent separations of husband and wife, a single-parent family, a common-law marriage, lack of furniture, apparent mental retardation, a dishonorable discharge from the military, or the arrest of one's child. These standards were not the result of *ad hoc* decisions made by tyrants; they were actually the legal regulations of public-housing authorities, and they gave housing officials unprecedented discretion—the early Americans would have called it *dominion*—over other people's lives. Private troubles became a reason for public punishment.

For people who needed money, the government provided welfare payments. But eligibility standards depended on morality. Every detail of a recipient's life was subject to scrutiny. Women were allowed different numbers of sanitary napkins each month, and men different numbers of razor blades, depending on whether they were employed or not. The same distinction governed the number of times one could have one's coat cleaned. There were no allowances for newspapers, and telephones were considered a luxury, even for the blind. A single woman with preschool-age children could have her children's benefits revoked if she were found to be sleeping with a man, and midnight raids by caseworkers became a common method of discovering such behavior. The abolition of privacy became a condition of survival.

For children who were in trouble and whose families did not have the resources to help, the government provided "services" through a system of family courts. Punishment was no part of the purpose of these courts, whose only function was to rehabilitate. But services that might have been purchased if a child's family were affluent enough—a governess, a tutor, a psychologist, a special school, a homemaker—were not provided. Instead, children were removed from their families and incarcerated, like criminals and often together with criminals, for truancy or sexual promiscuity, for running away from home, staying out too late, or using bad language, or even for vague reasons like "disobedience" or "incorrigibility." Whatever their problems, they did not usually come out of those institutions better off than when they entered, or even than they might have been had they been let alone. If their families had begun to break up under the pressure of poverty, the government's intervention often guaranteed and accelerated the breakup.

In institutions with lesser powers, such as public schools, intrusions and degradations were nonetheless substantial. Codes of dress and personal appearance were enforced with disproportionate intensity, as if the structure of public education itself would crumble if a boy were allowed another quarter-inch of hair or a girl permitted to wear pants. These conflicts were not trivial, because at the time they arose, personal appearance was strongly correlated with traditional sex roles. Boys wearing long hair or girls wearing pants threatened those traditional roles at precisely the time when they were beginning to be challenged elsewhere. Students were frequently suspended from school—denied their legal right to education—because they wore their hair long or dressed in a new way. Freedom of speech was often forbidden. While students were taught to revere James Madison and the First Amendment in their social-studies classes, they were swiftly suspended for applying those lessons to their own lives. Other students were suspended for truancy: their problem was that they were not attending school enough, and the school "helped" by not permitting them to attend at all. All of these actions were taken without giving the suspended student a fair procedural opportunity to explain or to contest the decision. Fair hearings were deemed unnecessary because it was assumed that everyone had the student's best interests at heart. Arbitrariness became the concomitant of benevolence.

CHALLENGING SOCIAL CONTROL

During the 1960s, many of these groups began to challenge the extraordinary powers of their benefactors. New York City high-school students began wearing buttons that exhorted FREE THE NEW YORK 275,000; groups such as the National Welfare Rights Organization and the Mental Patients' Liberation Front arose; unions were organized in prisons. By the mid-1970s, the movement was in full flower. In Syracuse, New York, a poster looking much like a traditional March of Dimes poster began to circulate, its legend announcing a new stance by the disabled toward charity: YOU GAVE US YOUR DIMES. NOW WE WANT OUR RIGHTS.

These movements displayed all the accoutrements of orthodox political organizations. There were meetings, rallies, leaflets, and newspapers. Often the response of the social-service professionals was unexpectedly repressive. Students peacefully handing out leaflets or homemade "underground" newspapers were suspended for distributing "seditious" literature, while welfare-rights advocates were arrested for handing out eligibility information to recipients in welfare centers. Not coincidentally, and concurrently, prisoners were being placed in solitary confinement for entries in their diaries critical of prison officials, and soldiers stationed in the United States were being court-martialed for criticizing the war in Vietnam. The analogy between service institutions on the one hand and the military and prisons on the other remained uncomfortably close.

Individual social-service employees who tried to defend their clients against these substantive and procedural depredations often discovered the adversarial nature of charity. If they persisted in defending their clients, they could be fired. Fighting for clients' interests became too risky, and not many took the risk. Clients learned that with few exceptions they could not rely upon those who served them. So they began to rely upon themselves. Encouraged by the general expansiveness of the Supreme Court toward the Bill of Rights in those years, and the suddenly larger availability of lawyers specializing in civil rights, civil liberties, and poverty law, client groups began to sue their benefactors. One by one during the 1960s, all these groups went to court to establish the principle that the Bill of Rights also applied to them, and to limit the power of those who governed their lives. The response of service professionals was almost always the same: they resisted attempts to place limits on their discretionary power, and they felt betrayed by those they had sought to serve.

School principals claimed that without the unfettered discretion to suspend students, they could not maintain adequate discipline in the schools. Family-court judges argued that it was necessary to "search" a welfare mother's house without a warrant in order to find out if her child was being abused. The New York State Department of Social Services supported solitary confinement in children's institutions as necessary to overall rehabilitative purposes. Housing officials defended evictions of entire families by claiming that such evictions were necessary to protect other residents from the drug-selling of individual family members. Psychiatrists in Florida justified the fifteen-year incarceration, without treatment, of a nondangerous "patient" in a mental "hospital" by claiming, in effect, that incarceration itself was therapeutic. They called it "milieu therapy."

In April 1977, the United States Supreme Court ruled that the beating of schoolchildren by teachers in public schools did not violate the Constitution. A spokesman for the American Federation of Teachers hailed the ruling by defending teachers' discretion and by emphasizing their benevolent intentions: "I shudder to think," he said, "that people will say that we are Nazis who want to beat up kids. That's not it; teachers want to maintain a healthy atmosphere and they need options." Another teacher spokesman added, "Teachers want corporal punishment retained as an option. No one likes to see their options limited."

Such justifications were not in principle different from those offered by the police. They, too, constantly clamor to be free of restrictions they perceive as hampering their ability to do their job. Yet it is precisely those restrictions that defend citizens' rights. From the police point of view, it might be easier to search whenever and whomever they want, without having to convince a judge that a search is both reasonable and lawful. Yet our Constitution recognizes—and nearly everyone agrees—that such unlimited police discretion would come at the expense of citizens' rights. Similarly, unlimited professional discretion—whether the professional is a teacher, a social worker, a housing official, or a psychiatrist—comes at the expense of the client's rights.

Yet until the rights revolution of the 1960s, no one saw it that way. Most professionals defended their own discretionary power—and therefore opposed the rights of their clients—with variations on the following argument:

1. I provide an essential and benevolent service. I am a helping professional: I teach, I heal, I rehabilitate, I provide shelter.

2. In order to provide the best possible service, I need broad discretionary powers. I am an expert. I know how to run schools, hospitals, children's shelters, housing programs, and I must be left alone to apply my special knowledge.

3. The adversary process is inappropriate to the service I provide. Lawyers are an intrusion. The Bill of Rights is disruptive. How can I get on with the difficult business of teaching if I am constantly forced to justify my actions to lawyers at hearings? How can I protect a helpless child from physical abuse if I am not allowed access to the home without having to go before a judge and get a warrant?

This attitude received the highest legal endorsement in a case that reached the Supreme Court in late 1970. The case involved Barbara James, a woman who was receiving welfare money for her dependent child, and who was notified that her home would be visited by a caseworker. Mrs. James offered to supply relevant information to welfare officials and to meet with them and be interviewed, but refused to permit the caseworker to "visit" her home. Officials of the Department of Welfare gave no specific reason for their desire to enter Mrs. James's home, except to say that they wanted to see whether there were "any changes in her situation" or any "social services" she "required." Mrs. James said no, and welfare aid to her children was terminated.

Mrs. James sued in federal court. She argued that the "visit" was a euphemism for a search, that the government had no legal power to search her home. The Fourth Amendment to the United States Constitution, she said, gave her the right to refuse such "visits." The Supreme Court disagreed. If Barbara James had resisted an effort by the police to enter her apartment she would have been successful. And, in fact, the first court to hear her case had ruled in her favor. But in a 5–4 decision, the Supreme Court ruled that the caseworker's visit was not constitutionally the same as a police officer's search. Justice Harry A. Blackmun, writing for the majority, ruled that "the caseworker is not a sleuth, but rather, we trust, is a friend to one in need." That the "one in need" had come before the Court to claim the right to reject such "friendship" seemed lost on Justice Blackmun and the four other justices who voted with him.

A closer reading of Justice Blackmun's opinion makes it plain that he drew such an easy distinction between welfare workers and police officers because of his belief that welfare workers meant well, while the police were rightly to be feared. The caseworker's "primary objective," wrote Blackmun, "is, or should be, the welfare, not the prosecution, of the aid recipient for whom the worker has profound responsibility." Nor was the Court moved by the testimony of a dozen other welfare recipients, who said that caseworkers often came to "visit" without notice or appointment, that such surprise visits could be "very embarrassing to me … when I have company" and that caseworkers sometimes asked "very personal questions" in front of children. None of this mattered. Bound by a benevolent vision of welfare, the Court failed to see the violation of rights which, had the police been involved, it would have been quick to see and quick to stop.

Of course, Barbara James could have stopped the unwarranted government searches anytime: all she had to do was decline welfare payments for her dependent children. Incredibly, in one federal lawsuit in Washington, D.C., a judge actually made that argument: a welfare recipient, he ruled, has "a perfect right to slam the door in the face of the investigator. Of course, he runs the risk then of being cut off the rolls." All dependents in public institutions faced similar "choices." Families in public housing could avoid official surveillance of their private affairs by moving out—except that they could not afford to. Students in public schools could avoid restrictions upon their personal appearance and freedom of political expression by leaving—except that they were compelled to attend or else pay high fees for private schooling. Children in foster-care institutions, patients in mental hospitals, and the aged in nursing homes often did not enjoy even that bleak alternative: incarcerated against their will, they could not avoid violations of their rights even by leaving.

In 1991, an especially cruel waiver of rights was forced upon poor women when the Supreme Court ruled, in *Rust v. Sullivan*, that doctors working at federally assisted family-planning clinics could not provide information about abortion to women, even if they requested such information and even if the doctors thought it was medically necessary. In effect, the Court said that medical clinics supported by government funds could be forced to tailor their medical advice to fit the government's ideological fashions. Many women were thus forced to accept such distortions, and abandon their right to an honest doctor-patient relationship, or else give up medical care entirely.

SOCIAL DEPENDENCE AND INDIVIDUAL LIBERTY

Social dependence thus frequently resulted in profound violations of individual liberty. These violations were not explicitly anticipated by those who wrote our Constitution and its Bill of Rights. Yet dependence upon government largesse or the institutions of caring has put millions of people in positions where they cannot defend themselves against the encroachments of power. It turned out to be naïve to hope that benevolent intentions could mitigate the mischief caused by that power so feared by those who wrote our Bill of Rights. Politically, we were not safe from the excesses of even so libertarian a man as Thomas Jefferson, once he became president; socially, we are not safe from the excesses of our service institutions or from the political ideologies of government benefactors. And just as the rights of the governed could not be assumed to be the concern of their governors, so the rights of the dependent could not be assumed to be the concern of their benefactors. Both meant to govern well, *but both meant to govern.* They both therefore had to be "bitted and bridled by a Bill of Rights."

By the late 1960s and early 1970s, the assumption of benevolence began increasingly to be seen as an insufficient reason to allow social-service professionals to exercise unlimited power over their clients, and lawsuits began to be brought to challenge that power. The kind of legal fiction endorsed by the Supreme Court in the Barbara James case began to be challenged everywhere. The caseworker whose job would be easier if he or she were allowed unwarranted access to an individual's home began to be seen as no different from the police officer whose job would also be easier if such access were allowed.

More and more, dependent clients and their lawyers began to argue that social-service professionals are, in constitutional terms, indistinguishable from police. Both serve important social ends, but both will violate rights in the course of their jobs if they think it is important enough — and therefore this is a decision that cannot be left to them. A revolutionary doctrine was thus advanced, and persistently put before the courts: no less than other government officials, service professionals were not the guardians of their clients' liberty, which only law could secure. During the decade between the mid-1960s and the mid-1970s, an immense amount of litigation was initiated to establish this general principle, and secure specific rights in a variety of institutional contexts. Though some of it was unsuccessful, many new rights were secured, and unprecedented limits imposed on institutions.

Students in public schools established their right to freedom of expression inside the schools. In a landmark decision, *Tinker v. Des Moines Independent School District,* the Supreme Court overturned the suspension of several teenage students who had peacefully publicized their objections to the war in Vietnam by wearing black armbands to school. The Court ruled that students do not lose their First Amendment right to free expression when they enter school, and explicitly rejected the claim that school officials ought to have the discretion to prohibit such expression. Other courts applied the same principle to different forms of expression, including homemade leaflets, buttons, and political clubs. In a later decision, the Supreme Court also ruled that a student has the right to a fair hearing anytime he is suspended from school. The Court established that right by limiting the discretion of school officials to suspend a student's entitlement to public education without adhering to the minimum procedures required by the Constitution to guarantee fairness. The traditional claim made by school officials that such procedures are not necessary because they have the student's best interests at heart was rejected. Limits were placed on their discretion despite their good intentions.

Welfare recipients established many new rights that restricted the discretion of social-service officials to determine or revoke benefits and intrude upon their private lives. In one case, the Supreme Court ruled that welfare officials could not revoke benefits to needy children because their mother had sexual relations with a man who was not her husband. In another case, the Court ruled that welfare benefits could not be revoked before a fair hearing. In a third, the Court prohibited local welfare officials from denying benefits to current residents, who were otherwise eligible, because they had not been residents for at least one year. Though the Supreme Court said (in the Barbara James case) that compulsory home visits did not require a search warrant, welfare officials were stopped by federal courts in other cases from conducting "unreasonable searches," such as midnight raids.

In housing, federal courts have said that "the existence of an absolute and uncontrolled discretion in an agency of government vested with the administration of a vast program such as public housing would be an intolerable invitation to abuse," and ruled that constitutional standards of due process required public-housing authorities to select tenants according to "ascertainable standards" and fair procedures.

In the area of juvenile justice, the Supreme Court rejected the notion that "the Bill of Rights is for adults only." In a case involving a minor from Arizona accused of making a lewd telephone call to a neighbor, the Court ruled that when a child faces the loss of liberty, he is entitled to a lawyer, notice of charges, the right to cross-examine witnesses, and the right to remain silent. All those rights had been denied by the Arizona juvenile court on the grounds that juvenile courts were not strictly courts, but rather were informal tribunals whose purpose was not to punish the accused minor, but to help him. The Supreme Court explicitly rejected such benevolence as insufficient justification for the denial of constitutional rights.

A few years later, another federal court struck down a statute that authorized reformatory sentences of up to four years for minors who had committed acts for which the maximum sentence was one year when committed by an adult. The government had claimed that the longer sentence for juveniles was justified because it was not intended to punish, but rather to rehabilitate, and more time was required for rehabilitation. The court explicitly rejected that claim. Similarly, another court later declared unconstitutional a statute authorizing incarceration of so-called wayward minors for the ostensible purpose of psychological and medical treatment. "Unbridled discretion," ruled the court, "however benevolently motivated, is frequently a poor substitute for principle and procedure."

Though cases like these established only partial limits on the discretion of institutions, leaving many rights still unprotected, they did make it clear that the mere claim of benevolence would no longer mean automatic exemption from the limits imposed by the Bill of Rights. Prison officials, mental-health officials, and child-care officials also saw their discretionary power limited during those years, though on varying matters and to varying degrees. It would be fair to characterize the results of such litigation as a legal revolution, but it would be inaccurate to suggest that the revolution was comprehensive, enduring, or complete. Many institutions today remain largely free of legal restrictions, and the Supreme Court in the *Rust* case has indicated its alarming willingness to allow the government to use funding as a means to restrict rights it could not restrict directly. The rights of individuals subject to the power of those institutions that are dependent upon government largesse therefore remain in jeopardy.

But in many cases the light of law had shone into the darkest corners of institutional life, and extended some of the traditional rights of free speech, equality, and fundamental fairness to people for whom such rights had previously been unthinkable. And their struggles—even those that were unsuccessful—taught the nation a new lesson: the midnight knock at the door is always implicit in government power. In one century, it comes in the form of a British soldier; in another, a caseworker or a federally funded clinic. Encroaching power wears many disguises.

TOWARD THE THIRD CENTURY

THE VISION OF LIBERTY UPON WHICH THIS NATION WAS FOUNDED WAS NOT static. Indeed, at its inception, the vision of liberty—of fundamental rights equally guaranteed to all—stood in sharp contrast to the political realities of American life. The Bill of Rights may have constituted a set of abstract legal guarantees, but those guarantees were not always enforceable: frequently they yielded to power, and in any case they failed to protect whole classes of people. But the Bill of Rights was more than a set of laws: it was also a beacon of hope to people who had little reason to hope; it was a set of ideals to which the vulnerable might aspire, something to strive for, even when the horizon seemed distant.

As we begin the third century of the Bill of Rights, therefore, we should honor more, much more, than the document itself or the wisdom of those who first wrote it down and steered it through to ratification. We should honor as well those who refused to accept the Constitution of 1787 and pressed for a Bill of Rights, even though their motives for doing so were not entirely pure.

We should honor the idea of an independent Supreme Court, even though we know how often that Court reflected majoritarian prejudice instead of curbing it, and deferred to government power instead of bridling it. Without an independent court system, no comparable legal gains could ever have been made, and many rights we take for granted today would be diminished.

But above all, we should honor the struggles of those who fought, and sometimes died, for their own rights, because it was their struggles that established our rights as well. We honor Newton Cantwell and those frightened Jehovah's Witness children; Frederick Douglass and Dred Scott and Homer A. Plessy and, later, Linda Brown, Rosa Parks, Martin Luther King, Jr., and the three young men who died that day in a Mississippi ditch. We honor Eugene V. Debs and Benjamin Gitlow and Eugene Dennis and the high-school students in Iowa who wore black armbands to express their religious and political convictions. We honor John Lilburne and those like him in America who insisted on fairness even as they faced disaster. We honor Myra

Bradwell and Helen Feeney and Jane Roe and the women in West Virginia and Wisconsin who came forward to test whether their employer could force them to be sterilized. We honor Michael Hardwick and all those who risked everything by declaring their homosexuality in order to keep the government out of their personal lives—and whose courage may help keep the government out of everyone else's personal life as well. And we honor Barbara James, who had little except a sense of her own dignity and the courage to assert it.

There is no need to assume that these people and thousands more like them were all wonderful or kind or noble. Many, perhaps most, were not. With major exceptions, they were just people who needed their own rights; they did not necessarily even think about the rights of others. But the legal principles they established protected us all. When they won, we all won, whether we knew it or not; when they lost, all our rights were diminished. And that remains true today.

If the Bill of Rights has developed from little more than a parchment barrier in 1791 to an enforceable set of legal restrictions today, it is to those who fought when the fight seemed hopeless that we owe the most gratitude. In this respect, the history of the Bill of Rights teaches us that those who are the most reliable guides when liberty is at stake are not necessarily those who cherish current values or hold fast to current norms, but rather those who challenge current values and seek to lead us beyond them.

Those who do not have liberty often see it more clearly. We could do worse than use them as our guides.

NOTES

In order to avoid hundreds of footnote numbers throughout the text, I've adopted a system of blind notes, wherein each note is identified by a key phrase or the name of the case being discussed, and separated from the next note by a bullet • ; the page number in the text is given, after the bullet, for the first reference on a given page.

Legal cases are customarily cited in compressed form, which I've used here. For example, in

Zurcher v. Stanford Daily, 436 U.S. 547 (1978),

Zurcher and *Stanford Daily* are the names of the opposing parties, the Supreme Court's decision in their case is reported in volume 436 of *United States Reports,* beginning at page 547, and 1978 is the year of the decision. Occasionally, Supreme Court decisions are cited from other collections, such as the *Supreme Court Reports* (abbreviated S.Ct.) or the *Lawyers Edition,* second series (L.Ed 2d). Even more occasionally, lower-court decisions may be cited from the *Federal Reporter,* second series (F.2d), or the *Federal Supplement* (F. Supp), or other collections. Very recent decisions are reported in a weekly publication called *U.S. Law Week;* and such cases are cited as 59 U.S.L.W. 4745 (June 21, 1991).

For fuller discussions of cases and issues and additional bibliography, I have often referred the reader to articles in the excellent *Encyclopedia of the American Constitution,* which was edited by Leonard W. Levy, Kenneth L. Karst, and Dennis J. Mahoney, and was published by Macmillan in 1988. It is abbreviated in these notes as *EAC.*

A PASSION FOR LIBERTY

8 "Patriotism is the last refuge of a scoundrel": Samuel Johnson, quoted in James Boswell, *Life of Johnson* (London: Oxford University Press, 1953), p. 615. • 11 The early American worldview summarized here derives entirely from Bernard Bailyn, *The Ideological Origins of the American Revolution* (Cambridge: Harvard University Press, 1967). The quotations are from p. 56. • "The wielders of power": ibid., p. 59. • 12 "Jefferson at one time or another": Leonard W. Levy, *Jefferson and Civil Liberties* (Cambridge: Harvard University Press, 1963), p. 18. • "the state must be bitted and bridled": ibid., p. 176 • 13 "Liberty lies in the hearts of men and women": Judge Learned Hand, "The Spirit of Liberty." Address, New York City, May 21, 1944.

I • THE BIRTH OF THE BILL OF RIGHTS

21–22 "In Europe, charters of liberty" and other quotations from James Madison are from a 1792 statement, as reported in Bailyn,

Ideological Origins, p. 55. • 23 Magna Carta generally: A.E. Dick Howard, "Magna Carta," *EAC,* vol. 3, pp. 1195–97. • 24 "All the free men of our kingdom": ibid., p. 1195. • 25 "You shall have the body": Paul J. Misklin, "Habeas Corpus," *EAC,* vol. 2, pp. 879–86. • 26 *United States v. Nixon,* 418 U.S. 683 (1974). • Petition of Right: Leonard W. Levy, "Petition of Right," *EAC,* vol. 3, pp. 1383–84. • 27 Footnote: The two recent Supreme Court decisions restricting the right to habeas corpus are *McCleskey v. Zant,* 59 U.S.L.W. 4288 (April 16, 1991), and *Coleman v. Thompson,* 59 U.S.L.W. 4789 (June 24, 1991). • 28 English Bill of Rights: Levy, "Bill of Rights (English)," *EAC,* vol. 1, p. 113. • 30 "Nothing is wanted at home": cited in Bailyn, *Ideological Origins,* p. 101. • "By loading the press": ibid., p. 101. • Louisiana tax on newspapers *Grosjean v. American Press Co., Inc.,* 297 U.S. 233 (1936). • 31 "Otis was a flame of Fire!": Leonard W. Levy, *Original Intent and the Framers' Constitution* (New York: Macmillan, 1988), p. 227. • 32 "Generally strangers to the provinces":

Benjamin Franklin, quoted in Bailyn, *Ideological Origins,* p. 102. • 33 "Thus our houses": from "The Rights of the Colonies," 1772, cited in Bernard Schwartz, *The Roots of the Bill of Rights* (New York: Chelsea House, 1980), vol. 1, p. 206. • "The enforcement of community consensus": Herman Belz, "Constitutionalism and the American Founding," *EAC,* vol. 2, p. 481. • 34 "Over himself, over his own body and mind": John Stuart Mill, *On Liberty,* 1859. • 35 Articles of Confederation: Levy, "Articles of Confederation," *EAC,* vol. 1, pp. 75–77. • 36 "Contemptibly weak": Levy, "Constitutional History, 1776–89," *EAC,* vol. 1, p. 382. • 37 "It would give great quiet to the people": Max Farrand, *The Records of the Federal Convention of 1787* (New Haven: Yale University Press, 1966), vol. 2, p. 587. • 38 "It is unnecessary": ibid., p. 618. • 38–39 James Wilson's arguments are cited in Robert Allen Rutland, *The Birth of the Bill of Rights* (Boston: Northeastern University Press, 1963), p. 132. • 39 "For universal experience": Judge Samuel Bryan, *Centinel No. 11,* 1787, cited in ibid., p. 135. • "Our situation is radically different": Edmund Randolph, cited in Jonathan Elliot, *The Debates in the Several State Conventions on the Adoption of the Federal Constitution* (Philadelphia: Lippincott, 1941), vol. 3, p. 191. • "Is itself, in every rational sense": Alexander Hamilton, *Federalist No. 84.* • **40** "An insult on the understanding of the people": Bryan, cited in Herbert J. Storing, *The Complete Anti-Federalist* (Chicago: University of Chicago Press, 1981), vol. 2, p. 144. • **40–41** "A bill of rights is what the people": from Thomas Jefferson's letter to James Madison, in Julian P. Boyd, *The Papers of Thomas Jefferson* (Princeton: Princeton University Press, 1950), vol. 12, pp. 339–42. • **41** "Serves to secure the minority": James Winthrop, cited in Storing, *Complete Anti-Federalist,* vol. 4, p. 111. • "Certain death to your liberty": Luther Martin, cited in Paul. L. Ford, *Essays on the Constitution* (Brooklyn, 1892), p. 289; also see Rutland, *Birth,* p. 153. • "A mad horse": Thomas Tredwell, cited in Rutland, *Birth,* p. 178. • **42** Madison's October 1788 letter to Jefferson is discussed in Levy, *Original Intent,* pp. 163–64. • **43–44** Madison's June 8, 1789 speech introducing his proposed Bill of Rights in Congress may be found in Schwartz, *Roots,* vol. 2, pp. 1023–34. His notes for the speech are on p. 1042. • **44** "The most valuable amendment": ibid., p. 1113. • **46** "When tyranny is abroad": Andrew Eliot, cited in Bailyn, *Ideological Origins,* p. 6. • "The principle of justifiable disobedience": ibid., p. 306. • "Found in the defiance of traditional order": ibid., p. 319. • **48** Judges as the ultimate arbiters: Gerald Gunther, "Judicial Review," *EAC,* vol. 3, p. 1057. • President Jefferson on judges: Levy, *Jefferson and Civil Liberties,* p. 81. • **49** *Marbury v. Madison:* Levy, "Marbury v. Madison," *EAC,* vol. 3, p. 1199. Decision reported at 1 Cranch 137 (1803). • **50** Activism and the Supreme Court: William W. Van Alstyne, "Judicial Activism and Judicial Restraint," *EAC,* vol. 3, pp. 1031–39. • **51** "The power [of states] to keep order": Paul L. Murphy, "Constitutional History, 1945–1961," *EAC,* vol. 1, pp. 452–54. • The Warren Court: for a brief general discussion, see G. Edward White, "Warren Court," *EAC,* vol. 4, pp. 2023–31. • **52** "The unamended Constitution": Ronald W. Reagan, "The Presidency: Rules and Responsibilities," *National Forum,* Fall 1984, p. 22. • **53** "Teach the lesson that democratic processes": Robert H. Bork, "Judicial Review and Democracy," *EAC,* vol. 3, pp. 1063–64. • *Griswold v. Connecticut,* 381 U.S. 479 (1985). See also Karst, "Griswold," *EAC,* vol. 2, p. 870. • **55** "No legal protec-

tion against the states": for a discussion of the legal doctrine that gradually applied the Bill of Rights to state and local government, see Levy, "Incorporation Doctrine," *EAC,* vol. 2, pp. 970–73. • *Barron v. Baltimore,* 7 Peters 243 (1833). • **56** "probably inconclusive": Levy, "Incorporation," p. 971; see also Michael Kent Curtis, *No State Shall Abridge* (Durham: Duke University Press, 1986). • Louisiana butchers: *Slaughterhouse Cases,* 16 Wallace 36 (1873). • **57** "American Indian" is used instead of "Native American" for several reasons. First, most Indians use the two terms interchangeably and most organizations, such as the National Congress of American Indians and the American Indian Movement, use "Indian" in their titles. Second, virtually all federal laws and agencies use "Indian." Finally, the term "Native Americans" includes others — Hawaiians, for example — and is therefore historically ambiguous. • "The absolute political evil": quoted in Bailyn, *Ideological Origins,* p. 232. • **58** "Being wholly under the power and control": ibid., p. 233. • "A force ... by which a man is obliged to act": ibid., p. 233. • "What is a trifling three-penny tax on tea?": ibid., p. 241. • "All men are born free": ibid., p. 235. • "The cause of our African slaves" and "advocates of American liberty": ibid., p. 239 • "Lighter than a feather": ibid., p. 244 • "Themselves own two thousand Negro slaves": ibid., p. 241. • "The abolition of domestic slavery": ibid., p. 236. • **59** "When an opportunity will be offered": ibid., p. 236. • "Meant to shield the consciences": John Hope Franklin, "Slavery and the Constitution," *EAC,* vol. 4, p. 1689. • **60** "The rich inheritance of justice": from a speech by Frederick Douglass, "What to the Slave Is the Fourth of July?" given Rochester, New York, July 5, 1882. • *Dred Scott v. Sandford,* 19 Howard 393 (1857); see also Don E. Fehrenbacher, "Dred Scott," *EAC,* vol. 2, pp. 584–87. • "Had no rights which the white man was bound to respect": ibid., p. 586.

2 • FREEDOM OF RELIGION

71 "The most mild and equitable establishment of religion": John Adams, *Diary and Autobiography,* vol. 3, p. 312, cited in Bailyn, *Ideological Origins,* p. 248. • **72** "From what we hear": ibid., p. 256. • "Spread a universal alarm": ibid. • **73** "You tell your governor": ibid., p. 268. • **74** "but your law of last June:" ibid., p. 270. • **75** Rehnquist's view is criticized in Levy, *Original Intent,* pp. 174–94. • "One religious sect or society": ibid., p. 181. See also Levy, "Establishment of Religion," *EAC,* vol. 2, pp. 653–55. • **76** The

Supreme Court case involving street solicitation by Jehovah's Witnesses was *Cantwell v. Connecticut,* 310 U.S. 296 (1940). • The case upholding religious parades in public parks and streets: *Cox v. New Hampshire,* 312 U.S. 569 (1941). • The right to distribute religious literature in bus and railroad terminals: *Jamison v. Texas,* 318 U.S. 413 (1943). • The right to make door-to-door solicitations: *Martin v. City of Struthers,* 319 U.S. 141 (1943). • **77** The New York permit law: *Kunz v. New York,* 340 U.S. 290 (1951). • Fred Shuttlesworth's case: *Shuttlesworth v. Birmingham,* 394 U.S. 147 (1969). • **78** "To profess a belief": *Torcaso v. Watkins,* 367 U.S. 488 (1961). • State laws disqualifying clergy from public office: *McDaniel v. Paty* 435 U.S. 618 (1978). • Sunday-closing laws were upheld in *McGowan v. Maryland,* 366 U.S. 420 (1961), and in *Two Guys From Harrison-Allentown v. McGinley,* 366 U.S. 582 (1961). • Saturday as Sabbath: *Gallagher v. Crown Kosher Super Market,* 366 U.S. 617 (1961), and *Braunfeld v. Brown,* 366 U.S. 599 (1961). • The Seventh-Day Adventist case: *Sherbert v. Verner,* 374 U.S. 398 (1963). • **79** Sacramental use of peyote: *Employment Division, Department of Human Resources v. Smith,* 110 S.Ct. 1595 (1990). • **79–80** "The very purpose of the BIll of Rights": *West Virginia Board of Education v. Barnette,* 319 U.S. 624 (1943). • **80** Churches and real-estate taxes: *Walz v. Tax Commission,* 397 U.S. 664 (1970). • **80–81** Amish employers: *United States v. Lee,* 455 U.S. 252 (1982). • **81** *Bob Jones University v. United States,* 461 U.S. 574 (1983). • Buddhist prisoner: *Cruz v. Beto,* 405 U.S. 319 (1972). • **82** Cadets and chapel: *Anderson v. Laird,* 409 U.S. 690 (1972). The lower-court decision is reported at 466 F.2d 283 (D.C.Cir.). • Military draft and the Thirteenth Amendment: *Arver v. United States,* 245 U.S. 366 (1918). • **83** The right of conscientious objection and non-religious believers: *United States v. Seeger,* 380 U.S. 163 (1965), and *Welsh v. United States,* 398 U.S. 333 (1970). • Opposition to all wars: *Gillette v. United States,* 401 U.S. 437 (1971). • Compulsory vaccination: *Jacobson v. Massachusetts,* 197 U.S. 11 (1905). • **84** Amish and compulsory school attendance: *Wisconsin v. Yoder,* 406 U.S. 205 (1972). • **86** Released-time programs: see Leo Pfeffer, "Released Time," *EAC,* vol. 3, pp. 1535–37. • **87** Religious instruction in public schools: *McCollum v. Board of Education,* 333 U.S. 203 (1948). • Released time for religious instruction off premises: *Zorach v. Clausen,* 343 U.S. 306 (1952). • **87–88** College students and on-campus religious clubs: *Widmar v. Vincent,* 454 U.S. 263 (1981). •

88 Equal Access Act: *Board of Education v. Mergens,* 110 L.Ed.2d 191 (1990). • 89 School prayer: *Engel v. Vitale,* 370 U.S. 421 (1962). • 90 School prayer: *Abington Township School District v. Schempp,* 374 U.S. 203 (1963). • 91 Ten Commandments: *Stone v. Graham,* 449 U.S. 39 (1980). • Silent prayer: *Wallace v. Jaffree,* 105 S.Ct.2479 (1985). • 91–92 Salute to the flag: *West Virginia Board of Education v. Barnette,* 319 U.S. 624 (1943). • 92 Earlier flag-salute case: *Minersville School District v. Gobitis,* 310 U.S. 586 (1940). • "pretended patriotism": Boswell, *Life of Johnson,* p. 615. • 92–93 West Virginia Jehovah's Witnesses: David Margolick, "Pledge Dispute Evokes Bitter Memories," *New York Times,* September 11, 1988. • 93 "The Monkey Trial": *State of Tennessee v. Scopes,* 289 SW 364 (1925). See also Michael E. Parrish, "Scopes," *EAC,* vol. 4, p. 1743. • 94 Arkansas anti-evolution case: *Epperson v. Arkansas,* 393 U.S. 97 (1968). • 95 Arkansas creationism case: *McLean v. Arkansas Board of Education,* 529 F.Supp. 1255 (1982). • Louisiana creationism case: *Edwards v. Aguillard,* 482 U.S. 578 (1987). • Church schools instead of public schools: *Pierce v. Society of Sisters,* 268 U.S. 510 (1925). • 96 Transporting children to religious schools: *Everson v. Board of Education,* 330 U.S. 1 (1947). This case was also the first to apply the First Amendment's establishment clause to the states. • 96–97 New York's textbook-loan program: *Board of Education v. Allen,* 392 U.S. 236 (1968). • 97 Salaries for teachers in religious schools: *Lemon v. Kurtzman,* 403 U.S. 602 (1971). • Tax deductions for religious-school expenses: The New York case was *Committee for Public Education and Religious Liberty v. Nyquist,* 413 U.S. 757 (1973). The Minnesota case was *Mueller v. Allen,* 459 U.S. 820 (1983). • 98–99 Little Axe incident: John M. Swomley, Jr., "Public Schools Embattled Over Prayer," *Christian Century,* July 20–27, 1983, pp. 681–83.

3 • FREEDOM OF EXPRESSION

115 "Hanged up by the neck": quoted in William O. Douglas, *An Almanac of Liberty* (New York: Doubleday, 1954), p. 17. • 116 "The liberty of the press is indeed essential": Sir William Blackstone, *Commentaries* (1769), cited in Thomas I. Emerson, "Freedom of the Press," *EAC,* vol. 2, p. 798. • 118 "False facts." For a general discussion of the early American view of freedom of the press, see Levy, Original Intent, pp. 195–220. • "It is time enough": ibid., p. 201. • "Actual freedom of the press": ibid., p. 211.

• "Scummy journalism": ibid. • 119 "Incompatible with social order": Douglas, *Almanac,* p. 12. • The 1798 sedition law: see Merrill D. Peterson, "Alien and Sedition Acts," *EAC,* vol. 1, pp. 43–44. • 120 "It would seem a mockery": cited in Levy, *Origins,* p. 215. • "Nobody to enjoy the Liberty of the Press": John Thomson, *An Enquiry, Concerning the Liberty, and Licentiousness of the Press* (1801; reprint New York: Da Capo Press, 1970. • 123 "Liberty of speech": Curtis, *No State Shall Abridge,* pp. 37–40. • Eugene V. Debs: see Levy, "Debs, In Re,", *EAC,* vol. 2, p. 544; also *In Re Debs,* 158 U.S. 564 (1895). • 126 *Schenck v. United States,* 249 U.S. 47 (1919). • The thirteenth Amendment and the draft: *Arver v. United States,* 245 U.S. 366 (1918). • 127 "Furnish the corpses": Michael E. Parrish, "Debs v. United States," *EAC,* vol. 2, pp. 544–45. See also *Debs v. United States,* 249 U.S. 211 (1919). • *Abrams v. United States,* 250 U.S. 616 (1919). • 128 The 1969 decision: *Brandenburg v. Ohio,* 395 U.S. 444 (1969). • "It is time enough": cited in Levy, *Original Intent,* p. 201. • 129 "Every idea is an incitement": from *Gitlow v. New York,* 268 U.S. 652 (1925). • 130 The Anita Whitney: *Whitney v. California,* 274 U.S. 357 (1927). • 131 Eugene Dennis: *Dennis v. United States,* 341 U.S. 494 (1951). • 132 "These petitioners were not charged," "If this were a case," and "Communism in this country": from the dissenting opinions in *Dennis,* ibid. • 133 The 1957 decision: *Yates v. United States,* 354 U.S. 298 (1957). • 134 "We don't need no damn flag": *Street v. New York,* 394 U.S. 576 (1969). • 136 Flag-burning in Texas: *Texas v. Johnson,* 105 L.Ed.2d 342 (1989). • Flag-burning in Washington: *United States v. Eichman,* 110 S.Ct. 2404 (1990). • 137 "No such thing as a false idea." *Gertz v. Robert Welch, Inc.,* 418 U.S. 323 (1974). • 138 "Purely private feuds." The quotes from Justice Black are in *Beauharnais v. Illinois,* 343 U.S. 250 (1952). • 140 Civil-libel suits by officials permitted, but made more difficult to win: *New York Times v. Sullivan,* 376 U.S. 254 (1964). • 141 The Minnesota prior-restraint case: *Near v. Minnesota,* 283 U.S. 697 (1931). • 142 Pentagon Papers: *New York Times Company v. United States,* 403 U.S. 713 (1971). • 143 The CIA and prior restraint: *Snepp v. United States,* 444 U.S. 507 (1980). • 144 Medical information and federal funds: *Rust v. Sullivan,* 59 U.S.L.W. 4451 (May 23, 1991). • 145 The right of reporters to attend criminal trials: *Richmond Newspapers v. Virginia,* 448 U.S. 555 (1980). • 146 The Supreme Court's first major consideration of the First Amendment and

"obscene" expression: *Roth v. United States* and *Alberts v. California,* 354 U.S. 476 (1957). • 148 "I know it when I see it": Justice Potter Stewart defining obscenity in *Jacobellis v. Ohio,* 378 U.S. 184 (1964). • *Stanley v. Georgia,* 394 U.S. 557 (1969). • The two decisions cutting back the scope of *Stanley: United States v. Reidel,* 402 U.S. 351 (1971), and *United States v. Thirty-Seven Photographs,* 402 U.S. 363 (1971). • 149 The movie theater and "obscene" film: *Paris Adult Theater I v. Slaton,* 413 U.S. 49 (1973). • The companion case: *Miller v. California,* 413 U.S. 15 (1973). • The dissents of Justices Brennan and Douglas are from *Miller,* ibid. • 150–51 Nude dancing: *Barnes v. Glen Theatre,* 59 U.S.L.W. 4745 (June 21, 1991).

4 • FUNDAMENTAL FAIRNESS

159 "Without being brought in answer": cited in Levy, "Due Process of Law," *EAC,* vol. 2, p. 589. • 160 "Though I be pulled to pieces": cited in Douglas, *Almanac,* p. 236. • "The law of the land and Magna Carta": ibid. • 160–61 John Lilburne: Levy, "Lilburne," *EAC,* vol. 3, p. 1160. • 161 For a discussion on the right not to testify against oneself, see Levy, "Right Against Self-Incrimination," *EAC,* pp. 1569–77. • The right against self-incrimination applied to the states: *Malloy v. Hogan,* 378 U.S. 1 (1964). • 162 The right against self-incrimination applied to noncriminal proceedings: *Murphy v. Waterfront Commission of New York Harbor,* 378 U.S. 52 (1964). • The 1956 "absolute immunity" case: *Ullman v. United States,* 350 U.S. 422 (1956). • *Kastigar v. United States,* 406 U.S. 441 (1972). • 163 Colonel North: *United States v. North,* 910 F.2d 843 (D.C.Cir.), *reh'g* granted in part and denied in part, 920 F.2d 940 (D.C.Cir. 1990), *cert. denied,* 59 U.S.L.W. 3793 (May 28, 1991). • 164 *Miranda v. Arizona,* 384 U.S. 436 (1966). • The American Bar Association survey: "Criminal Justice in Crisis," American Bar Association, Criminal Justice Section, 1988. • 165 "The poorest man may, in his cottage": cited in Levy, *Original Intent,* p. 222. See especially footnote 1, p. 441. • 166 "The Commencement of the Controversy": ibid., pp. 227–28. • "The right of the people to be secure": The Fourth Amendment to the United States Constitution. • 167 The exclusionary rule: *Weeks v. United States,* 232 U.S. 383 (1914). The later case applying this rule to the states was *Mapp v. Ohio,* 367 U.S. 643 (1961). • The annual number of crimes of violence and resulting arrests is cited in ABA, "Criminal Justice," p. 4. • The 1984

study by the National Center for State Courts: ibid. • **168** The 1988 study by ABA task force: ibid. • "Nothing can destroy a government more quickly": Justice Tom Clark in *Mapp*. • **169** Jailing for 48 hours without showing legal cause: *County of Riverside v. McLaughlin*, 59 U.S.L.W. 4413 (May 13, 1991). • **170** Warrantless search incidental to an arrest: *Warden v. Heydon*, 387 U.S. 294 (1967); *Chimel v. California*, 395 U.S. 152 (1969); and *United States v. Edwards*, 415 U.S. 800 (1974). See also Jacob W. Landynski, "Search Incident to Arrest," *EAC*, vol. 4, p. 1636–37. • Other exceptions to the warrant requirement: *Carroll v. United States*, 267 U.S. 132 (1925); *Schmerber v. California*, 384 U.S. 757 (1966); and *Terry v. Ohio*, 382 U.S. 1 (1968). • **171** Michigan roadblocks: *Michigan Department of State Police v. Sitz*, 110 S.Ct. 2481 (1990). • The bus search: *Florida v. Bostick*, 59 U.S.L.W. 4208 (June 20, 1991). • **172** Routine administrative inspections: *Camara v. Municipal Court*, 387 U.S. 523 (1967). • **173–74** Warrantless wiretapping: *Olmstead v. United States*, 277 U.S. 438 (1928). • **174** "Means of espionage" and "Experience should teach us": Justice Louis P. Brandeis, dissenting in *Olmstead*. • 1967 case that overruled *Olmstead*: *Katz v. United States*, 389 U.S. 347 (1967). • **175** "The sole end": Mill, *On Liberty*, p. 9. • **176** Electronic eavesdropping and political dissent: The two best books on the subject are by Frank J. Donner: *The Age of Surveillance* (New York: Knopf, 1980), about federal government activities; and *Protecters of Privilege* (Los Angeles: University of California Press, 1990), about local "Red squads." • **177** "an immolation of privacy": Justice Antonin Scalia dissenting in *National Treasury Employees Union v. Von Raab*, 109 S.Ct. 1384 (1989). • "The government could diminish": Anthony Amsterdam, cited in Wayne R. La Fave, "Search and Seizure," *EAC*, vol. 4, pp. 1632–33. • **178** "Unless a person is prepared to forgo": Justice Thurgood Marshall, dissenting in *Smith v. Maryland*, 442 U.S. 735 (1979). • **179** "No better instrument has been devised": Justice Felix Frankfurter, *Joint Anti-Fascist Refugee Committee v. McGrath*, 341 U.S. 123 (1951). • "The history of American freedom": Frankfurter, *Malinski v. New York*, 324 U.S. 401 (1945). • "It is procedure that spells much of the difference": Justice William O. Douglas, *Joint Anti-Fascist Committee*.

5 · RACIAL EQUALITY

191 "So perish all compromises": quoted in J.L. Thomas, *The Liberator* (Boston: Little, Brown, 1963). • **192** "Slavery will not be overthrown": ibid. • "Subordinate and inferior beings": *Dred Scott v. Sandford*, 19 Howard 343 (1857). • "The Supreme Court is not the only power": address on the anniversary of the American Abolitionist Society, May 24, 1857. • **196** "What does it all amount to?": speech to the Republican National Convention of 1876. • "All we say to America": Martin Luther King, Jr., Masonic Temple, Memphis, Tenn., April 3, 1968. • **197** The first case interpreting the Fourteenth Amendment: *Slaughterhouse Cases*, 16 Wallace 36 (1873). • White nightriders in Louisiana: *Cruikshank v. United States*, 92 U.S. 542 (1876). • **198** The case on the law barring blacks from juries: *Strauder v. West Virginia*, 100 U.S. 303 (1880). The case against two black defendants: *Virginia v. Rives*, 100 U.S. 313 (1880). • **198–99**: The five cases striking down the public-accommodations provisions of the 1875 Civil Rights Act are reported in *Civil Rights Cases*, 109 U.S. 3 (1883). • **199** The Thirteenth Amendment revived eighty-five years later: *Jones v. Mayer*, 392 U.S. 409 (1968). • "State action": see Charles L. Black, Jr., "State Action," *EAC*, vol. 4, pp. 1729–36; also Kenneth L. Karst, "State Action—Beyond Race," ibid., pp. 1736–38. • **200** Fugitive Slave Act upheld: *Ableman v. Booth*, 21 Howard 506 (1859). • **202** Homer A. Plessy and "separate but equal": *Plessy v. Ferguson*, 163 U.S. 537 (1896). • **203** "Grandfather clauses" in voting struck down: *Guinn v. United States*, 238 U.S. 347 (1915). Congress abolished literacy tests in 1965. • "Error in spilling": cited in Karst, "Literacy Test," *EAC*, vol. 3, p. 1169. • The Louisiana voting-registration statistics are from John Hope Franklin, *From Slavery to Freedom: A History of American Negroes*, 2nd ed. (New York: Knopf, 1956). • The lynching statistics are cited in Laughlin McDonald, *Racial Equality* (New York: National Textbook 1977), p. 39. • **205** The nine-point blueprint is from the 1920 NAACP Annual Report, pp. 87–90. • **206** *Buchanan v. Worley*, 245 U.S. 60 (1917). • ACLU and NAACP: For more on the their early relations, see Samuel Walker, *In Defense of American Liberty* (New York: Oxford University Press, 1990), p. 60. • **207** Mississippi allowed to maintain segregation in its schools: *Gong Lum v. Rice*, 275 U.S. 78 (1927). • "There was no real threat": cited in Karst, "Japanese American Cases," *EAC*, vol. 3, p. 1010. • **208** "The Japanese race is an enemy race": ibid. • On the workings of the Japanese-American "relocation" law: see Peter Irons, *Justice at War* (New York: Oxford University Press, 1983), p. 70. • **209**

"There would be Japs hanging from every pine tree" and other quotes in this paragraph: ibid., pp. 71–72. • Three Japanese-Americans challenged the program: Irons gives the best comprehensive account, ibid. • **210** Gordon Hirabayashi: *Hirabayashi v. United States*, 320 U.S. 81 (1943). • Fred Koremastu: *Koremastu v. United States*, 323 U.S. 214 (1944). • **211** Mitsuye Endo: *Ex parte Endo*, 323 U.S. 283 (1944). • **213** "Vicious circle of cumulative causation": Gunnar Myrdal, *An American Dilemma* (New York: Harper and Row, 1944). • **214** Racial segregation impermissible on interstate buses: *Morgan v. Virginia*, 328 U.S. 373 (1946). • Racially discriminatory contracts unenforceable: *Shelley v. Kraemer*, 334 U.S. 1 (1948). • **214–15** Segregation struck down in state law schools: *Sweatt v. Painter*, 339 U.S. 629 (1950); in graduate programs: *McLaurin v. Oklahoma State Regents*, 339 U.S. 637 (1950). • **216** *Brown* case: the best comprehensive account is Richard Kluger, *Simple Justice* (New York: Knopf, 1976). • "For me, the ultimate crucial factor": cited in Karst, "Brown v. Board of Education," *EAC*, vol. 1, p. 162. • **217** "To separate [children] ... solely because of their race": *Brown v. Board of Education*, 347 U.S. 483 (1954). For a complete text of the oral argument before the Supreme Court, see Leon Friedman, *Argument* (New York: Chelsea House, 1969). • **217–18** Confrontation at Central High School in Little Rock: see Daisy Bates, *The Long Shadow of Little Rock* (New York: David McKay, 1962). • **218** Delay of school desegregation rejected: *Cooper v. Aaron*, 358 U.S. 1 (1958). • **221** Public-accommodations provisions of the 1964 Civil Rights Act upheld: *Heart of Atlanta Motel v. United States*, 379 U.S. 241 (1964), and *Katzenbach v. McLung*, 379 U.S. 294 (1964). • The case outlawing racial discrimination in private contracts, as a violation of the Thirteenth Amendment, was *Jones v. Mayer*, 392 U.S. 409 (1968), discussed earlier. This case involved the buying and selling of homes; subsequent cases extending this ruling to the exclusion of black children from school and to employment contracts were, respectively, *Runyon v. McCrary*, 427 U.S. 160 (1976), and *Johnson v. Railway Express Agency*, 421 U.S. 454 (1975). • The voting-registration percentages are cited in Theodore Eisenberg, "Voting Rights Act of 1965 and its Amendments," *EAC*, vol. 4, 1987. • **222** The 1980 voting-rights case: *Mobile v. Bolden*, 446 U.S. 55 (1980). • **223** "Two increasingly separate Americas": *Report of the National Advisory Commission on Civil Disorders* ("Kerner Commission"), March 1, 1968,

p. 225. • **224** Compensatory opportunity: for a comprehensive defense, see Ira Glasser, "Affirmative Action and the Legacy of Racial Injustice," in P. Katz and D. Taylor, *Eliminating Racism* (New York: Plenum, 1988), pp. 341 ff. • **225** Racial harassment: *Patterson v. McLean Credit Union*, 109 S.Ct. 2363 (1989). • Rules of proof in employment-discrimination cases: *Wards Cove v. Atonio*, 109 S.Ct. 2115 (1989).

6 · INCLUDING ALL AMERICANS

240 Myra Bradwell: *Bradwell v. Illinois*, 16 Wallace 130 (1873). • **241** Oregon law limiting women's work hours upheld: *Muller v. Oregon*, 208 U.S. 412 (1908). • The case denying women the constitutional right to vote was *Minor v. Happersett*, 21 Wallace 162 (1875). • **242** Sally Reed given right to administer estate: *Reed v. Reed*, 404 U.S. 71 (1971). • **242–43** Sex differences in military benefits struck down: *Frontiero v. Richardson*, 411 U.S. 677 (1973). • **243** Utah case on supporting minor children: *Stanton v. Stanton*, 421 U.S. 7 (1975). • The case invalidating laws excluding women from required jury: *Taylor v. Louisiana*, 419 U.S. 522 (1975). • Louisiana property law modified: *Kirchberg v. Feenstra*, 450 U.S. 455 (1981). • **244** Tax benefits approved for women: *Kahn v. Shevin*, 416 U.S. 351 (1974). The naval officer case was *Schlesinger v. Ballard*, 419 U.S. 498 (1975). • **245** Social Security Act case: *Weinberger v. Wiesenfeld*, 420 U.S. 636 (1975). • Oklahoma law on 3.2 percent beer: *Craig v. Boren*, 429 U.S. 190 (1976). • Social Security death benefits: *Califano v. Goldfarb*, 430 U.S. 199 (1977). • **246** Alimony case: *Orr v. Orr*, 440 U.S. 268 (1979). • The 1980 Missouri death-benefit case: *Wengler v. Druggists Mutual Insurance Co.*, 446 U.S. 142 (1980). • Helen Feeney: *Personnel Administration of Massachusetts v. Feeney*, 442 U.S. 256 (1979). • **247** Military draft: *Rostker v. Goldberg*, 453 U.S. 57 (1981). • **248** Ohio case: *Cleveland Board of Education v. LaFleur*, 414 U.S. 632 (1974). • Unemployment benefits: *Turner v. Department of Employment Securities*, 423 U.S. 44 (1975). • Government disability insurance may exclude pregnancy: *Geduldig v. Aiello*, 417 U.S. 484 (1974). The same exclusion was permitted for private employers under Title VII of the Civil Rights Act of 1964 in *General Electric v. Gilbert*, 429 U.S. 125 (1976). • **249** Johnson Controls case: *International Union v. Johnson Controls*, 111 S.Ct. 1196 (1991). • **251** Religious belief about start of human life: in *Harris v. McRae*, 448 U.S. 297 (1980), plaintiffs made a major argument that religious liberty compelled the government to stay out of the issue of abortion, but the Court dismissed it. • **252** *Roe v. Wade*, 410 U.S. 113 (1973); *Doe v. Bolton*, 410 U.S. 179 (1973). • **254** Sexual activity between men: a good historical discussion may be found in Anne B. Goldstein, "History, Homosexuality, and Political Values: Searching for the Hidden Determinants of *Bowers v. Hardwick*," *Yale Law Journal*, vol. 97, 1988, pp. 1073–1103. • **255** The New Haven law, as well as Thomas Jefferson's attempt to modify Virginia's law, are described in Jonathan Katz, *Gay American History* (New York: Avon, 1976), pp. 36–37. • **256** The contraceptive case was *Griswold v. Connecticut*, 381 U.S. 479 (1965). The case extending the right to buy, sell and use contraceptives to unmarried people was *Eisenstadt v. Baird*, 405 U.S. 438 (1972). • **258** Virginia sodomy case: *Doe v. Commonwealth's Attorney*, 403 F.Supp.1199 (1976). • The Georgia case: *Bowers v. Hardwick*, 478 U.S. 186 (1986). • **260** "Men feared witches": *Whitney v. California*, 274 U.S. 357 (1927). • **262-63** The description of institutional life is from Erving Goffman, *Asylums* (New York: Anchor, 1961), pp. 1–125. • **266** "Milieu therapy": The Florida case went to the Supreme Court, which ruled, in *O'Connor v. Donaldson*, 422 U.S. 563 (1975), that the state could not merely confine a mentally ill person and give him nothing but custody. • "No one likes to see their options limited": *New York Times*, April 25, 1977, p. 24. • **267** Barbara James: *Wyman v. James*, 400 U.S. 309 (1971). • **268** *Rust v. Sullivan*, 59 U.S.L.W. 4451 (May 23, 1991). • **269** "Bitted and bridled by a Bill of Rights." Levy, *Jefferson*, p. 176. • *Tinker v. Des Moines Independent School District*, 393 U.S. 503 (1969). • **270** A student's right to a fair hearing: *Goss v. Lopez*, 419 U.S. 565 (1975). • Welfare officials could not revoke benefits because of sexual relations: *King v. Smith*, 392 U.S. 309 (1968); or before a fair hearing: *Goldberg v. Kelly*, 397 U.S. 254 (1970). • Residency requirement: *Shapiro v. Thompson*, 394 U.S. 618 (1969). • Housing cases: *Holmes v. New York City Housing Authority*, 398 F.2d 262 (2d Cir.1968), and *Escalera v. New York City Housing Authority*, 425 F.2d 853 (2d Cir. 1970), *cert. denied*, 400 U.S. 853 (1970). • "The Bill of Rights is for adults only" rejected: *In re Gault*, 387 U.S. 1 (1967). • Reformatory sentences: *United States ex rel. Sero v. Preiser*, 500 F.2d 1115 (2d Cir. 1974), *cert. denied*, 95 S.Ct.1587 (1975). • **271** Wayward minors: *Gesicki v. Oswald*, 336 F.Supp.371 (S.D.N.Y.1971).

INDEX

supremacy challenged by Massachusetts legislature 31
supremacy of, to crown 28
and taxation 25
as threat to civil and religious
liberties in colonial America 29, 72
Penn, William, first to print Magna
Carta in America 29
Pennsylvania
and Bible readings in public
schools 90
tax funds for teachers in religious
schools 97
Pentagon Papers (1971) 142
Peonage Act 195
Persian Gulf Crisis
and anti-Arab racism 212
and censorship 145
Petition of Right (1628) 26-27
Peyote, sacramental use of 79
Philadelphia Inquirer
and Pentagon Papers 142
Pitt, William
on general searches 165
Planned Parenthood, federal funds
dependent on restricting
information 144
Plessy, Homer A. 202
Plessy v. Ferguson (1896) 202, 215
Political dissent as target of electronic
eavesdropping 176
Poll taxes, used to restrict voting
rights 203
Power 11
of social-service professionals,
defended, 267
tendency to expand 33
versus liberty 33, 134
Power, congressional, limited in
Madison's amendments 44
Power, governmental
decentralized in America 77
limited in Madison's
amendments 43
need for limits on 28, 33
resisted in colonial America 29
Power, legislative, need to limit 34
Power, parliamentary
feared and opposed in colonial
America 29, 72
need for limits felt in colonial
America 32
Power, political
fluid in a democracy 122
Power, presidential, subject to rule of
law 26

Power, royal 22, 25
limited by Magna Carta 23, 24
limited by Petition of Right 26
limits in colonial America 29
versus parliamentary 28
Power, of states
Madison's "most valuable"
amendment to limit 44
unrestricted by first ten amendments 45
Powers, separation of
in U. S. Constitution 37
Prayer in public schools 89-92
Alabama law struck down 74
Preclearance of voting plans, required
under Voting Rights Act
of 1965 222
Pregnancy, stages, and abortion 252
Pregnant women, protection of 248
Prejudice, expression of 138
Presbyterians, New Light 75
and established churches in colonial
America 71, 73
Press, freedom of 114
and civil-libel suits 138-41
in early years of U. S. 118
in Louisiana 31
not mentioned in unamended
Constitution 37
and *Pentagon Papers* case 142
status debated under unamended
Constitution 39
See also Expression.
Press, taxation of
by Louisiana 30
by Stamp Act 30
Printing press and free speech 114
Prior restraint
generally impermissible 141
Privacy, marital
right to, implied in other constitutional rights 53
Privacy, right to
expectation of, as measure of Fourth
Amendment restrictions 177
presumption under Fourth
Amendment 166
"Privileges and immunities"
not to be abridged by states 55
clause held not to govern state
laws 56
"Probable cause": required for search
warrant 166
Procedural rights 159
defended by Fourth and Fifth
Amendments 178-79

See also Fair procedures; Rights,
procedural.
Prohibition of alcohol, as justification
for unconstitutional action 174
"Protective" legislation for women
seen as trap 244
Public accommodations, discrimina-
tion in, held not forbidden if not
done by state government 198-99
Public-interest law 207
as practiced by NAACP 205
Pullman Palace Car Company 123-24
Punishments in seventeenth-century
England 115

• R

Race: word omitted from
Constitution 190
"Race exception" to the
Constitution 190-91
Racial discrimination
held not to exist in absence of
explicit exclusion 198
in the North 204
Racial policies and tax exemption 81
Racial prejudice as determinant of
guilt 158
Racism during Persian Gulf Crisis 212
Railroads: held to be private, therefore
not subject to Bill of Rights 199
Randolph, A. Philip, demands
desegregation of defense
industries 213
Randolph, Edmund 39
Reagan administration
and restrictions on flow of information 143
efforts to overturn affirmative
action 225
Reagan, Ronald
attacks judicial review 52
increases scope of secret classifi-
cations 143
on Japanese-American
detention 211
nominates Robert Bork to Supreme
Court 52
praises unamended Constitution
41, 52
Red squads 176
Reed, Sally 242
Rehnquist, William
on nude dancing 151
supports nonpreferential aid to
religion 74-75